FINE F(

By the same author

Pâtés, Terrines and Potted Meats
Cook's Progress
Grandmothers' Lore
The Country Housewife
Effortless Entertaining

FINE FOOD

A directory of the best
and where to find it in
England, Wales and Scotland

Compiled by Simone Sekers

Hodder & Stoughton

LONDON SYDNEY AUCKLAND TORONTO

British Library Cataloguing in Publication Data
Sekers, Simone
 Fine food: a directory of the best
 and where to find it in England,
 Wales and Scotland.
 1. Food industry and trade – Great
 Britain – Directories
 I. Title
 338.7'6413'002514   HD9011.3
 ISBN 0-340-39071-9

Copyright © 1987 by Simone Sekers. First printed 1987. All rights reserved. No part of this publication may be reproduced or transmitted in any form or by any means, electronically or mechanically, including photocopying, recording or any information storage or retrieval system, without either the prior permission in writing from the publisher or a licence, permitting restricted copying, issued by the Copyright Licensing Agency, 7 Ridgmount Street, London WC1E 7AE. Printed in Great Britain for Hodder & Stoughton Limited, Mill Road, Dunton Green, Sevenoaks, Kent by T. J. Press (Padstow) Limited, Padstow, Cornwall. Photoset by Rowland Phototypesetting Limited, Bury St Edmunds, Suffolk. Hodder & Stoughton Editorial Office: 47 Bedford Square, London WC1B 3DP.

Acknowledgments

There are so many people who gave their time and support to the compilation of this book. Most notably I would like to thank the following: Jane Grigson, for her kindness in allowing me to make use of her book *The Observer Guide to British Cookery*, and for her further suggestions; Shona Crawford Poole, Sara Paston-Williams, Peter Bazalgette, Bobby Freeman, Michael Smith, Alan Porter and Lynda Brown. Also Ruth Goodwin of the British Goat Society, Jasmine Barley of the Goat Producers Association, and Olivia Mills of the British Sheep Dairying Association, Diana Zeuner of the Association of Independent Museums, Bridget Yates (Norfolk Rural Life Museum), Michael Thomas (Avoncroft Museum of Buildings), Pamela Sambrook (Staffordshire County Museum), Mark Suggit (York Castle Museum), Peter Brears (Leeds City Museum). Finally, but equally importantly, all my friends and relatives whose indefatigable observation and disinterested sampling made this book possible.

Contents

Introduction	9
How to use this book	13
Wine and beer	13
A note on prices	14
A note on terms	14
THE SOUTH-WEST	
Cornwall, Devon, Somerset and Avon, Dorset, Wiltshire, Gloucestershire	16
SOUTHERN ENGLAND	
Hampshire and the Isle of Wight, Berkshire, Oxfordshire, Buckinghamshire	59
LONDON AND THE SOUTH-EAST	
London, Surrey, Kent, Sussex	71
WALES	91
THE WEST MIDLANDS	
Hereford and Worcester, Warwickshire, Shropshire, Staffordshire	101
THE EAST MIDLANDS	
Northamptonshire, Leicestershire, Derbyshire, Nottinghamshire, Lincolnshire	122
EASTERN ENGLAND	
Essex, Suffolk, Cambridgeshire, Norfolk	137
THE NORTH-WEST	
Cheshire and Greater Manchester, Lancashire	159
THE NORTH-EAST	
Yorkshire and Humberside	174
NORTHERN ENGLAND	
Cumbria (including I.o.M.), Northumberland (including Tyne & Wear and Durham)	188
SCOTLAND	207
Useful organisations	223
Maps	224–34
Shops	235
Mail Order Index	235
Product Index	236

Introduction

This book is a personal guide to some of the best food producers in the country. It is based on an enormous amount of research, and a great deal of patience and time contributed by friends and colleagues. I myself shopped, tasted, judged, sought second and even third opinions, and then badgered others to do the same. My family ate their way through quantities of pork pies and sausages, grumbling about their expanding waistlines (although these grumbles were mysteriously set aside when it came to tasting chocolates) and complaining that the fridge and larder were always overflowing with dozens of different cheeses, or kippers, or even smoked salmon – but where was the milk for breakfast?

Fortunately, this back-up team of family and friends were familiar with the zealous gleam in my eye – it has appeared for my previous books on food, and appears regularly for the articles I write for *The Antique Collector* which involve trying out some very strange dishes indeed, in the interests of research. So they good-humouredly joined in the search for good food and we had happy weekends and holidays ferreting out shy ham-producers, flamboyant rare-breed farmers and delightful cider- and cheese-makers. We rejected twice as many as I have included in this book; those included range from small-scale goats' cheese producers to large-scale chocolate manufacturers – the only criterion is excellence.

Many of the food producers are reviving old regional foods. Some have been producing their particular speciality for years and generations, abiding by the old ways and traditions because there is clearly a market for them – albeit a purely local one. These producers were often surprised at an approach to appear in a book, feeling often that 'those in the area know about us already, and we don't feel that those outside the area would be interested', as one Yorkshire baker explained to me. But a source of dry-cured bacon is something to be shared, particularly among those who have little alternative to the wet mass-produced rashers that snivel, rather than sizzle, in the frying-pan. Others are producing 'new' foods, and it is these producers who often have a greater following outside their area. I found this to be especially true in the North, where traditional food is alive and well and appreciated by the locals, but unusual products such as smoked goats' cheese, venison sausages, gravad lax or taramasalata are often better known at the other end of the country. The visitors who come and holiday in the hotels and eat in the fine restaurants which serve the 'new' foods go away having developed a taste for them; a postal link is forged, the message spreads, but more often at a 100-mile radius than a five-mile one.

Some resourceful people are combining the regional traditional with new techniques. Bar Woodall, producer of very traditional Cumberland hams, found that this was being served raw and thinly sliced, like Parma ham, in one London hotel. He saw the potential at once, perfected a special cure and now produces a superlative air-dried ham. Vacuum-packing, as well as freezing, means that perishable foods can be sent safely from one end of the country to the other. This might mean that the term 'regional' loses some of its exclusivity, but at least it familiarises a wider public with the best food that Britain has to offer.

This book would have been very long indeed if I had included all the excellent wine-makers and brewers whose products we enjoyed on our trips round the country. But the growing number of English wine-makers deserve a book to themselves, written by someone particularly knowledgeable on the subject, and the brewers have their own *Real Ale Guide* already. Nor have I included shops and markets, although their role is a vital one in distributing good food – there are books which do this too. This is a book about the people who actually produce the food, who do their best to stem the tide of what the French so aptly term *banalisation*, or mass-production. It is this sort of banal food that most of us buy when we go on a weekly trip to the supermarket, when we want, or need, to eat cheaply and quickly. But it is a great deal more fun to combine a weekend shopping trip with a walk in the country, to stop in a market or at a farm shop and buy free-range eggs, farmhouse butter and cheese, organically grown fruit and vegetables, hormone-free meat.

I have gained enormous respect and admiration for those who work so hard to provide us all with real food in the face of much more profitable *banalisation*. It isn't easy to continue producing fine food on a small scale, when offered temptations by supermarket chains to produce not pounds, but tons of pâté, or cheese, or jam. Most refuse, however, knowing that there is a small but growing market for additive-free, flavour-full food. I hope that this book will help to enlarge the market still further.

Simone Sekers. Styal, Cheshire, November 1986

How to Use This Book

Britain has been divided into regions, and each region into counties – if you plan to visit a region, then simply reading that section should give you a reasonable idea of the food producers to be found in it, county by county. The introduction to each region will give an overall idea of what sort of thing to expect – and an asterisk * by a name denotes that that product is listed in the forthcoming pages. Each entry gives details of how to find the place described, and a telephone number, as well as a name to contact. It is *always* advisable to telephone first, to check on the availability of the product – many are seasonal – and on whether the producer is going to be there. And, also, to check on that producer's continued existence. Whilst every effort has been made to check this before going to press, it is a sad fact that not all these people will be able to weather the storms of a sometimes precarious method of earning a living. Where possible, or relevant, there is a short list of stockists, and whether or not you can buy by post. Vacuum packing and lightweight insulated containers have extended enormously the range of foods available by mail order. The cost of postage can be very high, but is still sometimes worth it, as I have discovered in buying truckles of farmhouse Cheddar – and you can often defray the cost by sharing an order with friends.

Indexes at the back list good food shops, useful addresses, and also list the entries by product type, by brand name, and by the producer's name.

Wine and Beer

I have not gone into any great detail about either of these; English wine is a growth area, and needs the sort of guide that I am not equipped to write. There are already good beer and pub guides and I don't think that this book needs to duplicate those – it is enough to say that there is a great deal of very good beer available, brewed by small breweries all round the country.

INTRODUCTION

A Note on Prices or the Absence Thereof

To give prices, or even price guides, in a book of this sort presents problems to everyone – producer, customer, publisher and author. They change quickly and changes can cause friction. Be prepared to find that the prices for most of the foods in this book are higher than for similar mass-produced items found in supermarkets, and then you will be pleasantly surprised. Good food costs more, but invariably represents better value for money.

A Note on Terms

Conservation grade – applied to flour and grain, refers to that not wholly organically grown, possibly by a farmer who is in the process of changing over to organic methods.

Cyder – is not an olde Englishe spelling of cider; it often refers to cider made from the first pressing of the apples; virgin cider, if you like, as in olive oil.

Extensive – as opposed to intensive; often used when referring to animals kept free-range and allowed to graze or browse at will.

Farm fresh – has specific meaning in relation to poultry. It means the fowl has been reared to fuller maturity, and therefore flavour, hung for at least a week before plucking, and processed by hand without added water or chemicals. Well worth paying a little extra for.

Farmhouse – I rarely refer to farmhouse with a capital F in this book, for the following reason. Along with words such as 'Heritage' and 'Traditional', 'Farmhouse' is used by Dairy Crest (the manufacturing and marketing arm of the Milk Marketing Board) to describe their own cheeses which are mass-produced, using milk from many herds in the area rather than the milk of a single herd belonging to the farm on which the cheese is made. In fact the MMB is charged by the British

Academy of Gastronomes (President Egon Ronay) with refusing to support the makers of traditional farmhouse cheeses, of refusing to market their products, and of claiming misleading names to describe their cheeses.

THE SOUTH-WEST

Cornwall
—
Devon
—
Somerset and Avon
—
Dorset
—
Wiltshire
—
Gloucestershire

If I could choose to settle in a part of the country simply for the food it produces, then I should pick the south-west. It is not surprising that this area should contain so many fine restaurants: Riverside at Helford in Cornwall, the Carved Angel in Dartmouth, the Horn of Plenty near Tavistock, the Hole in the Wall in Bath, Thornbury Castle near Bristol and Beechfield House near Melksham form a chain of excellence the length and breadth of this large region, which helps and encourages the good food producers to be found here.

The rich pastures produce rich milk, which is turned into clotted and ice cream, and some of the best of the British farmhouse cheeses, both new and traditional. These same pastures also produce good meat, and several farmers are working hard to produce superlative meat, often from old breeds, without using additives of any sort. Allowed to roam freely, Anne Petch's* rare breed pigs – Tamworths, Gloucester Old Spots, Middle Whites, Large Blacks, Berkshires – are turned into outstanding hams, bacon and sausages. Seeing the pigs, you are not surprised that they should yield good meat – a Tamworth with the sunlight picking out the red-gold glow of its hide is one of the finest sights you can imagine. These animals all possess the proper proportion of fat to lean, to achieve tenderness, and are allowed to grow on slowly, at their own pace, to develop flavour. Mrs Petch sends her pigs to a small local abattoir to avoid stress; apart from the obvious benefit to the animal, this lack of stress improves the quality of the meat. Anyone who has deplored the intensively reared fatless pork which is sold on the mass market should try a joint from a Large Black (don't be put off by the colour of the rind, it makes superb crackling), or chops from a Tamworth. Trim off the fat before eating, if you must, but it *should*, indeed *must*, be there while the meat cooks. Christopher Murray*, near Barnstaple, sells his hormone-free lamb, beef and pork by mail order only, but encourages parties of schoolchildren to visit his farm to learn that agriculture, conservation and humane conditions can go together; in Wiltshire, the Guys* have formed an admirable group, called the Real Meat Co.*, to act as an umbrella organisation for both farmers and butchers.

Cheese is one of the glories of this area, which boasts good goats' and ewes' milk cheeses as well as new cheeses like those made by the Charnleys of Park Farm, Umberleigh*. Robin Congdon is making Beenleigh Blue* from ewes' milk, near Totnes, and Tony Udall and Peter White are making Coleford Blue* from ewes' milk near Taunton. Vulscombe goats' cheese* is made from unpasteurised milk, the goats browsing on old permanent pastures near Tiverton. But perhaps the finest cheeses of all are those truly traditional farmhouse (note the small 'f') Cheddars, made on small farms in Somerset where the milk from the farms' own herds is unpasteurised, and the cows graze on undisturbed pastures – I make no apologies for including five such producers in this chapter. Each of the cheeses is subtly different, as the soil and herbage change from mile to mile; here you can indulge in a real Cheddar treasure hunt.

The problem many of these small food producers have is that of marketing their products. Devon Fare is a group formed by the producers themselves, to promote and distribute their excellent products. Anne Petch is a member, so are Peter and Hilary Charnley, who make Devon Garland and Satterleigh cheeses, the Stapletons*, who produce, among many good things, live unsweetened fresh fruit yoghurt, and Gillian Pearkes* with her Devon red wine, and cyder. The address of Devon Fare is on page 223.

In Cornwall, one of the champions of the small food producer is Alan Paston-Williams, the National Trust's catering manager for Cornwall (the only Trust region to boast such a position); he takes particular trouble to use good local products in the Trust's Cornish restaurants and tea-rooms, which has helped them gain entries in the good food guides. The trifle at Trerice is one of the best I have ever eaten, and Cotehele's cream teas are as idyllic as the place itself.

It is sad, however, that such a region is cursed with the fast-buck mediocrity of tourist catering, despite the number of superlative restaurants, which are accessible to the 'serious' eaters, prepared to book in advance and pay the rather higher prices that such excellence deserves. For the casual visitor with children in tow, things are very different – cream teas are often the best meals on offer, but why are there so few fish suppers? Or lobster lunches? Fish abounds here, but it is usually best to buy it and take it home to cook in your caravan or holiday cottage, rather than to look for a simple lunch of fresh grilled mackerel washed down with local cider. There are a few gleams of hope, however – try morning coffee elegantly served in Bath's beautiful Assembly Rooms, with Bath Buns freshly brought in from Cobbs'* bakery, or tea at the American Museum at Claverton, where the queue can be tedious, but the cakes and cookies freshly baked to traditional American recipes are absolutely wonderful, and can be eaten outside on the terrace overlooking one of the best landscapes anywhere.

CORNWALL

Bersey's ewes' milk cheeses

Sheviock Barton, Torpoint, Cornwall
Tel. St Germans (0503) 30793
GEOFFREY T BERSEY

Mr Bersey has developed these ewes' milk cheeses for two reasons – the difficulties of making a living from cow dairying since the milk quotas were introduced, and, more importantly, his commitment to organic principles. *Sheviock* is a full fat hard cheese, subtly flavoured with cider; *Ladywell* is a soft textured cheese. Neither contains any artificial additives or flavourings, and both are made with non-animal rennet. The cheeses are available from major delicatessens and food stores, from the farm dairy, and from: Bersey's Rural Shopping Centre, Tideford, Saltash, Cornwall, Tel. Landrake (075 538) 777. Visitors are welcome to watch the sheep being milked, a process which takes place between 8 and 10a.m., from January to August. Although the milking is seasonal, the cheese is available throughout the year. The dairy is in the middle of Sheviock village, which is on the A374 Torpoint road.

Apple Blossom Cider

*The Cornish Cider Co.,
Trevean Farm, Coombe Kea,
Truro, Cornwall
Tel. Truro (0872) 77177*
JOHN WATT

John Watt learned wine-making in Tuscany and Bordeaux during the 1960s, then, as he says, 'returned to my native Cornwall in the early 70s complete with new wife and French cider press.' He believes that the cider industry, like the wine industry, produces quantities of 'plonk' for the undiscerning drinker, but that the good name of the industry is preserved by the small producers who make a traditional farmhouse cider for those interested enough to seek them out.

His *Apple Blossom Cider* is made from a variety of cider apples including Kingston Black, and he keeps the output under 20,000 gallons a year: 'I consider that gallonage in excess of 20,000 gallons is of the "industrial" variety, and unlikely to be so good!' His cider is sold in the National Trust restaurants in Cornwall, and can be bought in local shops, off-licences and pubs. But for the discerning cider drinker who is prepared to buy 4½ gallons or more, the cider is sold from Beach Cottage, Coombe Kea, Truro – take the A39 road from Truro to Falmouth, then take the first left to Calenick, follow signs to Combe; Beach Cottage is 200 yards along the foreshore road on the right.

The Cornish Scrumpy Co. Ltd

*Callestock Cider Farm,
Penhallow, Truro, Cornwall
Tel. Truro (0872) 573356*
DAVID HEALEY

Mr Healey's own words best describe the evolution of his cider: 'My wife and I used to own an off-licence in Mevagissey. We used to buy hogsheads of cider from the local farmers and bottle it into our own containers in the courtyard behind the shop. However, one summer we completely dried out our suppliers, and in order to maintain both quantity and quality we decided to make it ourselves.' Their first brew was made in barrels bought from a bankrupt whisky firm. 'The resultant cider was pretty heady stuff. Our logo was thus coined – "legless but smiling!"' The cider is still and very strong, filtered but not pasteurised, and it's best when treated like a wine. Distribution is mainly wholesale to the local Cornish market, but there are retail outlets as far afield as Cumbria, the Shetland Isles, and Cleveland. Or the cider can be bought directly from the farm – the pressing season is obviously linked with the apple harvest: September to December. Opening times are 9a.m.–6p.m. from March to

December; the cider farm is ½ mile off the A3075, Newquay to Truro road. Turn off at the Mithian/Callestick crossroads at Penhallow towards Callestick.

The Cornish Smoked Fish Co. Ltd

*Charlestown, St Austell,
Cornwall PL25 3NY
Tel. St Austell (0726) 72356*

MARTIN PUMPHREY

The company was formed in 1971 to smoke the mackerel which was then plentiful off the Cornish coast. As the mackerel supply dwindled, so the company has gradually diversified and now smokes salmon, trout, cod's roe, kippers, chicken and pheasant. Available to order are scallops, smoked salmon pâté, smoked sprats, smoked trout pâté, and cold-cured and smoked trout and mackerel, both of which can be served in thin slices, like smoked salmon. A mail order service is available (telephone the ansaphone service), and personal callers are welcome at the retail shop, open Monday to Friday, 8a.m.–5p.m., 100 yards north of the dock at Charlestown.

Furniss's Cornish Fairings

*Furniss & Co. Ltd,
15 New Bridge Street, Truro,
Cornwall TR1 2AB
Tel. Truro (0872) 72064/71425*

J V SMITH (MANAGING DIRECTOR)

All those who have ever spent a holiday in Cornwall must have brought tins of Cornish Fairings back with them. For me, the first taste revives memories of those holidays at once – we used to eat them spread with clotted cream (we used to eat *everything* spread with clotted cream). It's nice to know that these spicy ginger biscuits are still made to the same 40-year-old recipe, and still come in the same packaging. They contain no additives at all, and nor do any of the other biscuits and sweets made by Furniss & Co. Production is on the site of the company's original bakery, opened in 1886. Once out of the south-west, you might find these easier to buy in Europe and the Middle East than in the rest of the UK, unless you go to specialist grocers in London, like Harrods or Fortnums. This adds to their charm; they really are a local treat. Available in local supermarkets and grocers, in National Trust and other gift shops.

Lynher Valley Dairy

*Netherton Farm, Upton Cross, Liskeard,
Cornwall DL14 5BD
Tel. Liskeard (0579) 62244*

D E HORRELL

Although the three cheeses made on Netherton Farm are relative newcomers, they have been developed using traditional processes. *Cornish Yarg* is a mould ripened cheese which is wrapped in nettles – an old English method which gives the cheese a particular identity and a lovely 'green' flavour. *Cornish Pepper* is a full fat soft cheese coated with cracked black peppercorns, and *Cornish Herb & Garlic* is the same cheese mixed with six herbs and garlic – both cheeses are full flavoured in their own right, and this combined with the flavourings gives them great character. All three are made from the milk of the farm's pedigree Friesian herd, and a vegetable coagulant is used instead of animal rennet. The farm itself is on the estate of the Duchy of Cornwall, and has been farmed by the Horrells for three generations. The cheeses are sold through good cheese shops round the country, including Paxton & Whitfield, Neal's Yard Dairy, and Harrods in London, and in Wells Stores, Streatley, Berkshire. They are also available by mail order. Callers are welcome at the farm, which is near Upton Cross on the B3254 between Liskeard and Launceston.

M & C Provis – sausages

Leat House, Church Hill, Port Isaac, North Cornwall PL29 3RW
Tel. Port Isaac (020 888) 0258
MARK AND CAROL PROVIS

The friends who recommended the Provis's sausages said quite simply that they were the best in the world – certainly people travel long distances to buy them. Hand-made, with a high pork, low fat content, the recipe is a family secret, but additives are kept to a minimum. The Provis's also sell their own cured ham, beef and tongue. They supply the local hotels, cafés, restaurants and inns, and have a country round. The shop is open from 9a.m.–5p.m. Monday to Saturday in the winter, with half days on Wednesday and Saturday. From Easter to the end of September, the hours are 8a.m.–6p.m. all week, with no half days. The shop is forty yards' walk from the harbour to the bottom of Church Hill, on the left.

Rodda's Clotted Cream

The Creamery, Scorrier, Redruth, Cornwall TR16 5BU
Tel. Redruth (0209) 820526
PHILIP RODDA

Although this is one of the largest independent creameries in Cornwall, it is still run in the traditional family way, by Willie and Eric, the sons of the founder, and their wives. Methods have changed a great deal since the Rodda family made clotted cream in their farmhouse kitchen in the 1870s, and modern methods of production ensure that the cream stays fresh for long enough for it to be sent in perfect condition all over the country. Despite these new methods, the only ingredient is the pure milk from local farms, and the flavour is rich and buttery. One friend, flying to America recently, was delighted to find the cream he had just been enjoying while on holiday was being offered to him on board the aircraft. But Mr Rodda told me that marketing his cream in the USA had proved almost impossible – the Americans didn't like the word 'clotted' and the patriotic Cornish were unwilling to call it by any other name. And clotted cream apparently does not sell well in the north of England either – why, I can't think, since nothing goes better with a piece of freshly baked parkin. Rodda's cream was served at the wedding breakfast of Prince Charles and Lady Diana Spencer, and is sent weekly to one of the Royal households. Fortunately for the rest of us, clotted cream travels well packed in insulated containers, and Rodda's will send their cream anywhere in the country, and even organise a standing order for you if you would like to make a habit of enjoying this truly Cornish treat. It is widely distributed throughout Cornwall and Devon, and can be bought from the farm itself between 8a.m.–4.30p.m. Scorrier is just off the A3047, about 4 miles north of Redruth.

Roskilly Clotted Cream

Tregellast Barton, St Keverne, Helston, Cornwall TR12 6NX
Tel. St Keverne (0326) 280479
J B ROSKILLY

I make no excuse for including another clotted cream producer. The Roskillys' cream is produced on a much smaller scale than that of the Roddas, and from the sort of farm we all like to imagine when we think of the product – 130 acres of the Lizard peninsula, where the herd of eighty Channel Island cows ('Guernseys for the deep golden colour, Jerseys for the rich cream') graze on 'beautiful green Cornish pastures, unadulterated by any artificial fertilisers or weed killers'. It is to these pastures that Rachel Roskilly attributes the deliciously nutty flavour of the cream. One of the best

ROSKILLY CREAM
Available direct from the farm
TREGELLAST BARTON,
ST. KEVERNE.
Tel: St. Keverne 280479
Or from most shops on The Lizard Peninsula

ways to enjoy it is to stay in one of the cottages which are to let on the farm, and watch the cream being made. It is widely distributed to local shops, there is a very good mail order service, and callers are welcome at the farm, *except* between 2p.m.–5p.m. daily. To find Tregellast Barton, take the Lizard road from Helston, turning off to St Keverne (B3298) at the roundabout at the end of Culdrose Naval Airstation. Follow this road for 8 miles. Go through St Keverne Square, leaving the war memorial on your left. Immediately out of the square turn up to the right, past the school. After ¼ mile take a right turn, the farm is on the left.

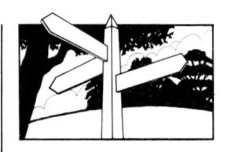

DEVON

Beenleigh Blue and Harbourne Blue ewes' and goats' milk cheeses

*Lower Sharpham Barton,
Ashprington, Totnes, Devon
Tel. Harbertonford (080 423) 702
(evenings)*

ROBIN CONGDON AND SARIE COOPER

Robin Congdon has been milking sheep on his steep, 100-acre grassland farm on the banks of the River Dart for nine years, and has been making *Beenleigh Blue* for five of them. It is only available in limited quantities, between August and December, and its rarity has gained it a following well outside its locality. *Harbourne Blue*, made with bought-in goats' milk, is made all the year round, although again in limited quantities. Both these cheeses, and their soft cheeses and yoghurt, are made in the couple's own shop in Totnes, where they also promote the sale of fresh locally produced food with an emphasis on farmhouse cheeses. Their own dairy products are all organically produced. Buy the cheeses from: Dartington Farm Food Shop, Cider Press Centre, Dartington, Totnes; Country Pannier (market stall), Newton Abbot; James's, 188 Beckenham High Street, Beckenham, Kent; Wells Stores, Streatley, Berkshire; Cookery Nook, Church Street, Pershore, Worcestershire. Or from Robin Congdon and Sarie Cooper's own shop – 1 Ticklemore Street, Totnes, Tel. Totnes (0803) 865926.

Blackdown Farm goats' dairy produce

*Loddiswell, Kingsbridge, Devon
Tel. Gara Bridge (054 882) 387*

RICHARD MARTIN

Richard Martin is helped by his parents in producing goats' dairy products which are well distributed in South Devon. Fresh goats' milk, yoghurt, both soft and hard cheeses are available at any time from the farm, where the Martins also have rare breeds of cattle. Kid meat is also available to order. Look for Blackdown Farm products at the following Devon shops: Maid Marian, Fore Street, Kingsbridge; Salcombe Health Foods, and Lindy's, Salcombe; Cookes (delicatessen), Walnut Road, Chelston, Torquay; Crisp & Green, Foss Street, Dartmouth; Cranks, High Street, Totnes. Blackdown Farm itself is 2½ miles north of Loddiswell on the B3196 which connects Kingsbridge with the A38 – there is a sign at Blackdown Cross.

Budleigh Salterton Pâté

*Perriams Place, Budleigh Salterton,
Devon EX9 6LY
Tel. Budleigh Salterton (039 54) 3487
(Ansaphone)*

GRAHAM AND BERYL WORRALL

This small company has made a name for itself in the few years since the

Worralls bought the business in 1979. It all started with chicken liver pâté made to a Strasbourg recipe and brought to Budleigh by Major R G Scott in 1947. He made the pâté in his own house, and it rapidly gained popularity in the area. Graham Worrall trained as a food technologist, and gained experience with several large food companies before setting out in partnership with his wife to produce high quality foods without additives or preservatives. Their range

BUDLEIGH SALTERTON
POTTED CHICKEN LIVER WITH BUTTER

Major R. G. Scott's Original Strasbourg Recipe

Ingredients: Chicken Liver, Butter, Herbs & Spices

2¾ lb 1.25 Kg

SERVE COOL   KEEP REFRIGERATED
MADE IN DEVON
TO MAJOR SCOTT'S ORIGINAL RECIPE

BUDLEIGH SALTERTON PÂTÉ
Perriams Place, Budleigh Salterton
Devon EX9 6LY   Tel. (039 54) 3487

now includes, as well as the *chicken liver pâté* still made to Major Scott's recipe, *crab* and *mackerel pâtés* and, marketed under the name of 'Otter Vale', some delicious chutneys and jellies. *Onion and Pineapple Chutney* is Graham's own recipe and is particularly good with cheese or ham;

Spiced Fruit and *Honey and Peppers* are both interesting and original. The jellies include *Quince and Orange* and *Elderberry*. The Worralls also make traditional, round, muslin-wrapped *Christmas puddings*. All these products are available by post (via the Kitchen Shop, Fore Street, Budleigh Salterton), and from good delicatessens in most towns in Devon and neighbouring counties. There is no distribution to supermarkets, as the Worralls prefer to stay small and keep the quality high.

Capton Vineyard fruit liqueurs

Dittisham Fruit Farm, Capton, nr Dartmouth, Devon TQ6 0JE
Tel. Blackawton (080 421) 452

MR & MRS D J LLOYD

Mr and Mrs Lloyd started the production of their pure fruit liqueurs in 1979 when a sudden thunderstorm rendered 300lbs of raspberries, ready for market, useless for resale: from these they made the initial batch of *Framboise* liqueur. Since then they have developed *Cassis* and *Fraisia* from their own blackcurrants and strawberries. All the liqueurs are hand-made, without preservatives or colourings, and the fruit is cold-pressed as heating destroys the flavour and vitamin content. The Lloyds also grow a wide range of fruit and vegetables for distribution to high quality restaurants and shops, and for callers who pick their own in the summer. Asparagus, herbs (including Mediterranean parsley), globe artichokes, Italian spinach, French lettuces, broad, runner and French beans, new and maincrop potatoes,

THE SOUTH-WEST

raspberries, strawberries, tayberries, loganberries, gooseberries, red and blackcurrants are all available in their respective seasons. Various specialist vegetables are also available on request. But perhaps the most interesting of their fruit is the famous *Dittisham Plum*, reputedly brought to the area from Germany by a retired seaman in the early eighteenth century, and which has flourished here now for 250 years. Mid-August is the time when visitors come from far and wide to collect the plums, which make the most delicious jam, and freeze well. Add to this cornucopia the Capton Vineyard table wine, and perhaps a visit to their prehistoric hill settlement museum, and you have the perfect day out. The fruit farm is open seven days a week, 9.30a.m.–7p.m., from May to October. The village of Capton is signed from the Sportsmans Arms on the Totnes to Dartmouth road.

DEVON RASPBERRY LIQUEUR

Produced and Bottled at
Capton Vineyard Dartmouth
South Devon

Contents 35 cl.   43° Proof

Crowdy Mill stoneground flour and grain products

Crowdy Mill, Harbertonford, Totnes, Devon TQ9 7HU
Tel. Harbertonford (080 423) 340

MARTIN WATTS (MILLER)

Martin Watts has a background in architecture and building conservation, with a long-standing interest in wind and water mills, and in natural sources of power. He spent three years as curator at Worsbrough Mill Museum in South Yorkshire, and

Stoneground Flour
85% BROWN FLOUR

Crowdy Mill   Harbertonford   Totnes   Devon

1.5 kg   3.31 lbs

Best before:

was then given the opportunity to repair Crowdy Mill, and put it to work again after twenty-eight years of disuse. It has now been in production for two years, providing a growing market with stoneground flour from locally grown English grains, ground by the original millstones. Once the repair work is finally completed, the three sets of millstones, grain cleaning and flour dressing machinery will all be water-powered: 'all the equipment used is traditional, as I believe that conservation and commerce on this scale can go hand-in-hand'.

Wholemeal, brown flour, unbleached white flour, semolina, bran and *100% rye flour* are all available from the mill, where customers are welcome during the working week, and particularly welcome on weekday afternoons (at other times by prior arrangement). The mill is located downstream of the village of Harbertonford, along Bow Road (on the A381, about 4 miles south of Totnes).

Dart Valley preserves and marmalades

Dart Valley Foods,
Unit 3, Cadleigh Close, Lee Mill,
Ivybridge, Devon PL21 9PE
Tel. Plymouth (0752) 794795
DAVID HAWKES

The business began by chance, following a delivery of eggs to a local farm food shop; David Hawkes and his partner were asked to make lemon curd, which they did, on the kitchen cooker. The demand outgrew the kitchen's capacity, so a small industrial unit was leased. With this extra space came the creation of more products and more varieties, and now, ten years after that first batch of lemon curd, Dart Valley Foods is housed in a factory unit built to its own specifications. Despite this and 'a lovely filling machine and a machine for putting the caps on', it is still a hand-made product free from artificial preservatives, colourings or any other additives. The marmalades and preserves are 'still cooked the same as on the kitchen stove, hand stirred with lots of love'. I particularly liked the *Orange Marmalade with Cider* and the *Cider Apple Jam*, and, of course, the lemon curd. The packaging is charming. Sales are wholesale, mail order, and to personal callers Monday to Friday, 9a.m.–5p.m. Ivybridge is about 7 miles from Plymouth towards Buckfastleigh on the A38.

Devon Herbs

Thorn Cottage, Burn Lane, Brentor,
Nr Tavistock, Devon PL19 0ND
Tel. Mary Tavy (082 281) 285
H F AND S A WETHERBEE

The Wetherbees started to grow herbs originally because Sally Wetherbee, a home economist and cookery demonstrator, was unable to find fresh herbs locally for her work. They realised that there was a real need for such a service in the area, and grew to meet it, providing both herb plants and fresh-cut herbs, all organically grown, fragrant and culinary, to many retail outlets in the Tavistock area, including the National Trust shop at Lydford Gorge. But they also do a small amount by mail order, and sell to personal callers from 1 April to 30 September, Thursday, Friday and Saturday, 2–6p.m. They are situated 1 mile north-east of Brentor village on the road to West Blackdown.

Devon Larder Recipes

Granary Cottage, Whitehall, Hemyock,
Devon (Head Office)
Tel. Hemyock (0823) 680347
MRS KATHLEEN THOMAS

The story of Country Larders is an interesting and a heartening one, demonstrating just how much demand there is for traditional country pies, freshly baked, using the best available ingredients. Mrs Thomas started the business fifteen years ago 'to try and put country food back on the market'. It quickly became so successful that demand spread far beyond the area which a fresh pie can reasonably expect to travel, so the idea of licensing other people to set up 'Larders' in other parts of the country was born. The company is now in the middle of a major expansion and hopes to have at least a dozen more units opening in the very near future, with a new central kitchen at Bradninch, near Exeter, where prospective entrants to its franchise group will be trained. Mrs Thomas herself was for ten years cookery editor of *Farmers' Weekly*, during which time she was able to gather a mass of knowledge about traditional country recipes. One of Country Larders' most popular products is *Figgy Sly*, an old West Country recipe in which mixed fruit, walnuts and chopped figs are packed into a sweet pastry case and topped with a thin sugary crust. *Stuffed Chicken Pie*, *Game Pie* and *Clovelly Chicken* are included in the range, as well as sweet and savoury flans, fruit tarts, cheesecakes, regional sausages and English country desserts. Ring Mrs Thomas on the above number if you would like to find out if there is a *Country Larder* in your area (and see page 162). The central kitchen address is: Halthaies, Bradninch, Exeter, Tel. Exeter (0392) 881187.

Eveleigh Jersey dairy produce

Eveleighs, Cruwys Morchard, Tiverton, Devon EX16 8LB
Tel. Tiverton (0884) 257510
NORA M BISHOP

Miss Bishop established her cream business in 1983 as a means of achieving her ambition to own a herd of Jersey cows and have a farm-orientated way of life. The untreated Jersey cream is produced by separating the top quality Jersey milk by means of an electrically-powered cream separator; in turn this can be processed one step further by scalding and cooling to produce clotted cream (thus in effect heat-treating the product to obtain a more distinctive flavour and improved keeping qualities). No additives are necessary. The cream is produced all year round with little seasonal variation, except in the demand, which is greatest during the summer holidays and around Christmas, so Miss Bishop subsidises her farming activities by her part-time job with a local firm of auctioneers. She is happy to progress slowly at building up a pedigree herd, expanding the cream market at every opportunity, but always striving to maintain the production of her top quality product. Personal callers are welcome 'at all reasonable times', but telephone orders are appreciated; otherwise Eveleigh Jersey cream can be bought from: Nomansland Stores, Nomansland, Tiverton; Thelbridge Cross Inn, Thelbridge, Crediton; Garden Centre Tea Rooms, East Street, Tiverton, all in Devon. Eveleighs is located on the A373 approximately 6 miles from both Tiverton and Witheridge.

Foxfire ewes' milk yoghurt

*Waterloo Farm, Clayhidon,
Cullompton, Devon EX15 3TN
Tel. Hemyock (0823) 680273*

COMMANDER AND MRS A G TROTTER

Commander Trotter, a veteran of the Falklands War, retired from the Navy in 1983 to follow a more peaceful career – that of farming dairy sheep. He and his wife, Yvonne, had always been interested in farming, and now combine a livery service, bed and breakfast, and haymaking on ten acres with their ewes' milk and yoghurt production. Such is the demand for these products that the Trotters recently went to considerable trouble and expense to improve the milk yield of their British Friesland herd by importing two Friesland rams from Holland (the first to be imported for over twenty years). Ewes' milk freezes well – 'people come here and buy a hundred pints at a time to put in their deep-freeze' – and the demand for ewes' milk yoghurt has grown since people have developed a taste for it while on holiday in Greece and Turkey – it is wonderfully rich and creamy and goes very well indeed with Devonshire honey. Mrs Trotter used to take Foxfire yoghurt to London, where stores like Fortnum & Mason 'sold it at a premium', but now the trip has become so expensive, and local demand so good that such distribution is no longer economic or necessary. It is now distributed to thirty retail outlets within the Trotters' delivery area on the Somerset/Devon border. Personal callers are welcome, but preferably by appointment. Waterloo Farm is 4 miles from Junction 26 on the M5.

Head Mill Trout Farm

*Head Mill, Umberleigh, Devon EX37 9HA
Tel. Chulmleigh (0769) 80862*

ROBIN AND CAROLINE BOA

The Boas are refugees from London, where Robin was an accountant and Caroline a public relations consultant. They were both disenchanted with working for other people, and with food which was full of additives, so decided to combat both evils by farming trout in this beautiful corner of North Devon. The trout are reared in water which comes straight from Exmoor, and the Boas feel that the granite gives the fish especial flavour. Some of the trout are slowly *smoked* over oak, and the *pâté* made from these smoked fish contains quark cheese from the local farm dairy; the *smoked trout fillets* are entirely boneless. *Potted trout* consists of fresh cooked trout covered with a layer of sorrel, tarragon and parsley, sealed with clarified butter. The products are available by mail order, from the farm shop itself, and supplied to hotels locally, and in London. There is also a wholesale service to shops. However, the Boas feel that the future for the small producer of high quality food lies in selling direct to the public, and to this end have formed a group of eight food and drink makers committed to humane farming techniques, traditional growing methods and high standards of production, using natural ingredients. Details of this group, called *Devon Fare*, can be obtained from Robin and Caroline Boa at the address above. Christmas hampers are available, containing products from all the Devon Fare producers (see pages 18,

223 for other members of this group). The Mill itself is open from 9a.m.–6p.m. every day except at Christmas. To find it, see details for Heal Farm, below.

Heal Farm Quality Traditional Meats

Heal Farm, Kings Nympton, Umberleigh, Devon EX37 9TB
Tel. South Molton (076 95) 2077
ANNE PETCH

While doing the research for this book, I and my family and our friends tasted hundreds of different makes of sausage, ham and bacon and found that our tastes varied widely – but we were unanimous about the quality of all the products from Heal Farm. Mrs Petch's secret lies in the meat which goes into her products, as well as the natural flavourings and the total lack of additives. All the pork comes from the Heal Farm traditional breeds of pig – Middle Whites, Gloucester Old Spots, Tamworths and Berkshires – which are reared non-intensively, without the aid of growth-promoters, and fed on specially mixed food which contains no hormones or antibiotics. Furthermore, the pigs are taken to a small local abattoir, where great care is taken to avoid the stressful slaughtering conditions involved in long journeys to large abattoirs. The fresh pork has a proper proportion of firm fat to meat, so that the meat is succulent and the crackling crisp – a revelation to those accustomed to over-lean, intensively reared pork. The hams and bacon are naturally of equal quality, and are brine-cured and smoked in the farm butchery, without water retainers or colouring, which aren't necessary as the long slow smoking over oak gives a good rich colour. Heal Farm is one of the members of *Devon Fare*, and provides an excellent mail order service for those of us who are far from such quality pork ourselves. The product range is wide and varied, so send for details. For personal callers, the farm shop is open from 9a.m.–5p.m. on weekdays, 10a.m.–4p.m. on Saturdays, and on Sundays by appointment. It is situated very near Head Mill Trout Farm (see previous entry), so it is very well worthwhile making a special journey to stock up with products from both farms at once. Kings Nympton is the place to head for – about 13 miles from Barnstaple taking the A377 to Exeter. Turn left on to the B3226 to South Molton by the Fortescue Arms. *Head Mill* is about 1 mile on the left; *Heal Farm* is beyond the Grove pub in the middle of Kings Nympton, on the left.

HEAL FARM
QUALITY TRADITIONAL MEATS
Kings Nympton, Umberleigh, Devon EX37 9TB
Tel. South Molton (STD 076 95) 2077
SMOKED BACK BACON

lb.	oz.	Naturally cured in brine and smoked over oak chips.
		KEEP REFRIGERATED

Hele Mill stoneground flour

Hele Mill, Hele Bay, Ilfracombe, Devon
Tel. Ilfracombe (0271) 63162 (home number)

MR AND MRS C L LOVELL

Hele Mill dates from 1525, and has now been completely restored, after thirty years' dereliction, to full operation as a flour mill. It has an 18-foot overshot water wheel, and Mr Lovell is justly proud of the exhaustive study he has made of milling since his retirement from the Merchant Navy. 'Hele Mill is often praised as the most educational mill there is.' In a beautiful setting, the mill produces *stoneground 100% wholemeal flour*, coarse, medium and fine, with nothing added and nothing removed; *kibbled or cracked wheat, wheatflakes*, and a *granary type flour* of kibbled wheat and fine flour without malt. Personal callers are welcome from Easter to 1 November, 10a.m.–5p.m. on weekdays, 2–5p.m. on Sundays. The mill is closed on Saturdays. During the rest of the year, it can be visited by appointment, 'or if the miller happens to be there'. It is situated on the A399 Combe Martin–Ilfracombe road, 1 mile east of Ilfracombe opposite Allcock's Garage.

Inch's Cider

Inch's Cider Co,
Western Barn, Hatherleigh Road,
Winkleigh, Devon EX19 8AP
Tel. Winkleigh (0837) 83560

DEREK INCH

We got through a wet summer holiday once on Inch's cider and Rodda's clotted cream (see page 22), and the best plums I have ever bottled were in a syrup made from Inch's sweet cider (the sweeter the cider, the redder the colour, so the plums looked as well as tasted good). The redness of Inch's cider is said to come from the red sandstone soil which is such a feature of that part of Devon on which the apple stock is grown; and the flavour is due to the strict adherence to a seventeenth-century recipe which the company has used for seventy years, ever since Sam Inch decided to turn the apples which were his wages for working on a local farm into cider.

Inch's

Devonshire Scrumpy

The Traditional Taste of the West Country

INCH'S CIDER COMPANY
Western Barn, Winkleigh, N. Devon.
Telephone: Winkleigh (083783) 363/560

Cider, in the same way as sherry, becomes paler and drier with age, and stronger too. So the sweet red cider is about 6% proof, while the pale, three-year-old *Harvest Scrumpy* is over 8%. Inch's still deliver cider to Sam Inch's first customers, the White Hart at North Tawton, and the Kings Arms at Winkleigh. Personal callers can buy the cider locally from such firms as Peter Dominic, The Victoria Wine Co, and Threshers as well as from Inch's themselves – Monday to Saturday, 9a.m.–5p.m. Winkleigh is on the B3220, off the A377 from Exeter to Barnstaple (turn off at Morchard Road).

Leworthy Mill ice cream

Leworthy Mill, Woolsery,
Nr Bideford, Devon
Tel. Clovelly (023 73) 445
MARK AND CAROLINE LUCAS

The Lucas's small dairy farm, a few miles from the beautiful North Devon coast, is run on traditional lines. After seven years of selling milk to the Milk Marketing Board, they decided that their high quality Jersey milk could be used more efficiently. For the past six years they have been making all their milk into quality dairy products, filling a gap in the local market for an ice cream made with real cream. Mark and Caroline Lucas now make 1500 litres of ice cream and 400lbs of clotted cream in an average month (between March and October), but do not plan to expand any further as they feel that both the quality and personal service might suffer. They have taken considerable trouble to find an emulsifier and stabiliser, necessary to give the freezer life needed to sell the ice cream commercially, of vegetable rather than chemical origin, and now use Alginade, a natural derivative of seaweed, from Scotland. They use no artificial colours or flavours, and 2lbs cream go into each gallon of Jersey milk. Their ice cream is available from

FROM THE MILK & CREAM OF OUR PEDIGREE JERSEY HERD
FREE FROM ARTIFICIAL FLAVOUR AND COLOUR

LEWORTHY MILL

DAIRY ICE CREAM

½ LITRE   REAL VANILLA

Neal's Yard Dairy, Covent Garden, London WC2, and both the ice cream and clotted cream are available in shops in the Bideford/Barnstaple/Clovelly area. Callers are not encouraged, not because they are unwelcome, but because the farm is isolated, difficult to find, and down nearly a mile of very narrow lane.

Michaelmas Fare – geese and preserves

Indiwell, Swimbridge, Barnstaple, Devon
Tel. Barnstaple (0271) 830715
MRS MARIAN WOOD

Mrs Wood specialises in very seasonal produce – *preserves* made from *fruits growing wild* on the farm, as well as her *superb lemon curd*. She also rears *geese*, which are allowed to mature naturally, grazing on the farm pastures, and gleaning among the stubble. These are usually available for the traditional feast of Michaelmas (29 September), and her *damson pickle* goes very well indeed with any cold goose left over. Her products are marketed from the farm gate, and by Linacres, Pilton, Barnstaple. Open from September to Christmas, Indiwell is on the A361 east of

> 350 g. 12 oz.
> **HEDGEROW JELLY**
> Ingredients:
> Apple, Blackberry, Elderberry & Sloe Juice; Sugar.
> MICHAELMAS FARE
> Swimbridge, N. Devon

Swimbridge. Mrs Wood also supplies goslings to many parts of the country, so may well be able to put you in touch with a local supplier if a visit to her farm is impracticable. She can also tell you the name of a supplier of Dorset Camphorated Goose Grease, for all those who swear that there is nothing like goose fat to protect the chest from winter cold.

Murray's Meat

West Rock, Broadhempston,
Nr Totnes, Devon TQ9 6BH
Tel. Totnes (0803) 813172
CHRISTOPHER MURRAY

From the age of three, Christopher Murray wanted to farm, despite his non-farming background. His stepfather was an early member of the Soil Association, and brought Christopher up on the adage 'you are what you eat'. So, three years ago, as partner and manager of Sharpham Stock Farm, he introduced organic farming on the major part of Sharpham's hundred acres. The intention of the business is to supply the very best quality produce to the customer from livestock that have had a stress-free life and are naturally reared without the use of chemical implants, growth promoters and artificially fertilised pastures. Now, Christopher Murray's *lamb*, *beef* and *pork* are available by mail order only, at very competitive prices considering the cost of sowing the pastures with the grasses, clovers and herbs which give the meat its flavour. Visitors are not encouraged, but farm visits can be arranged for primary school children – Christopher Murray is keen to help them understand from an early age the relationship between commercial and responsible use of the countryside.

Park Farm cheeses

Park Farm, Umberleigh, Devon
Tel. Chittlehamholt (076 94) 237
PETER AND HILARY CHARNLEY

The Charnleys run their small farm on organic lines and make their cheeses from the unpasteurised milk from their own herds of Jersey cows and Anglo-Nubian goats. *Devon Garland* is a Jersey milk cheese with a band of herbs running through it; *Satterleigh* is a mild goats' milk cheese, made to an old Dales recipe. My own favourite is the *Exmoor* – small Jersey milk cheeses that ripen deliciously later in the year. All are ripened for six to eight weeks before selling. The Charnleys supply most of their cheeses to wholesalers, but will sell direct to shops who are outside wholesalers' areas. They will also sell to 'enthusiastic callers' who will take whole cheeses, but only by prior arrangement. So, find Park Farm cheeses at the following top quality cheese shops: Neal's Yard Dairy, Covent Garden, London WC2; James's, 188 Beckenham High Street, Beckenham, Kent; Wells Stores, Streatley, Nr Reading, Berkshire; The Real Cheese Shop, High Street, Barnes, London SW13; Humble Pie, Market Place, Burnham Market, Norfolk; Country Pannier, Newton Abbot Market Hall, Newton Abbot, Devon; Bea's Pantry, 182 Bath Road, Cheltenham, Gloucestershire; Barnstaple Delicatessen (Wilson & Elmer), Barnstaple, Devon.

Quicke's Cheddar cheese

J G Quicke & Partners,
Woodley, Newton St Cyres, Exeter,
Devon EX5 5BT
Tel. Newton St Cyres (039 285) 222
TOM LANGDON-DAVIES

The Quicke family's *Cheddar* ranks amongst the best of the traditionally made Cheddars on the market, and is stocked by quality supermarkets as well as good cheese shops all round the country. The secret of the consistent quality of their cheese is due in no small measure to the storing of the cheese during its maturation; a cheese store, built in 1980, ensures that the cheese can be sent out properly matured, with quality control in the hands of the dairy itself. *Double Gloucester* is made here too, and *Smoked* and *Herb* cheeses, *cream*, *butter* and *ice cream*, and a *Cheddar* made with vegetarian rennet. Quicke's Cheddar and their other cheeses are stocked by good cheese shops all over the country, and can be bought direct from the dairy, too, which is open from 9a.m.–5.30p.m., Monday to Friday, and 9a.m.–1p.m. on Saturdays. Newton St Cyres is on the A377, just outside Exeter on the way to Crediton.

Salcombe Dairy ice cream

Salcombe Dairy Ltd,
Shadycombe Road, Salcombe,
Devon TQ8 8DX
Tel. Salcombe (054 884) 3228
PETER HOWARD

Peter Howard founded his ice cream business in 1979, after a training in marketing which made him aware of the gap in the market for high quality ice creams and sorbets. Salcombe Dairy ices are now on the menus of some of the best known restaurants in the West Country; the recipes are pre-war, made to the highest standards 'regardless of cost', with small batch production to preserve the quality. 'We have survived recession, and will only survive by maintaining *quality* above all else,' Peter Howard told me. The flavours are genuine – I found the *Whole Apricot* particularly good – the ingredients cream, butter, fresh milk.

Two recent additions to the range are *Praline Bombe* and *Apple and Cider Sorbet*. Distribution is wholesale only to about 200 good food shops in the Devon/Somerset area, and to restaurants, hotels and theatres. Sales from the factory gate are during normal working hours five days a week, half day on Saturday.

Salcombe Smokies

*Salcombe Smokers,
54 Fore Street, Kingsbridge,
Devon TQ7 1NY
Tel. Kingsbridge (0548) 2006*

J J M BARRON

Mr Barron has only just taken over the running of this long-established firm which made its reputation with *Salcombe Smokies* (hot smoked mackerel fillets) and smoked salmon. Helped by the expertise of the previous owner, Mr Barron is currently researching into the question of additives and colourings used for smoked fish in this country. He feels there is a demand, steadily increasing but still very much a minority one, for the 'natural' uncoloured products. *Smoked prawns, whiting cutlets, roe, haddock* and *pollack fillets* are all smoked on the premises, and Mr Barron has reduced by up to 50% the permitted colouring added to the normal run. It will be very interesting to see the results of his experiments to persuade local people that less colour still equals good food. He also sells the complete range of locally landed fresh white and shellfish, together with a range (limited at the moment) of good quality French wines suitable for drinking with fish. The smoked fish is supplied wholesale to various retail outlets, including: The Taste Bud, High Street, Totnes, Devon, and Lockes Delicatessen, Jewry Street, Winchester, Hampshire. A mail order service operates from Clarksons of Devon, Alansway, Ottery St Mary (040 481) 3581. The shop is open from 8a.m.–1p.m. and 1.45–5p.m. each weekday, but closes on Thursday and Saturday afternoons *except* in the busy holiday season, and at Easter and Christmas.

Stapleton Farm yoghurts, cream, fudge and wholewheat biscuit bars

*Stapleton Farm, Langtree,
Nr Torrington, Devon
Tel. Langtree (080 55) 414*

PETER AND CAROL DUNCAN

Stapleton Farm is another member of the *Devon Fare* group – which alone gives some idea of the quality of their products. I found their live, *unsweetened yoghurts* absolutely delicious, and am glad to say that the Holland & Barrett chain of health food shops stock this under their own label. In addition there is *Greek style, Bulgarian recipe breakfast yoghurt*, and *low fat fruit yoghurt* using raw cane sugar. None contains any artificial additives at all. As well as the range of yoghurts, *clotted cream* is available by post, with *double* and *whipping cream* distributed throughout Devon, Cornwall and Somerset. Some of the double cream goes into *fudge*, and their *wholewheat biscuit bars* accompany their yoghurt very well. The Stapletons buy in fresh yoghurt culture each week all the way from Denmark, to maintain the delicate balance between the two types of bacteria which work on the skimmed milk. It took three years to perfect their yoghurt production and over the last ten years they have brought their output from a single churn a day to 1000 litres (or 3000 pots) daily. Marketing has been the biggest problem: convincing people that the most-advertised brands are not always the best has been very hard. But their products are now stocked by Harrods, and with the current wave of interest in all additive-free food, most of their problems should be over. Personal callers should telephone first to arrange a time and to receive directions. Also telephone for details of your nearest retail outlet.

Vulscombe Devon goats' cheese

Higher Vulscombe, Cruwys Morchard, Tiverton, Devon EX16 8NB
Tel. Tiverton (0884) 252505
G J AND MRS J M TOWNSEND

Four years ago the Townsends risked exchanging the security of a successful academic career for the challenge of a small, run-down Devon farm. With the milk from their single goat they experimented, as have so many others, with cheese-making. With much patient trial and error, they have succeeded, where others have failed, in making a rich, creamy goats' cheese which has none of the rankness which so often mars the flavour. The Vulscombe herd of goats grazes old permanent pastures rich in plant species, the milk is unpasteurised, and the unrennetted cheese is made entirely by hand, daily, from curd obtained by a uniquely slow process. As a result of all this care and

attention, the three flavours – *plain*, *fresh herbs and garlic*, and *garlic and peppercorns*, have won places on the 'serious' cheese-boards of restaurants in Bristol and the south-west, and on the counters of good cheese shops in Surrey, Sussex and Kent, as well as Paxton and Whitfield in London, and several outlets in Tiverton itself. Personal callers are welcome 'at any reasonable time all the year round'. Cruwys Morchard lies just off the A373 from Tiverton to South Molton, about 5 miles out of Tiverton.

Welcombe Country Fayre culinary and medicinal herbs

Darracott Farm, Welcombe, Nr Bideford, Devon EX39 6HG
Tel. Morwenstowe (028 883) 322
MIKE AND SALLY ST JOHN HOLLIS

The experience that the Hollis's gained during their time working for the agri-chemical industry has been put to good use in their own horticultural business. While developing the nursery side (heathers and conifers), and their farm shop, which stocks as many of their own fruits and vegetables as possible together with *Devon Fare* products and crafts by local craftspeople, their real interest is in herbs. They now produce a wide range of *fresh and dried herbs*, and *herb plants*, for culinary, medicinal and decorative purposes. *Culinary herbs* are supplied wholesale to hotels, restaurants and caterers, and retail sales are either via the farm shop, or by mail order. Opening times for the farm shop and nursery are as follows: April to October, 9.30a.m.–6p.m. daily. October to

March, Monday, Wednesday, Friday and Saturday, 10a.m.–2p.m. with other times by arrangement. Welcombe lies 2 miles from the A39 towards the coast on the south side of Hartland Point, with Darracott Farm on the right as you approach Welcombe, next door to the Pottery.

Yearlstone Vineyard wines and cyders

Yearlstone Vineyard, Chilton, Bickleigh, Tiverton, Devon
Tel. Bickleigh (088 45) 450

GILLIAN PEARKES

The vineyard at Yearlstone was planted on its steep, exceptionally warm, south-facing slope in the Exe valley in 1976, after intensive research into the viability of growing grapes for wine-making. The long history of wine-making in England convinced Gillian Pearkes that it was possible, and she has been proved right so far. Her three white wines (*Madeleine Angevine*, *Seigerrebe* and *Special Reserve Chardonnay*), and her *Red Deer* (like a red Bordeaux in character, and a rare product for England, but made possible by the superb vineyard site) are now available in a dozen good shops in the area, and in La Vigneronne, 105 Old Brompton Road, SW7. The *cyders* are made from unsprayed apples from local orchards – *Gold Vintage Cyder* is still and dry; *Cyder Royale* is medium sweet, made from the cyder apples from a single Exe valley orchard of great antiquity. *Yearlstone Perry* – of which there is only a limited supply – is made from local perry pears, and has

a particularly delicate flavour. Gillian Pearkes' considerable knowledge and expertise of viticulture has led her to write V*inegrowing in Britain*, an invaluable book to help and encourage more people to plant vineyards despite the problems of the British climate. Visitors are welcome by appointment – 'to make sure we are here'.

yearlstone
FINE ENGLISH TABLE WINE
devon

MADELEINE ANGEVINE
Estate Grown and bottled in the Exe Valley by Gillian Pearkes.
Chilton, Bickleigh, Tiverton, Devon, United Kingdom.
70cl minimum contents

SOMERSET AND AVON

Arne Herbs

Limeburn Nurseries, Limeburn Hill, Chew Magna, Avon BS18 8QW
Tel. Bristol (0782) 333399

ANTONY LYMAN-DIXON AND HELEN LEE

Antony Lyman-Dixon, originally an expert in Renaissance studies, and unhappy with the debasement of Italy's gastronomic heritage by the fast food industry, began making fresh pasta to redress the injustice.

Pasta-making ceased last year, when the business moved from its old address at Compton Dundon to Chew Magna, but the fresh herbs flourish. Telephone first, before calling, as Mr Lyman-Dixon does not welcome the casual visitor. But he is a mine of information on old recipes, and has a large reference library to help those genuinely interested. When telephoning, please ask for directions.

Brown & Forrest smoked eel and salmon

Brown & Forrest,
Thorney, Langport, Somerset TA10 0DR
Tel. Langport (0458) 251520
MICHAEL BROWN

One of the delights of compiling a book of this sort is that you not only widen your taste in food, but you also come across people of tremendous imagination and resourcefulness. Michael Brown was in the elver business – that is, he was a supplier of baby eels for restocking – and this led him to try smoking eel. The general response was minimal – we are a very conservative race – but a small connoisseur market was reached via advertising and a mailing list. The Browns found the English recipes for smoking eel were unsatisfactory, so they went to Germany, where the smoking methods are very different. As a result of their research there, Michael Brown has developed a natural wood-fired smoker, using beech; the results are delicious – borne out by the 80% growth in sales in a year. Although you can buy the *eel filleted ready for the table,* the true gourmet prefers the flavour of the *whole smoked eel in the round.* There is *smoked eel pâté* too. Brown & Forrest also supply *smoked Scottish wild salmon,* traditionally cured and oak-smoked. Personal callers are welcome, but sales are all by mail order. 'We enjoy the very special mail order relationship that builds up between supplier and customer – invisible friends made by the quality of the product and reliability of service,' as Michael Brown told me.

BROWN
and
FORREST

Purveyors of the finest
fresh-smoked Eel & Salmon
by post to your door.

Burrow Hill cider and cider mulling spices

Pass Vale Farm, Burrow Hill, Kingsbury Episcopi, Martock, Somerset
Tel. South Petherton (0460) 40782

JULIAN TEMPERLEY

The apples which go into *Burrow Hill cider* have curious names – Foxwhelp, Sweet Coppin, Brown Snout, Chisel Jersey – traditional varieties which are among the 4000 trees at Pass Vale Farm. Mr Temperley points out that his cider, fermented in oak vats and sold draught from wooden barrels, is for 'the discerning 10%', and is not 'the mass-market sticky pop which often masquerades under the same name'. It regularly wins the top prizes at the large shows like the Royal Bath & West, and the Devon Country Show. One of the best ways to enjoy cider in the winter is to mull it, and Burrow Hill sell special sachets of *mulling spices* that you can use like tea-bags to produce a hot, spiced drink. (Mr Temperley also recommends it iced in the summer.) You can buy the spices by mail order, but for the cider itself you must visit pubs in the area, or better still, visit the farm itself, which has an outstanding view of the Somerset Levels: 'There is normally someone available to sell cider until 6p.m. on weekdays, and we are open all day on Saturdays, but never on Sundays. But if you are coming from a long way away it is best to phone first; we are a working farm and staff may be involved elsewhere.' Kingsbury Episcopi is off the B3165, between A303 and Long Sutton.

Capricorn goats' cheese, see *Lubborn Cheese*

Carolina ewes' milk cheese and yoghurt

Higher Holditch Farm, Holditch, Chard, Somerset TA20 4NL
Tel. South Chard (0460) 21066

MR J A NORMAN

Carolina is a full fat hard matured cheese, rather like a Pecorino, and one of our favourites of all those we have been tasting and testing for this book. Not surprisingly, it has been winning prizes – First in the Sheep & Goat Cheese class at the Royal Bath & West, and Second in the open class against an international entry of traditional cows' cheeses. All this is good going for Mr Norman, who only recently retired from the animal feed and veterinary pharmaceuticals industries. The Normans also run a farm guest house, and visitors are encouraged to try ewes' milk products as part of the gourmet cooking which is a feature of the establishment. The future looks good for Carolina cheese – although the aim is to stay small, exclusive and hand-made, it is also to double the quantity of cheese made to 35kg a week. But *yoghurt* sales (and the yoghurt, too, wins prizes at the local large shows) will not be expanded

HIGHER HOLDITCH

CAROLINA DAIRY SHEEP
Higher Holditch Farm, Holditch, Chard, Somerset.

beyond the present outlets: Manor Court Delicatessen, Chard; Country Fayre, Chard; Ganesha Health Foods, Axminster and Honiton. The cheese is stocked by good cheese shops including Neal's Yard, Covent Garden, London WC2 and James's, 188 Beckenham High Street, Beckenham, Kent. Personal callers are welcome, but do telephone first to avoid disappointment, and to be given directions – Holditch is deep in the country 5 miles south of Chard, east of the A358.

Charlton Orchards

Creech St Michael, Nr Taunton, Somerset TA3 5PF
Tel. West Monkton (0823) 412979/412959/412928
MATTHEW FREUDENBERG

Charlton Orchards pride themselves on growing a range of flavourful apples and pears, including old or unusual varieties – *Orleans Reinette*, for example, and *Glou Morceau* pears. There are now thirty-five acres of fruit, where there were only six twenty years ago – a measure, as Mr Freudenberg points out, of their faith in the future of English tree fruit in the face of competition from the Continent. They belong to the 'Taste of Somerset' marketing group, and sell part wholesale, and part through the farm shop. From *late August* to the *end of February* they are open from 3.30–6p.m., Monday to Friday, 10a.m.–5p.m. Saturday and Sunday. Charlton Orchards are located approximately 6 miles east of Taunton at the Creech Heathfield end of Creech St Michael, 1 mile down Charlton Road.

Chewton Cheddar

Chewton Cheese Dairy,
Priory Farm, Chewton Mendip,
Bath, Somerset BA3 4NT
Tel. Chewton Mendip (076 121) 666
MRS MARIAN SHAW (MANAGER)

You can see *Chewton Cheddar* being made at the dairy, which of course adds interest – the cheese is the traditional, cloth-bound, fully matured (for up to a year) Cheddar of the area, made from the milk of the estate's own herds; *butter* is made here too. The Waldegrave estate has been owned and farmed by the Waldegrave family ever since it was given to them by Queen Mary in 1553, and is presently owned and run by Viscount Chewton, heir to the estate. Chewton Cheddar is available from good cheese shops everywhere: The Cheesery, Regent Road, Altrincham, Cheshire; Larners of Holt, Market Place, Holt, Norfolk; Saltmarsh & Druce, Market Square, Witney, Oxfordshire; Chatsworth Farm Shop, Pilsley, nr. Bakewell, Derbyshire; Wells Stores, Streatley, Berkshire; Neal's Yard Dairy, Covent Garden, London WC2 and from the dairy itself – 8.30a.m.–5p.m. Monday to Friday, 9a.m.–5p.m. Saturday and Sunday. *Closes at 4p.m. in January, February and March.* Chewton Mendip is at the junction of the A39 with the B3114, about 5 miles north of Wells.

Cobb's Bath Buns

Cobb & Co.,
11 Westgate Street, Bath
Tel. Bath (0225) 66158
R N COBB

The best way to enjoy these is with the excellent coffee served in the Assembly Rooms, Bath. This is a wonderfully elegant place, with chamber music chiming peacefully in your ears as you read the newspapers arranged on poles, and try to limit yourself to only one of these delicious buns. Cobb's recipe dates from 1679, and uses a rich brioche-type dough (so rich that it can only be worked by hand), fragrant with lemon and spices and stuffed with lumps of sugar, with sugar nibs and currants sprinkled on the top – quite different from any other so-called Bath bun. Cobb & Co. have been making Bath buns since they were founded in 1866, and still make the best. They are served in the Pump Room, too, and can be bought from their other branches: 1 Lower Borough Walls; 37 Moorland Road; 30 Bathwick Street; 30 Wellsway – all in Bath, and 15 High Street, Melksham, Wiltshire.

Cricket St Thomas ice cream

Cricket St Thomas,
Chard, Somerset TA20 4DD
Tel. Winsham (046 030) 755
MRS R TAYLOR

Cricket St Thomas is a lovely house, familiar to many since its use for the BBC TV series 'To the Manor Born', and set in a thousand acres of farmland which also contains a wildlife park. The 250,000 visitors who flock here every year have had an ice cream developed especially for them, which has proved so popular outside the estate that it is now on general sale. The cream used comes from the estate herds, the flavourings (real fruit, and no additives) come from Italy, so they are interestingly sophisticated, ranging widely from *Walnut* to *Brandy and Orange*. Sales are mainly wholesale, unless you are a visitor to the Park. Cricket St Thomas is on the A30 between Chard and Crewkerne.

Cromwell's chocolates

15 Pulteney Bridge, Bath BA2 4AY
Tel. Bath (0225) 66876
ALAN GLOVER

See main entry on page 162.

Jane Croswell-Jones' ewes' milk products

Manor Garden Cottage, Mells,
Frome, Somerset
Tel. Frome (0373) 812876

JANE CROSWELL-JONES

After Jane's return home from Wye College in 1979, she was determined to carry on the family dairying tradition, but with sheep rather than cows. Currently she is producing *milk, yoghurt*, and a *thick strained yoghurt*. Where possible the fruit for the flavoured yoghurt is prepared by hand, and honey rather than sugar is used as a sweetener. The *Hunza apricot and honey* 'must be tasted to be believed – pure ambrosia', and there is a *roast hazelnut and honey* version, and a *blackcurrant and honey*. The extra rich and creamy *strained yoghurt* comes either flavoured with *herbs*, or with a *sweet white wine* (Beaumes de Venise, lemon juice and sugar). Remember that ewes' milk is much more easily digested than cows' milk, so even the richest yoghurt is easily tolerated by those who are allergic to bovine dairy products. Personal callers are welcome from 10a.m.–6p.m. throughout the year. Mells is 3 miles east of Frome. Manor Garden Cottage is the last cottage on the left going towards the church.

Duckett's Caerphilly cheese

R A Duckett & Co. Ltd,
Walnut Tree Farm, Heath House,
Wedmore, Somerset BS28 4U
Tel. Wedmore (0934) 712218

CHRIS DUCKETT

Caerphilly cheesemaking has been a tradition in the Duckett family for at least three generations. The milk for the cheese comes from the farm's Friesian herd, which spends the summer months grazing on the famous Somerset Levels, where there is a wide variety of grass species (over sixty on some pastures). Chris Duckett feels this must contribute to the unique flavour of the cheese; made with unpasteurised milk, it does indeed develop a much creamier flavour than the mass-produced Caerphillys, as Patrick Rance notes in *The Great British Cheese Book*. There is a *chive-flavoured* variation, and other flavours, such as *cumin, caraway*, and *chive and garlic*, are currently being experimented with, as well as *smoked cheese*. The cheese is sold in Patrick Rance's shop, Wells Stores, Streatley, Berkshire; for other retail outlets, please telephone the farm. Personal callers are welcome, preferably in the morning, and please telephone first. Wedmore lies at the junction of the B3151 with the B3139, about 7 miles west of Wells (call at Walnut Tree farmhouse).

SOMERSET AND AVON

The Elms farmhouse produce

*The Elms, Lower Westholme, Pilton,
Somerset BA4 4EL
Tel. Pilton (074 989) 371*
C D STONE

The Stones' business venture is designed to provide quality healthy products in as natural a way as possible, and to enable visitors to see and appreciate some aspects of rural life. All the dairy products (*goats'* and *ewes' milk, yoghurt and cheese*) are additive-free, as is the *cider*, which is made using traditional equipment. All the *soft fruit* (which includes some of the less usual varieties such as white currants, tayberries, sunberries and worcesterberries) and *vegetables* are grown using minimal chemicals – information on any chemicals used is available in the shop. The *poultry* is free-range. Retail sales are mainly through the farm shop, with some wholesale to local wholefood shops. Visitors are very welcome, from 10a.m.–5.30p.m. daily *except Tuesday*. The Elms is situated just outside Pilton on the A361 – take the Wells turning in Pilton itself, then the first turning left to Westholme – the farm is 500m on the left at the bottom of the hill.

Exmoor ewes' milk cheeses

*Willett Farm, Lydeard St Lawrence,
Taunton, Somerset
Tel. Lydeard St Lawrence (098 47) 328 or 391*
ANNE AND PETER WHITE

Coleford Blue is a traditional blue-veined farmhouse ewes' milk cheese not unlike Roquefort, which takes three months to mature; *Colwick* is a soft curd cheese which is sold fresh, within a few days of making. Although this is a new enterprise for the farm, the cheese recipes and methods are traditional, and combine the interests of the gourmet and the allergy sufferer. The milk is produced on the farm, and any extra is bought in from other Exmoor farms – neither cheese contains any additives. Sales are mainly wholesale to good cheese shops in London and the south-east, and to a few local Somerset shops: Pauline's (Wholefood) Larder, The Pig Market, Taunton; M. Baxter, Higher Folly Farm, Crewkerne. Visitors to the farm are welcome, but a prior arrangement is appreciated – Lydeard St Lawrence lies between the B3224 and the A358, west of Taunton.

Grant's traditional farmhouse Cheddar

*Hamwood Farm, Trull, Taunton,
Somerset TA3 7NX
Tel. Blagdon Hill (082 342) 248*
HUGH GRANT

Mr Grant is one of the few Cheddar makers using unpasteurised milk, from the 400-acre farm's Friesian herd, and this, together with the upright presses which are still in use here give this cheese a special texture which I found very attractive. Mr Grant was trained as a cheesemaker, and made cheese on several farms before going into business in his own right forty years ago. He moved to Hamwood Farm in 1952. The sole agents for his cheese are: Mendip Foods Ltd, Keward Farm, Glastonbury Road, Wells, Somerset. Or you can buy it (and *butter*, which is hand-rolled here) Monday–Friday, 9a.m.–5p.m., from the farm, which is 1 mile south of Taunton, between the M5 and A38.

Keen's traditional farmhouse Cheddar

Moorhayes Farm, Verrington Road, Wincanton, Somerset
Tel. Wincanton (0963) 32286
MRS D M KEEN

Another of the select band of unpasteurised Cheddar cheesemakers, the Keen family have been making Cheddar at Moorhayes Farm since the turn of the century. The original dairy is still in use, part of the sixteenth-century farmhouse, and the methods are traditional, with up to twelve months' maturing time allowed to bring the cheese to full flavour – 'using unpasteurised milk the flavour is always more exciting'. The cheesemaker, Jack Parsons, has a lifetime's experience, and makes eight 60lb cheeses daily, which find a ready market via the wholesale Mendip Foods Ltd (see previous entry); James's, 188 Beckenham High Street, Beckenham, Kent; Harvey & Brockless, 17–23 Linford Street, London SW8. Small quantities are also sold from the farm, between 9a.m.–4p.m. on weekdays. To find Moorhayes Farm, leave Wincanton along Bruton Road, turn left on leaving town into Verrington Road – the farm is 1 mile along on the right.

Lubborn cheeses – Capricorn goats' cheese; Somerset Brie

Lubborn Cheese Ltd,
North Street, Crewkerne, Somerset
Tel. Crewkerne (0460) 76102
PIERS FEILDEN

Piers Feilden set up his company specifically to manufacture mould-ripened soft cheeses (of the Brie and Camembert type), feeling that there was a demand for quality cheeses of this type which was unlikely to be satisfied by the major companies in the dairy industry. *Somerset Brie* is a traditional type Brie made from local milk, largely hand-made, and hand wrapped. *Capricorn* goats' cheese is a mould-ripened chèvre type soft cheese made in two sizes – 100g and 1kg. The milk for this is from local herds of British Saanen goats, and vegetable rennet is used. Sales are wholesale only, and the cheese is widely distributed in the south of England ('and in Celtic outposts') via speciality cheese shops, delicatessens, restaurants and some supermarket groups. For further details contact Mr Feilden.

Montgomery's traditional farmhouse Cheddar

J, A & E Montgomery Ltd,
Manor Farm, North Cadbury, Yeovil,
Somerset BA22 7DW
Tel. North Cadbury (0963) 40243

J, A & E MONTGOMERY

I have to admit that this is my own favourite Cheddar, and one which I have been buying – by post when there has been no other way – for many years. It has an individual character and a full, nutty flavour. This flavour undoubtedly comes from the milk, which is unpasteurised and from the Montgomerys' own herd. The cows only graze part of the day on newly grown grass fields; they are then moved for the rest of the day on to old permanent pastures where there is a great mixture of varieties of grasses and clover as well as wild plants and herbs. The cheesemaker, Harold Chase, 'lover of classical music as anyone within earshot of the cheese room would know', has been a maker nearly all his life, and takes great pride in his product. 'Good cheese must start with pure clean milk from well-fed cows, so the cowman also has an important part to play.' Cheese has been made at Manor Farm for more than fifty years. There is an old West Country saying, 'you can't make good cheese from pastureland where there are no hares',

and perhaps where hares don't like the pasture there is something missing from the milk used for cheesemaking; fortunately, Manor Farm has plenty of large wild brown hares. Sales are largely through Mendip Foods (see p.168), who are specialists in marketing farmhouse cheese; some is sold at the farm during office hours, and some is posted to those willing to pay what the Montgomerys feel is excessive postage. Sales are also through the Women's Institute Shop in Yeovil on Wednesday, Friday and Saturday. Personal callers are welcome on an informal basis, as there is neither the space nor time to receive parties.

Roundoak Dairy ewes' and goats' milk cheeses

Roundoak Dairy, Upper New Road,
Cheddar, Somerset BS27 3DL
Tel. Cheddar (0934) 743238

MRS ROSEMARY LATHAM

Mrs Latham began cheesemaking in 1976 on a domestic scale, which grew from doorstep sales to local shops and beyond. Cheesemaking is not one of her many professional qualifications, but she finds the combination of art and science fascinating. While accepting there is a growing demand for 'wholesome hand-crafted' cheeses, she is sceptical about the commercial future, which is limited by the difficulty of distribution, and the maintenance of standards where so much hand work is involved. And the hours are demanding – 'seven long days a week'. Mrs Latham's range of cheeses is wide – both *hard* and *soft*, both *ewes'* and *goats' milk*, some flavoured with *garlic*, some with *herbs*, and some *smoked*. They are well distributed by Harvey and Brockless, 17–23 Linford Street, London SW8, and are available at Harrods and Selfridges, and as far afield as Harrogate (The Cheeseboard, 1 Commercial Street), and Gloucestershire (J & P Langman Ltd, Perrots Brook Farm, Cirencester), as well as from local shops. Farm door sales are strictly limited by space, so please telephone for an appointment, especially as there are no regular opening hours.

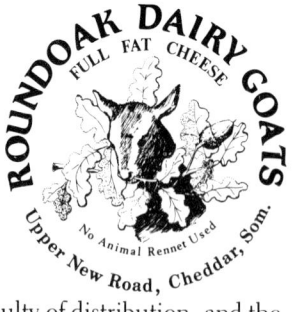

Sheppy's farmhouse cider

Three Bridges, Bradford on Tone, Taunton TA4 1ER
Tel. Bradford on Tone (082 346) 233
MR R J SHEPPY

This is a family business, built on a tradition of cider making which stretches back almost 200 years. Forty acres of the 370-acre farm are devoted to cider apples, growing varieties such as Dabinett, Kingston Black and Tremlett's Bitter. Richard Sheppy takes great pains to keep up with modern trends in marketing and presentation, whilst maintaining a traditional farmhouse type of cider as the end product – this combination of the old and the new is apparent when you visit Sheppy's. There is a good farm and cider museum showing the antique methods of production alongside the modern press room, where the apple crop is processed each autumn. The cider is sold mostly to personal callers, and some to the wholesale trade. Both the excellent *draught*, and the *Gold Medal vintage* ciders can be sent by National Carriers to retail customers. Several free houses in the area sell the draught cider by the glass. Sheppy's is well signposted on the A38 midway between Taunton and Wellington, and only 2½ miles from exit 26 on the M5. Opening hours are complicated, as follows: Monday to Saturday, 1 April to 31 May: 8.30a.m.–7p.m. 1 June to 31 August: 8.30a.m.–8p.m. September: 8.30a.m.–7p.m. 1 October to 31 March: 8.30a.m.–6p.m. Sundays 12–2p.m. only, Easter to Christmas.

Somerset Brie, see Lubborn Cheeses Ltd, page 44

Somerset Ducks

*Greenway Farm, North Newton,
Bridgwater, Somerset TA7 0DS
Tel. Bridgwater (0278) 662656*
MRS GILL DURMAN

Mrs Durman's delicious duck products have won her a following as far afield as Yorkshire, where Alan Porter stocks them in his shop in Boroughbridge. The *boned* and *cooked ducks* come with a range of stuffings, including *apple and cider with a cider and honey glaze*, and the traditional *sage and onion*. *Duck and orange pie, duck liver pâté*, and *duck portions cooked with orange and honey glaze* are also available, all made with natural ingredients and without preservatives. *Oven-ready birds* are farm fresh. Retail sales are available from the farm, but please telephone first; or look for Somerset Duck products at the Women's Institute Market in Taunton. North Newton is about 1 mile south of North Petherton (on the A38).

Stawell Fruit Farm

*Stawell, Bridgwater, Somerset TA7 9AE
Tel. Chilton Polden (0278) 722732*
CHARLES GRAHAM

Stawell Farm was established in 1916 by Mr Graham's grandmother as one of the first commercial dessert and culinary apple growers in Somerset. The farm specialises in producing *Cox's Orange Pippins* of the highest quality, among the twenty varieties on sale. *Ashmead's Kernel* is available later in the season, and I very much liked the *Cherry Cox*, crisp, juicy, with a hint of the Cox flavour which I had never tasted before and which was at its best when I visited the farm in early October. The apples are supplied wholesale, through the farm shop, and on a pick-your-own basis. The season starts in mid-August, when Stawell is open between 11a.m.–5p.m. from Wednesday to Sunday. After the pick-your-own season is over, apples are available from the packing shed until Christmas at the same times as before. The Christmas break extends from 25 December to the second weekend in January, when the opening times are from 11a.m.–4p.m. at weekends only.

Tatworth Fruit Farm

*Tatworth Fruit Farm Ltd,
Tatworth, Chard, Somerset TA20 2SG
Tel. Chard (0460) 20272*
ARTHUR DAVIES

Mr Davies has been growing fruit at Tatworth for over thirty years – ever since he left school, in fact, apart from two years' National Service. After retailing from the farm began in the early sixties, further expansion has resulted in the development of a flourishing farm shop. The farm grows seventeen different varieties of apple, which are available from August until May, and specialises in unusual varieties which are seldom seen in shops. There is also plenty of soft fruit available on a pick-your-own basis. Tatworth is open 7 days a week, from 9a.m.–5p.m. (Sundays 10.30a.m. 5p.m.), and is 2 miles from Chard just off the A358 Axminster road.

Thatcher's cider

Myrtle Farm, Sandford, Bristol BS19 5RA
Tel. Banwell (0934) 822862
MR J THATCHER

This is a traditional farmhouse cider made from cider apples grown on the farm, where cider has been produced and sold since early this century by three generations of the Thatcher family. My own preference is for the *cloudy cider* sold at the farm itself to personal callers. The cider is also available in local pubs and clubs. Telephone for your nearest retail outlet. Opening times are 8a.m.–6p.m., Monday to Saturday throughout the year. Sandford is on the A38, 4 miles SE of exit 21 on the M5.

DORSET

Dorchester Chocolates

Poundbury West Industrial Estate,
Dorchester, Dorset DT1 2PG
Tel. Dorchester (0305) 64257
RICHARD UNGARETTI, MARTYN SPICE

Richard Ungaretti has been involved in chocolate and confectionery making for forty-five years, apart from the war years, and has trained a work force who share his pride and dedication. All the chocolates are hand-made, using the best couverture, fresh fruit, pure essential oils, and full-strength liqueurs. No artificial additives or preservatives are used, even for the *fresh cream truffles*. Chocolates can also be produced to V*egan* specifications by special order. Dorchester Chocolates' sales are very often 'own-brand'; presentation boxes can be individually printed with the customer's name, in quantities as small as twenty-five, and even as one-offs in some cases. Visit the factory shop (at the above address) particularly at Easter and Christmas for the *hand-moulded eggs decorated with sugar flowers,* or the *Father Christmas* figures more than two feet high, intricately detailed, made using old-fashioned metal moulds. Hours are 8a.m.–5p.m. on weekdays.

Dorset Blue cheese

Farmer Bailey's Cheese Centre,
Shorts Green Farm, Motcombe,
Shaftesbury, Dorset
Tel. Shaftesbury (0747) 2260
I C BAILEY

Mr Bailey is the sole agent for Mike Davis's *Dorset Blue cheese*. Mr Davis has taken over three years to develop this cheese to its present stage, a challenge he could not resist. So many had tried and failed in their experiments to reproduce this original regional cheese which shares some characteristics with Stilton. There are still seasonal difficulties in maintaining quality and uniformity, but Mike Davis's perseverance is winning through and he now feels able to cope with a modest expansion of production, while still keeping it very much a farm-made product. Sales are mainly wholesale, with distribution throughout Dorset, Hampshire and

Wiltshire; carriers are used for retail outlets further afield. Some sales are through the specialist cheese shop on the farm – please telephone Mr Bailey for further details.

Dorset Farm sausages

Manor Farm, Little Windsor,
Broadwindsor, Dorset
Tel. Broadwindsor (0308) 68822
H V M BIRCH

Dorset Farm sausages are all made on the farm premises, are low fat, without preservatives or colouring, and come in four types – *plain pork*, *herb*, *Cumberland* and *chipolata*. They are widely distributed to high-class butchers – thirty in and around London and eighty in the Dorset, Somerset and Avon areas. They are also sold through the farm shop, which sells *beef, lamb and pork* too, and by November 1986, Manor Farm was completely organic. Times for the shop are as follows: Monday to Friday, 9a.m.–5p.m., Saturday 9a.m.–12p.m. Broadwindsor is at the junction of the B3164, B3163 and B3162 about 6 miles north of Bridport.

Dorset spring water

Lower Brimley Coombe Farm, Stoke
Abbott, Beaminster, Dorset DT8 3JZ
Tel. Broadwindsor (0308) 68792
ANTHONY FRIEND

Dorset spring water is bottled at source by the Friends on their farm – an enterprise started in order to augment their income from dairy farming, and, equally important, to provide some competition to foreign imports. The water is still, naturally filtered through the deep Jurassic rocks of Lewesdon Hill at the western end of the North Dorset Downs. It is distributed wholesale to health food shops throughout Southern England, South Wales, London and East Anglia. Please telephone for further details.

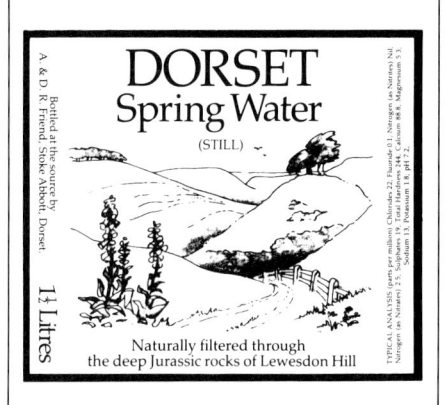

The Mary Ford Cake Artistry Centre Ltd

28–30 Southbourne Grove, Southbourne,
Bournemouth BH6 3RA
Tel. Bournemouth (0202) 431001
G A GRIFFITH (SALES AND MARKETING)

Michael and Mary Ford are both qualified bakers and confectioners, and formed the centre in 1970, to teach cake decoration on a part-time basis. As the interest and demand grew, they expanded into larger premises and full-time teaching. Just over ten years ago the Fords started their own bakery which now produces a wide variety of bread, cakes and pastries for local hotels and restaurants, and for sale to the public.

They specialise in making unusual cakes for State occasions, and many of their products feature as special offers in women's magazines. I first came across them as makers of marzipan fruits sold by the National Trust, and they also make their chocolates and Christmas cakes. For cake decorators they offer an invaluable mail order service, supplying everything from artificial flowers to icing utensils and colours. Their retail shop at the above address is open Monday to Saturday 8.30a.m.–5.30p.m.

Horn Park Farm ewes' dairy produce

Horn Park Farm, Broadwindsor Road, Beaminster, Dorset
Tel. Broadwindsor (0308) 862311

EVE AND ANGUS NICOLL

The Nicolls began with a beef herd sixteen years ago, and then changed to a flock of dairy sheep as they discovered the need for an alternative to cows' milk for all those who suffered bovine allergies. Their *ewes' milk, yoghurt,* and two types of *cheese* (a *soft yoghurt-based variety, flavoured* or *plain,* and a *full milk variety with vegetable rennet*) are offered to those who come to courses on natural health and holistic therapy held on this lovely farm, set in Hardy country. They are also distributed wholesale to wholefood shops in Dorchester, Sherborne, Yeovil, Ilminster, Crewkerne, Bridport, Swanage, Wareham, Lyme Regis, Parkstone, Bournemouth, Glastonbury and London (The Organic Shop, Neal's Yard, London WC2), or to personal callers who are welcome at any time if they telephone first. Horn Park Farm is 1 mile from Beaminster, on the Broadwindsor road (B3163).

Moores' Dorset Knobs

S Moores, The Biscuit Bakery, Morcombelake, Bridport, Dorset DT6 3ES
Tel. Chideock (0297) 89253

R K MOORES AND G M MOORES

Moores' Dorset Biscuit Bakery began baking Dorset Knobs in the 1860s, using wheat grown on the farm, milled in the farm's own water-powered mill, and baked in the farm bakehouse. Since then, Moores have moved from Stoke Mills to Litton Cheney, to Stoke Abbott and finally to Morcombelake, always taking the Dorset Knobs recipe with them. These small, round, rusk-like biscuits are still baked today, in essentially the same premises to which Samuel Moores moved in 1879. They are not economical to make (which has meant that all other local bakers stopped making them many years ago), and so can only be made when there are staff and oven space to spare, in the quiet season. Although *Dorset Knobs,* packed in tins with a highly decorative red and gold label, are the speciality for which Moores are best known, the range of

MOORES
Dorset Knob Biscuits

biscuits produced here is very large, and includes *Dorset Shortbread* and *Dorset Gingers, Easter Cakes* and *Cherry Biscuits*, all made without additives. These are available from the Dorset Shop (adjoining the bakery), open from Monday to Friday, 9a.m.–5p.m. throughout the year. Dorset Knobs, however, are only available during *December to March*.

Paradise goats' cheese

Paradise Farm, Lower Row, Holt, Wimborne, Dorset
Tel. Wimborne (0202) 882210
RUPERT HARRISON-HALL

The Harrison-Halls use a Poitou recipe – Chabichou – for their *goats' cheese logs* and *small soft cheeses*, which gives them a distinctive and delicious character that I liked very much. The cheeses come *plain*, or covered in *crushed peppercorns, celery seeds, cumin, paprika* or *charcoal*. Distribution is via Duff & Trotter, 47 Bow Lane, London EC4, and 13–15 Leadenhall Market, London EC3, and you can buy Paradise cheese from Spill the Beans, 7 West Street, Wimborne, although not from the farm itself. But as production increases, so will the number of stockists – please telephone for further details.

'Puddings'

Welgoer Farmhouse, Poyntington, Sherborne, Dorset
Tel. Corton Denham (096 322) 293
MICHAEL AND WENDY HORNE

When the Hornes retired from running their restaurant, they found that their erstwhile customers bemoaned the loss of 'the puddings' more than anything else. So they started Puddings to counteract the mediocrity of Black Forest gâteau and apple pie with ice cream served with monotonous regularity in most pubs and restaurants in the area. After two years of hard crusading, Puddings is having to expand to meet demand, and they have added pies and quiches to their range. This now includes nineteen puddings, ranging from the 'Light and Fluffy' to the 'Old-Fashioneds and Extra Specials', including *Soufflé Monte Cristo* (brandy-soaked macaroons surrounded by vanilla soufflé), *Dorset Tipsy Cake, Almond and Apricot Tart* and *Gâteau Diane*. There are *vegetarian quiches* and rich, *meaty pies* too, and *pâtés, soups* and *cocktail savouries*. No additives or preservatives are used, and it has been a problem, as the Hornes admit, trying to persuade shopkeepers to go for quality rather than long shelf-life. However, they seem to be winning, and deliver to many restaurants, pubs, golf clubs and good food shops in the area, with the delivery area expanding as their premises extend and production increases. Please telephone them for further details.

Riversdale Farm crayfish

*Riversdale Farm, Stour Provost,
Gillingham, Dorset
Tel. East Stour (074 785) 495*
KEN RICHARDS

Mr Richards' venture as crayfish farmer began in order to meet a need which had existed ever since plague wiped out the native crayfish from Europe in 1860. Crayfish farming has been successful in Europe for some time, but little was done in this country. *Signal Crayfish* (so called because of the white blotches on their claws) are being introduced because of their resistance to the plague, and because they are both larger and better flavoured than the native species. Ken Richards can supply stock of these should you wish to set up your own crayfish farm, but he also supplies the shellfish themselves to the best restaurants (the Roux Brothers', and The Neal Street Restaurant, among others), or you can buy from the farm gate, although it is advisable to telephone first. The farm is open all day, every day, and is 1½ miles from the junction of the A30 with the B3092 (between Shaftesbury and Sherborne), in Stour Provost.

WILTSHIRE

Beechenlea goats' dairy produce

*11 Sherington Mead, Pewsham,
Chippenham, Wiltshire
Tel. Chippenham (0249) 658898*
ANNE TURNER

Miss Turner stresses that her goats are fed entirely on natural feedstuffs, including natural concentrates – she feels that any fish or animal proteins present in concentrates are bound to alter the levels subsequently produced in the milk. She has kept goats since the age of ten, and has researched the subject carefully, first as a hobby, then more formally, studying the breeding of fine dairy animals, and taking a course in farm management. Anne feels that the future for goat products is very good, and that the marked increase in interest bodes well for the future. All her products – *fresh and frozen milk, yoghurt, cheese, ice cream and fudge* – can be bought from Causeway Health Foods, 4 The Causeway, Chippenham, Wiltshire, as well as from the dairy itself. *Kid meat* is available, but to order only, and she will also make up any special orders required. The dairy is open seven days a week, 8a.m.–6p.m., and is off the A4 Chippenham–Calne road. From Chippenham, turn right down Pewsham Way, take first right, then first left, and first right again into Sherington Mead.

Hosken's stoneground flour

Mill Farm, Blackland, Nr Calne, Wiltshire SN11 8PR
Tel. Calne (0249) 814507
DERREK HOSKEN

Derrek Hosken comes from a long line of Cornish millers, who were finally bought out by Spillers Ltd in 1931. He continued with the new management for thirty-two years, though always with an ambition to start his own mill. The opportunity came three years ago when redundancy freed him to restore the traditional water mill at Blackland. Milling is done with French burr stones, whose slow action ensures that the maximum goodness is retained within the flour, making it rich both in flavour, and in bran, protein, calcium, iron and vitamins B and E. Most of the mill output goes to bakers via the distribution network of a major milling group, but it is sold at the door in *1.5 and 15kg bags.* The mill is open most weekdays, from 8a.m.–5p.m. *if it is working.* If not, then there is always someone on the farm. Blackland is just south of Calne on the B3102.

The Real Meat Co.

East Hill Farm, Heytesbury, Warminster, Wiltshire BA12 0HR
Tel. Warminster (0985) 40436/40060
RICHARD AND GILLIAN GUY

Two Wiltshire farmers have formed this enterprising company to sponsor good farming practices, and to give the public a better chance of obtaining 'real' meat – i.e. meat from animals kept in a humane manner, and not given growth promoters, hormones or routine antibiotics. Farmers supplying the Real Meat Co. are obliged to follow the company's welfare code, based on the mandates of 'Compassion in World Farming', and on the Ministry of Agriculture's own good, but unenforced code. Some of the meat is produced on the Guys' own farm, and callers are welcome by prior arrangement. Open days are in the process of being arranged – ring the Guys for the latest information. Meanwhile, stockists of 'Real' meat in the area are: Gordon Bond, High Street, Lyndhurst, Hampshire (042 128) 2864; W Morgan, Lavant Street, Petersfield, Hampshire (0730) 62160; Artingstall Ltd, High Street, Corsham, Wiltshire (0249) 713253; Jarrat & Son, Alderholt, Fordingbridge, Hampshire (0425) 55053; Birdham Stores Ltd, Birdham, Chichester, W. Sussex (0243) 512888; A J Meredith, Target, 2 The Colonnade, Hawkhurst, Kent (0580) 53558.

Sherston Earl Vineyards cider, apple juice and English wine

The Vineyard, Sherston, Nr Malmesbury, Wiltshire SN16 0PY
Tel. Malmesbury (0666) 840716
NORMAN AND LINDA SELLERS

Only seven years ago, the Sellers were living in a mobile home on the thirteen acres they had just planted with vines and traditional cider apple trees. They now produce 20–30,000 gallons of cider and 6000 bottles of wine a year, and they and the production units are decently housed in stone and timber buildings built to blend in with this area of outstanding natural beauty. They specialise in '*single apple ciders*', from such varieties as Kingston Black and Dabinett. Bottled in champagne bottles, they produce a natural sparkle.

Their most famous cider is '*Sherston Scorcher*', medium dry, and renowned for its flavour and strength; at the other end of the scale, there is *Pipsqueak* apple juice. The products are well distributed by wholesalers in the south, or they can be bought from the vineyard, open every day between 10a.m.–6p.m., except Tuesdays, and Sundays 12–2p.m. Sherston is about 8 miles west of Malmesbury on the B4040.

Sherston Quail

St Catherines, Sandpits Lane, Sherston, Malmesbury, Wiltshire SN16 0NN
Tel. Malmesbury (0666) 840387
MRS ANN MASLEN

Mrs Maslen feeds the quail on game-bird mix, which gives them a good 'natural' flavour, and her quail eggs have a good reputation for size and flavour. She sells *oven-ready birds, fresh and pickled eggs*, and has *smoked quail* to order. Her quail products are stocked locally by: Tuck's (butcher), Sherston, Malmesbury (0666) 840695; Tyler's Traditional Meat, Tetbury, Gloucester (0452) 52892; Bartlett's (butcher), Green Street, Bath (0225) 66731; Walker's (butcher), Market Cross, Malmesbury.

Sherston Quail
12 QUAILS EGGS
Pickled to a traditional recipe
in distilled malt vinegar, water and spices
ANN MASLEN—St. Catherines, Sherston, Wilts. SN16 0NN. Tel: Malmesbury 840387

Wiltshire Tracklement's English mustards

The Wiltshire Tracklement Co. Ltd, High Street, Sherston, Wiltshire SN16 0LQ
Tel. Malmesbury (0666) 840851
WILLIAM TULLBERG

I well remember buying my first jar of Urchfont mustard (as it was then called) – it was a revelation after the smooth, flavourless condiment we had grown used to. William Tullberg started the English coarse-grain mustard business single-handed fourteen years ago, and the distinctive labels, written in his own elegant italic hand, appeared on the shelves of high class grocers and delicatessens all over the country. Today they are still the best, although much imitated, and their range has widened to include *vinaigrettes, horseradishes, and fine ground mustards*. I like their dry mustard powders, mixing them myself with sherry, or cider, or red or white wine depending on what they are to accompany. Asked about stockists, William Tullberg replied that 'you will find our products in the kind of retail outlet that concerns itself with reliable long-term quality – delicatessens, health and wholefood shops, good retail groups and that rare and splendid bird, the good grocer'. Or you can call at their own shop in Sherston (on the B4040, about 8 miles north-west of Chippenham), which is open Monday–Friday 9.30a.m.–12.45p.m., 1.45–5p.m.; Saturday 9.30a.m.–1p.m. Closed Bank Holiday Mondays *and the following Tuesdays.*

GLOUCESTERSHIRE

Clare's Kitchen chutneys and preserves

Aycote Farm, Rendcomb, Cirencester, Glos. GL7 7EP
Tel. North Cerney (028 583) 463 or 555
MRS CLARE BENSON

I have never enjoyed making chutney, and on buying my first jar of *Clare's Kitchen Orange Chutney*, I realised with relief I need never bother with burnt pans and vinegar fumes again. Not only is the flavour convincingly 'home-made', but there is a welcome lack of sugar which suits my non-sweet tooth very well, and there is an interesting range of flavours, which includes *Banana, Orange and Apple*, and an extra-hot *Mango Chutney*. There are also seven *marmalades*, fourteen *jams* (including a delicious *Wild Plum*, and *Peach and Orange*), five *mustards* (*Summer Herbs* tastes as delightful as it sounds), five *nut spreads*, and *humous*, and a *suet-free mincemeat with brandy*. The firm is very small, but with a staff of part-timers it manages to supply fifty shops, including all the major wholefood shops in central London,

THE SOUTH-WEST

and many of the better ones in the suburbs, and in Bath, Bristol and Cheltenham. Visitors to the farm are very welcome but please telephone

CLARE'S KITCHEN
HOMOUS
A chick pea spread or dip
Ingredients:
chick peas,
tahini, lemons
olive oil, garlic,
herbs and
sea salt.
net. wt. **340 g.**
Aycote Farm Cottage, Rendcomb, Cirencester, Glos

first as Mrs Benson is often out buying from the fruit and vegetable markets in the company of her baby daughter, Emma. Rendcomb is just east of the A435 between Cirencester and Cheltenham.

Donnington Fish Farm

Stow-on-the-Wold, Gloucestershire

See page 68 for further details.

J & P Langman dairy products and English farmhouse cheeses

Perrotts Brook Farm, nr Cirencester, Gloucestershire GL7 7BS
Tel. North Cerney (028 583) 283 or 632
MR T W WRIGHT

The famous Churnside herd of pedigree Jersey cows was founded by

Sir John and Lady Langman, and Perrotts Brook Farm has long held a reputation for preservative- and additive-free dairy products – all pastures on the farm are free from pesticides and herbicides. The products include *unpasteurised Jersey cream*, *live yoghurt (plain*, and *fruit flavours)*, *Greek-style ewes' milk yoghurt*. In addition to these, they also distribute British farmhouse cheeses, many of which are described elsewhere throughout this book. Their own products are widely distributed throughout the south of England including Harrods, and Sainsbury's. Delivery is via their own vans.

Martell's farmhouse cheeses

Charles Martell & Son,
Laurel Farm, Dymock, Gloucestershire
CHARLES MARTELL

The Martells began cheesemaking in 1972 to try to save the critically rare Old Gloucester breed of cattle by putting it back to its original use. They make *Single Gloucester*, a cheese

CHARLES MARTELL & SON
Farm
SINGLE GLOUCESTER
Cheese
Includes milk
from "Old Gloucester" cows
LAUREL FARM · DYMOCK · GLOUCESTERSHIRE · ENGLAND

originally considered inferior to its rich relation as it was kept to be eaten at home, while the Double Gloucester was sent to market to provide income. It is uncoloured, softer, and eaten younger than Double Gloucester – it has a wonderfully fresh flavour, which is particularly noticeable in the *Single Gloucester with Nettles*, a herb once much used in cheesemaking (see also Yarg, pages 21–2). The Martells are also reviving *Double Berkeley*, a golden marbled cheese originally made in the Vale of Berkeley; *Cloisters* is a creamy cheese made to a recipe previously used by thirteenth-century Cistercian monks in the Dymock area. Finally, *Nuns of Caen* is curiously named after the founders of Minchinhampton, again in the thirteenth century, and is a semi-soft ewes' milk cheese, which I would travel a long way to buy. The Martells would rather not have visitors – they are very much occupied with their cheese-making and cattle rearing. But they sell their wonderful cheeses from their own stalls at Cirencester Market on Mondays and Fridays, and Ledbury Market on Saturday mornings. Many of their cheeses are now stocked by good cheese shops round the country.

Minola smoked salmon and other foods

Kencot Hill Farmhouse, Filkins, Nr Lechlade, Gloucestershire
Tel. Filkins (036 786) 391 or 544

HUGH AND JANE FORESTIER-WALKER

The Forestier-Walkers began their career by experimentally smoking the excess large rainbow trout from a trout hatchery which they were both running. Jane then studied salmon smoking under Richard Pinney at the Butley Oysterage at Orford in Suffolk (see page 145), and in November 1984, Hugh and Jane started Minola Smoked Foods. Only a year later, their *smoked salmon* won very high praise in a *Sunday Times* smoked salmon tasting article. This isn't surprising; it is smoked over oak which retains its

Minola
SMOKED PRODUCTS
Home Oak Cure Fish, Poultry & Game

bark, and therefore the acids which produce the true smoked flavour. Their range of products is large, and includes such delicacies as smoked

Barbarie Duck Breast, *pheasant*, *almonds*, *cashews* and the *bacon* and *salamis* which are proving especially popular at the moment. They use pure salt, without magnesium, and no additives or colourings, relying on careful smoking to provide all that's necessary. Most of their sales are via mail order (by telephone or letter, three days notice is required), and the rest are via wholesalers, with their own van delivering to retailers, including fishmongers, weekly, within a 50-mile radius. Personal callers should ring in advance, as the produce is smoked and prepared freshly to order, with only very small amounts held in stock. Kencot Hill Farmhouse is 3½ miles south of Burford on the A361, ¼ mile north of the North Filkin turning.

SOUTHERN ENGLAND

Hampshire and the Isle of Wight
—
Berkshire
—
Oxfordshire
—
Buckinghamshire

Southern England combines the sophistication of outer London with the encroaching rurality of the West Country. This is a good apple area; apple tastings are held at Blackmoor* in October, or you can buy the less usual Ashmeads Kernel and Red James Grieve apples at Swanmore*. Swanmore also has cherries in the early summer, and is the only Hampshire fruit farm to grow them. The Isle of Wight, in its small area, shelters a number of resourceful producers, including the largest commercial grower of garlic* in Britain.

Near Winchester, the chief architect of the revival of sheep dairying in this country, Olivia Mills*, rears her sheep on the old salt levels. She has inspired many a good cheesemaker with the courage and optimism to branch out into this relatively uncharted territory.

Up in Buckinghamshire, at beautiful Nether Winchendon House, Robert Spencer Bernard* is engaged in breeding wild boar crossed with Tamworth pigs, in order to produce a lean, gamey meat as near to wild boar meat as possible. Oxford now offers one of the best places for informal eating that I've come across for a long time – The Oxford Brew-house is a microbrewery which uses its beer yeast in the bread baked in the adjacent bakery. You can buy this to take home, or eat it there with salt beef or a herring and beetroot salad for lunch, sometimes with live jazz as an accompaniment. At the other end of the scale, the Maison Blanc bakery in Woodstock Road (and in the covered market) makes French pâtisserie and bread; although I found my *baguette* disappointing, the small *tartes aux prunes* were exceptional.

Berkshire contains one of Britain's best cheese shops, now run by Hugh Rance, but started by his father Patrick – almost the patron saint of British cheese. He has done more to revive interest in cheese generally, and in British traditional farmhouse cheese in particular, than almost anyone else. His inspiring book *The Great British Cheese Book*, reminded those who were old enough to have forgotten and instructed those too young to know, that the mouse-trap doldrums are over, and great cheese is still being made in this country, although not without difficulty. Things can only continue to improve – he has told us what to look for and what we should expect – we must learn to ask for it.

HAMPSHIRE AND THE ISLE OF WIGHT

Blackmoor Apples

Blackmoor Apple Shop, Blackmoor, Liss, Hampshire GU33 6BS
Tel. Bordon (042 03) 3576/7 Shop: Bordon (042 03) 3782
SUE LORRAINE (RETAIL SALES MANAGER)

The Blackmoor Estate grows a wide range of apples, as do many similar orchards in the area. It does, however, organise *Apple Tastings* each October, which are a wonderful way to introduce people to the less well-known varieties, *Chivers Delight*, for instance. We found, when travelling through New England one October, that apple growers offered tastings of their crops in much the same way that good wine merchants hold wine-tastings (and often with the same amount of seriousness, too); we managed to try many different kinds before committing ourselves to buying any one variety. The Blackmoor Apple Shop also sells *locally made jams and cakes*, and *meat without hormones*, either frozen or vacuum packed; it is open from Tuesday to Thursday, 9a.m.–4p.m., Friday and Saturday, 9a.m.–5p.m., Sunday 11a.m.–4p.m.

Telephone for further details of their October apple tastings. Blackmoor is just to the west of the A325 Farnham to Petersfield road, 4 miles north of Liss.

Ewe Tree Farm ewes' milk products

The Firs, Embley Lane, nr Romsey, Hampshire SO5 0DN
Tel. Romsey (0794) 523099/523812
MR AND MRS G CORLASS

The Corlass's make a very original dessert from their ewes' milk: *Caillé de Brébis* is a sort of crème caramel, ewes' milk infused with a bay leaf, then renneted with a vegetable rennet and poured into small glass jars which contain a sauce – chocolate, honey, caramel. The result is rich and delicious, blander than yoghurt. They also produce *live yoghurt*, with fruit flavours made by request, and *soft cheese*, either plain or with various flavourings, both sweet and savoury. They supply health food shops, delicatessens and restaurants in the area, and visitors to the farm are very welcome, especially so if preceded by a telephone call. To find The Firs, take the A27 from Romsey to Salisbury – Embley Lane is the second road on the left after about 2 miles; The Firs is on the right after approximately ½ mile.

Hartley's 'Country Cousins' fruit wines

C J Hartley Ltd,
Hillgrove, The Meon Valley Vineyard,
Swanmore, Southampton SO3 2PZ
Tel. Droxford (0489) 877435
CHRISTOPHER AND KATHLEEN HARTLEY

The Hartleys make a wide range of country fruit wines, meads and English wines, drawing on Christopher Hartley's inherited and acquired skills as a wine and cider maker. The *English wines* are made from grapes grown at Hillgrove – Müller-Thurgau, Madeleine Angevine, Seyval Blanc, Pinot Meunier, Chardonnay, Triomphe d'Alsace. The *fruit wines* are all made from pure fruit juices with the addition only of sugar and yeast, using traditional recipes to produce *Blackberry & Elderberry*, *Strawberry*, *Gooseberry*, *Apple & Morello Cherry*. The *meads* are of honey with additional fruit juices – *Sparkling Mead*, *Sparkling Mary Rose* (described as '*a Melomel of English Strawberries and Pure Honey*', and *Hippocras*, made as the mead, but with added spices. There is also a super quality *fudge*, and *Grape Jelly*, made from their own grapes to an American recipe (a very good idea, and a change from the more usual vineyard by-product, mustard). Retail outlets include: Peter Dominic, High Street, Southampton; Riber Castle, nr Matlock, Derbyshire; James Grant Wines, 8 Wentworth Crescent, Penistone, Sheffield; Essentially English, 10b West Street, Oundle, Northamptonshire; Vitis Wines, 29 Kingsway, Banbury, Oxfordshire, as well as wine shops in the area. Sales also from the vineyard, but please phone first to make an appointment, as the Hartleys themselves are not always there. Shop hours: daily 9a.m.–6p.m., Sundays 12–2p.m. Swanmore is to the east of the A32 between Fareham and Alton, about 9 miles north of Fareham.

Hill Farm Orchards

Droxford Road, Swanmore,
Southampton SO3 2PY
Tel. Droxford (0489) 878616 (office);
877225 (shop); 878570 (ansaphone)
PETER BARWICK

Hill Farm Orchards pride themselves on their range of apples – which includes such varieties as *Egremont Russet*, *Lord Lambourne*, *Ashmeads Kernel* and *Red James Grieve*. They also grow *pears*, and *cherries* (the only orchard in Hampshire to do so). They also have a pick-your-own area near Chichester (Pagham Road, Tel. Chichester (0243) 787849). The cherry season is in early July, after the gooseberries and strawberries, and at the same time as the raspberries. The apple season lasts through September to mid-October, with pears in October. The farm shop is open all year round, Monday–Saturday 9a.m.–5p.m., Sunday 10a.m.– 5p.m., and sells farm-pressed apple juice, amongst other local produce.

Swanmore lies west of the A32, about 2 miles north of Wickham.

Island Country Foods pork products

Asheybrook, Ashey, Ryde, Isle of Wight PO33 4AT
Tel. Ryde (0983) 65686
J H AND S H FISHER

The Fishers noticed, while they were living in Germany, the part that traditional food played in the pattern of family life, and felt that it was sad that it no longer played such an important role in this country. On their retirement from the Forces they decided to set up on their own to produce the sort of food they felt was so often lacking in England. Combining this with their interest in rare breeds of farm animal, and their family traditions of farming and horticulture, they now produce *pork products* from a herd of *Tamworth pigs*, reared outside on a high-vegetable diet. *Suckling pigs*, and *marinated barbecue packs* are the specialities – the marinade is a secret blend of home-grown herbs to a mixed old English and Hanoverian farmhouse recipe. Organically grown fresh fruit and vegetables and pure fruit juices are also sold through the farm shop. The pork is prepared to order, so please telephone first for this. Open seven days a week in the summer, *closed on Sunday mornings in the winter*. Leave Ryde on the Ashey road, past the Shell petrol station; take the second turning left signed Nunwell and Brading – it is the first house on the left.

Kingcob vacuum packed garlic

Mersely Farms, Newchurch, Sandown, Isle of Wight PO36 0MT
Tel. Sandown (0983) 865229
COLIN BOSWELL

Those of us who live too far north to grow good garlic have probably often depended on Colin Boswell's *Kingcob garlic*, which sells all over the country in supermarkets as well as via independent retailers. He started growing garlic in 1976, and growing it commercially in 1979, and is now the largest commercial grower in Britain. His newest venture – greeted with relief by lovers of dishes such as Chicken with Forty Cloves of Garlic – is *fresh peeled garlic*, vacuum packed without preservatives. Kingcob products are available through the Mersely Farms shop, at *Langbridge Farm*, Newchurch, Isle of Wight, open May to October 9a.m.–5p.m. and at weekends. Take the Newport road (B3056) at Sandown – the Newchurch turning is on the right after about 3 miles.

Ruth Liversedge hand-made chocolates

Hidden Cottage, High Street, Beaulieu, Hampshire SO4 7YA
Tel. Beaulieu (0590) 612279
RUTH AND ALAN LIVERSEDGE

The Liversedges began making chocolates for their tea shop in Beaulieu four years ago. The chocolates are now so popular that the tea shop has become a chocolate factory, and the major part of the business, where the chocolate production and packing are on view to the public. The recipes are secret, but the ingredients are top quality Belgian couverture and natural flavours. Packaging is a speciality – apart from the elegant maroon and gold boxes, the chocolates can be packed in decorative tea caddies or biscuit tins, in a 'box camera' which afterwards doubles as a photo file, or a model of 'Hidden Cottage', which becomes a jewellery box with a secret opening. Sales are wholesale to top London shops such as Harrods and Fortnums, and abroad to Saks 5th Avenue, New York; Marshall Fields, Chicago, and Wannermakers of Philadelphia, as well as outlets in Japan, Germany, the Middle East and Scandinavia. There is some mail order, and of course visitors are welcome at the shop, which is open seven days a week all year round (with the exception of Christmas week), 10a.m.–5p.m.

Meadow Cottage low-fat and real dairy ice cream

Meadow Cottage, Headley, Bordon, Hampshire GU35 8SS
Tel. Headley Down (0428) 712155
HUGH BLACKBURNE, PETER AND CELIA HAYNES

Hugh Blackburne, his sister Celia and her husband Peter began farming twenty years ago on twenty-three acres, with two Jersey cows. Now the acreage has grown to 150 acres, and the herd to ninety-five pedigree Jersey milkers and sixty youngsters. The farm has been selling untreated milk and cream locally for a number of years, with ice cream production beginning only two years ago. The *dairy ice cream* is made solely with the cream and milk from the home herd in order to maintain quality and hygiene, plus raw cane sugar, egg-yolk and natural flavourings, with no artificial colour. Five flavours are produced including a particularly delicious *Honey, Hazelnut and Almond*. The *Skimline Milk Ice* is very popular with those who prefer a lighter ice cream, and sells well to health food shops and nursing homes, as well as to hotels, and stores such as Harrods. It is made mainly from skimmed milk, with only 2.5% added butterfat, and also comes in five natural flavours, without artificial colourings. Telephone for further details of retail outlets. Visitors are very welcome, and can see the cows and calves 'at work'. Hours are from 6.30a.m.–6.30p.m., seven days a week! From Farnham or Hindhead take the A287 to Churt, and once there take the Headley road. After 1¼ miles, the farm is signed 'Weydown Jerseys' on the right hand side of the road.

Millers Damsel Wheat Wafers

Lower Mill, Newbridge, Yarmouth, Isle of Wight PO41 0TZ
Tel. Calbourne (098 378) 228
JOHN PRETTY

John Pretty began milling Isle of Wight wheat at Lower Calbourne in 1973, in the water mill he had bought as a weekend retreat five years earlier, while on the main board of Watney's. After the takeover of Watney Mann in 1973, John Pretty decided he would rather run his own small enterprise than be part of a larger one. His first product was wholemeal flour, which then developed into bread baked in a wood-fired oven. Another bakery was bought in 1976, and biscuit baking began to augment the bread baking, still using the mill's own flour. Now, *Millers Damsel Wheat Wafers,* their most popular and most original product (they have taken the place of Bath Olivers, to my mind, as being one of the best biscuits to complement the new British cheeses), along with

WHEAT WAFERS
SLIGHTLY SAVOURY

Millers Damsel Enterprises Ltd.

their range of *Calbourne Crunchies,* are widely distributed throughout the country. As customers are being added every week, it's best to telephone for further details of your nearest stockist – or you may be able to make arrangements for mail order, too.

Phillips smoked salmon

Wight Farm, Quarr Hill, Binstead, Isle of Wight, PO33 4EH
Tel. Isle of Wight (0983) 65100
RICHARD PHILLIPS

Mr Phillips is proud of the quality of his *smoked Scotch salmon,* which is without additives, and hand-sliced. It is available by mail order, and wholesale, for export as well as nationally. However, personal callers to Wight Farm shop are also able to buy *fresh seafood, live lobsters* and *trout, venison* and *venison sausages, smoked salmon pâté* and *taramasalata.* Open Thursday, Friday and Saturday 9a.m.–5p.m. all year round. Binstead is on the Ryde to Newport road (B3054), about 2 miles outside Ryde.

Wield Wood Sheep Dairy

Wield Wood, Nr Alresford, Hampshire SO24 9RU
Tel. Alton (0420) 63151
MRS OLIVIA MILLS

Mrs Mills is the doyenne of sheep dairying in this country, and as founder of the British Sheep Dairying Association has inspired and helped many ewes' milk producers to gain experience and recognition (Mrs Corlass, see page 61, was inspired by seeing Mrs Mills on television). She herself began by selling up her herd of dairy cattle, and turning her back on thirty years' experience of milking. Since her farm is on thin chalk, sheep farming was the only alternative, but it was extremely hard to make it viable. So Mrs Mills researched, then began milking her ewes. Her book is the definitive work in English (and now translated into Russian too), *Practical*

Sheep Dairying, published by Thorsons. The Wield Wood products are *fresh and frozen milk*, *yoghurt*, a *drained yoghurt curd* called *Petit Friese* (plain, or with chives), and *Walda*, a semi-hard cheese, which takes three to six months to mature, and has green peppercorns, or caraway seeds added sometimes for variety. These are stocked by such shops as Cranks, Marshall Street, London W1, Selfridges, Harrods, and Wells Stores, Streatley, Berkshire. Visitors are welcome at the farm any afternoon between 2.30 and 5p.m.

BERKSHIRE

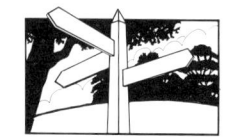

Culham Harvest foods

Culham Farms, Frogmill, Hurley, Maidenhead, Berkshire SL6 5NJ
Tel. Littlewick Green (062 882) 3155

MRS H STOKES

Mrs Stokes started a farm shop eight years ago, when the stock consisted mainly of local vegetables. The range gradually expanded to include prepared dishes – *casseroles*, *quiches*, *desserts* and *dinner party dishes* – which also sold to several outlets in London. This proved uneconomic, as the delivery costs ate into the profits, and so now the outlets are local, with one or two exceptions – Hobbs of South Audley Street, London W1, for example. The range also includes the well-known *Culham Hams*, which Mrs Stokes has been producing for more than twenty years, to an old recipe; and *marmalades*, including a new malt whisky flavour, using Macallan 10-year-old malt. Sales are by telephone orders, as there is now no retail outlet on the premises. Mail order by Datapost can be arranged too. Please telephone Mrs Stokes for details.

Denton's Dairy farm shop

17 High Street, Lambourne, Berkshire
Tel. Lambourne (0488) 72484

C G DENTON AND FAMILY

The Dentons have been selling the *unpasteurised milk* and *cream* from their own pedigree herd of Jerseys for five years, in the belief that it is the best way to utilise their milk production. They also sell their own organically grown vegetables and farm-produced lamb, chicken, turkeys, pheasants and free-range eggs. They supply wholesale as well as to their own farm shop, which is open 9a.m.–5.30p.m. on weekdays (closed 1–2p.m. for lunch), except Thursdays, when they close at 1p.m. On Saturdays the hours are 9a.m.–4.30p.m. (closed for lunch) and Sundays 9.30a.m.–12.30p.m. Lambourne is on the B4001 about 6 miles north of Hungerford.

Rock's country wines

*Loddon Park Farm, New Bath Road,
Twyford, Berkshire
Tel. Twyford (0734) 342344*

HUGH ROCK

Hugh Rock feels that people are frequently unwilling to try country wines since they are so often sweet and heavy. He is now working at dispelling these prejudices by applying modern wine technology to a long-standing country craft. The *Elderflower Wine* is made once a year in June, July and August from a fermentation of fresh elderflowers, with gooseberries and grape juice. It is then matured in casks and bottled at Christmas for drinking the following year, to produce a light table-wine. The champagne-method sparkling *Gooseberry Wine* is a much stronger party wine, completely dry, and made by the process of refermentation in the bottle which gives 'such a wonderful bubble'. Sales are mainly wholesale to restaurants, hotels and wine bars, and some wine merchants; also by mail order direct from the farm – please apply for full lists of retail outlets. Visitors are welcome by prior appointment. Loddon Park Farm is on the A4 at Twyford.

OXFORDSHIRE

Abbey Farm ewes' milk products

*Abbey House Farm, Goosey,
Faringdon, Oxfordshire
Tel. West Hannay (023 587) 705*

R C WHITWORTH

A packet of French-made Greek feta cheese made Mr Whitworth feel that if the French could make Greek cheese and sell it at a profit in England, then it was high time that the English started to make their own ewes' milk cheese. Mr Whitworth's career experience, from a jackeroo in Australia to salesman for a large assurance company, more than fitted him for such an enterprise, and although the feta-making is still a proposed development, he distributes fresh and frozen ewes' milk and yoghurt to twenty-three shops in the area. Farm gate sales are limited to milk only at the moment, and please telephone first to avoid disappointment, and to find out more about about the proposed cheesemaking. Abbey House Farm is situated on the right hand side of Goosey Green as you approach from Goosey, ¼ mile from the main Wantage–Faringdon road (A417).

Clearwater trout

Ludbridge Mill, East Hendred, Wantage, Oxfordshire OX12 8LN
Tel. Abingdon (0235) 833732/833798
PETER AUSTIN

Peter and Rachael Austin run a partnership which specialises in producing food from good ingredients – their *smoked trout pâté* is very good indeed, made to their own secret recipe and entirely without additives or preservatives. The *pâté, fresh* and *smoked trout* are available to personal callers either at the above address, or The Donnington Fish Farm, Stow-on-the-Wold, Gloucestershire. But there is a mail order service for their *smoked Scotch salmon*. Opening times for Ludbridge Mill: Tuesday to Sunday, 10a.m.–5p.m., November to March; Tuesday to Sunday, 10a.m.–6p.m. April to October *and* Bank Holidays. East Hendred is just south of the A417 to the east of Wantage. Opening times for Donnington: 7 days, 10a.m.–5p.m., November to March; 7 days, 10a.m.–6p.m., April to October. About 3 miles north of Stow-on-the-Wold, to the west of the A429.

Oxbridge marmalades and conserves

Unit 11, Oxford Business Centre, Osney Lane, Oxford OX1 1TB
Tel. Oxford (0865) 246510
MRS MAUREEN KEENAN

Mrs Keenan's experience in production and marketing, gained while she was working for a manufacturer of jams and marmalades, led her to set up her own business. Her products are high quality, traditional and with much appeal for export as very English gifts. The *marmalades, jams* and *chutneys* are all hand-prepared and cooked in small batches; the *Christmas puddings* are entirely free of preservatives, artificial colourings and additives. Her choice of name for the products has led her into trouble with a rival marmalade firm, and gives some indication of the success of her marketing. You can buy Oxbridge products from the John Lewis Group, Lewis's/Selfridge group, Harrods and House of Fraser stores, and Liberty & Co. Look for the jars wearing mortar boards.

Meg Rivers fruit cakes

Lower Brailes, Banbury, Oxfordshire OX15 5HT
Tel. Brailes (060 885) 584
MEG DORMAN

This is the sort of enterprise which we all feel we could start, but never do. Luckily for the rest of us, Meg Dorman has, based on the simple idea of feeding family and friends delicious cakes which do not break the healthy eating rules, and then making enough to sell to a wider and wider and ever more appreciative public. This is how Meg Dorman started, and she has continued to make her fruit cakes to the highest possible standards. They contain masses of fruit and nuts, all are made in a choice of either *white* or *organically grown wholemeal flour*, *butter* or *Granose margarine*; there is also a *vegetarian Christmas pudding*. The cakes are sold by mail order, with plans for a small retail shop in Brailes and wholesale to good grocers and health food shops. Write or telephone for details of such things as *Sailing Cake, Australian Fruit Loaf,* and *Summer Fruit Cake.*

Autumn & Winter 1985/86

Meg Rivers Cakes
Lower Brailes
Banbury, Oxon. OX15 5HT
Tel. Brailes (060885) 584

MAIL ORDER

Enjoy the exceptional taste of delicious fruit cakes individually baked in the traditional way.

BUCKINGHAMSHIRE

Chiltern beef and kid meat

*Chiltern Beef Ltd,
Chalcombe, 13 Highwoods Drive,
Marlow Bottom, Marlow,
Buckinghamshire SL7 3PU
Tel. Marlow (062 84) 2653*

DR J M WILKINSON

Dr Wilkinson has written two books on the subject of grass-produced beef, and is currently writing another on commercial goat production (he is Chairman of the Goat Producers Association), so Chiltern beef and goat meat are naturally quality products. The grass/clover pastures and silage in the Chiltern Hills result in good flavour, combined with leanness – it is this last quality which is particularly relevant for today's cholesterol-conscious consumer. Hence the production of goat meat too, very low in fat. The kids are reared for four to six months, and fed on grass, hay and cereal/protein supplements. Sales are direct to the public, and Chiltern Beef will deliver. Please telephone before calling, to check on availability. Marlow Bottom is about 2 miles north of Marlow.

Nether Winchendon Farms cross-bred wild boar

Estate Office, Nether Winchendon, Aylesbury, Buckinghamshire HP18 0DY
ROBERT SPENCER BERNARD

While compiling this book, I saw a photograph in *The Times* of Mr Spencer Bernard's wild boar and Tamworth crossbreed. With no more information than his name and 'a farm near Aylesbury', I sent a letter off into the blue – and was eventually rewarded, first by a telephone call, then with a letter explaining his fascinating work on his wild boar enterprise. The idea for this came while staying with friends in Austria who rear these crossbreeds as 'Waldschwein' rather than 'Wildschwein'. The pure-bred wild boar at Nether Winchendon have to be kept virtually imprisoned, subject to the provisions of a Local Authority licence under the Dangerous Wild Animals Act. Crossbreeds, however, are not subject to the same provisions, so the answer is to breed 75% pure. These are reared slowly out of doors in woodland where they forage largely for themselves, living off whatever they root out of the ground, as well as off drops of wild cherries, acorns, beech mast and sweet chestnuts. They are not fed chemicals. The resulting meat is tender and gamey 'which seems to attract universal approval' – but the animals take far longer to reach a suitable size for slaughter. The experimental nature of Mr Spencer Bernard's work means that it isn't possible to sell less than half a pig at a time at the moment. Eventually he hopes to increase production and produce a cured and smoked ham in the German manner. Meanwhile, enquiries *in writing* are welcomed. Nether Winchendon House, which has been in Mr Spencer Bernard's family since the mid-sixteenth century, is open to the public, and lies off the A418, approximately 7 miles north-west of Aylesbury.

Springhill Bakery

Springhill Farm Foods Ltd, Gatehouse Close, Aylesbury, Buckinghamshire HP19 3DE
Tel. Aylesbury (0296) 25333/32300
JAMES DIXON

The founders of Springhill Foods, Hugh and Nadya Coates, are keen to develop products that make a positive contribution to health rather than to simply avoid harmful additives. To this end, Springhill Bakery products contain no animal fats, or artificial additives, colourings or preservatives. Most of the organic grain used is grown on their own farms and milled fresh every day in the bakery. Wherever possible natural leaven is used, and most products have reduced sodium and one or two are low-gluten, too. The *Sprouted Grain Bread* is delicious, as is the *Country Gristy Bread*, although I must admit to having eaten both thickly spread with butter. Springhill Bakery products are available through Holland & Barrett and other leading health food shops – telephone Mr Dixon for your nearest stockist.

LONDON AND THE SOUTH-EAST

LONDON

SURREY

KENT

SUSSEX

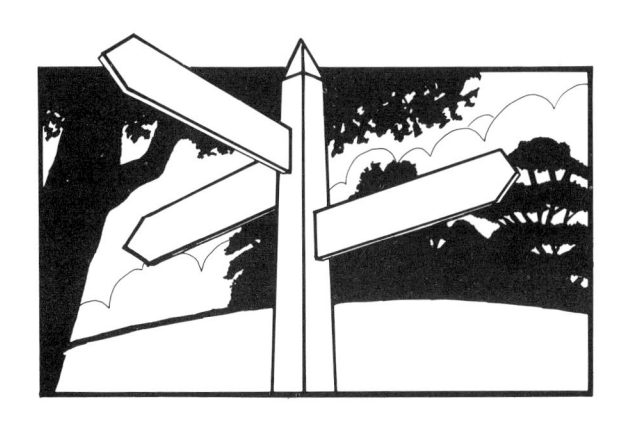

T his is the area in which I grew up, at a time when rotund Southdown sheep still cropped the thymey turf on the South Downs, and provided many a memorable Sunday roast – now the Downs are largely submerged under fields of superfluous grain, and what sheep remain are as often bred for their milk as for their meat. It is the area of the Channel ports, too, where people can take ferries on day trips to French supermarkets while ignoring the wonderful food being produced on their doorsteps, or rather, almost in their own gardens. Good wine is being made here, some good cheeses too and how much more comfortable it is driving down a Sussex lane to buy some of Mrs Flintan's* superb humanely-reared veal, than to battle with queues and strike threats at the Channel ports.

Kent has always been famous for its orchards, and there are many fine producers of cider, apple wine and apple juice here. Penshurst Vineyards* apple wine and juice are both excellent; I like Andrew Helbling's* approach to apple juice, made on his farm near Canterbury. He makes it by variety, not by blending, and uses wine language to describe the character each apple gives to the juice. I wish all these Kent apple juices were marketed more widely; it is sad to note that in my local supermarket, in Cheshire, almost all the apple juices are imported.

London is, as it always has been, the home of sophisticated food; much is imported, but now more is being produced at home too. Fresh pasta shops have sprung up like fungi over the past few years, but James Talbot's Pasta Factory* was one of the first, and is still one of the best. In Winchmore Hill, Geoffrey Hazzan* is making fresh cream truffles which equal anything from Belgium. At La Maison des Sorbets*, Paris-trained Julian Tomkins has the wonderful idea of making sorbet cakes for summer weddings, and Mrs Gill's Indian Kitchen* can supply you with first class authentic dishes which you can take away and reheat with the minimum of fuss. Should you prefer to do your own Indian cooking from scratch, then join The Curry Club*, which supplies almost everything you need by post (except the perishables, of course). At Rococo* in the King's Road, Chantal Coady produces gloriously frivolous colour-co-ordinated confectionery in an enchantingly pretty shop decorated in wedding-cake colours. But if it is traditional London food you want, then Cooke's* eel and pie shop has hardly changed for a hundred years, and it still serves just that, eels and pies.

LONDON

Cooke's eel and pie shop

F Cooke & Sons, 41 Kingsland High Street, London E8 2JS
Tel. 01-254 2878

FRED AND CHRIS COOKE

Fred and Chris Cooke's eel and pie shop is almost the last of its kind, although there's no sign of its being a dying breed, to judge by the queues on a Saturday night, and the volume of pies baked and sold (about 2000 on a Saturday). It is as much visited by

Pie Manufacturers and Eel Merchants

F. COOKE & SONS

41 KINGSLAND HIGH ST., E8 2JS

Phone: 01 254 2878

tourists as by locals, not for gastronomic reasons – many of us might find the *hot eels with parsley liquor* a bit bland – but for the splendid Edwardian premises virtually unchanged since the shop was built in 1908. The food is simple: *live, jellied* or *hot eels, pie and mash* and by way of dessert, *fruit pie and custard*. All the pies are made on the premises. The eels come from all over England, collected in the Cookes' own tanker to ensure they don't suffer from mishandling en route, or sometimes from Spain and Greece when necessary. They are kept in tanks, constantly aerated to keep the eels alive and healthy. Live eels are supplied to fishmongers, Chinese supermarkets and London Zoo – and you can buy them over the counter. Pubs and restaurants are supplied with jellied eels. Open Mondays, Thursdays 10a.m.–8p.m.; Tuesdays, Wednesdays 10a.m.–6p.m., Fridays, Saturdays 10a.m.–10p.m. Closed on Sundays and Bank Holidays.

Geoffroi's fresh cream truffles

Geoffroi & Co.,
65 Station Road, Winchmore Hill, London N21 3NB
Tel. 01-360 8289
GEOFFREY HAZZAN

A husband and wife team, the Hazzans began their truffle-making when Geoffrey was made redundant from his job in the plastics industry in 1983 – his wife still works as a pharmacologist. Not surprisingly, they felt that making hand-made truffles in small batches with the best ingredients, would provide a pleasant contrast to their careers. The truffles are wonderful – I fell for the *Amaretto* flavour covered in dark chocolate – and beautifully boxed in dark green, red and gold. The sales are retail through the shop, with some work done for special functions. The delivery area is limited by the truffles' short shelf life; the Hazzans like to deliver them personally – special arrangements can always be made. The shop is open Tuesday to Friday, 10.30a.m.–7p.m., Saturday 10a.m.–5p.m., and is opposite Winchmore Hill station.

Mrs Gill's Indian Kitchen

144 Bowes Road, London N13
Tel. 01-886 0424
CHRISTOPHER AND DAMAN GILL

The Gills run a valuable service for all lovers of Indian food – they provide traditionally prepared and carefully cooked food in clear plastic pouches, which can be reheated by immersing in boiling water, as well as in a microwave oven. The advantages are obvious; you can see what you are buying, and the reheating process is simple even for those who only possess one gas ring and a saucepan. Best of all, the food is very good indeed, cooked to recipes passed down through generations of Mrs Gill's family – her mother, Mrs Shanti Bahl, is a member of the team. The ingredients are fresh, the list of spices (clearly indicated on the labels) is long and expensive spices such as green cardamom and black cumin are used wherever the recipe dictates – no corners are cut.

Furthermore, there are no additives in any form. There is a range of nineteen dishes, including several vegetarian items such as *Brinjal Curry*, *Gobi Aloo*, and V*egetable Samosas*. Sales are both retail and wholesale, and there is a wonderful freezer-filling service, with deliveries to your home. Retail outlets include Neal's Yard Wholefood Warehouse, Covent Garden, London WC2; The Curry Shop, Covent Garden, London WC2; and Humble Pie, Burnham Market, Norfolk, and from 144 Bowes Road (10a.m.–5p.m. on weekdays), on the North Circular Road, due north of Muswell Hill.

Leatham's Larder gravad lax and game

1 Bethwin Road, Camberwell,
London SE5 0YJ
Tel. 01-703 7031

MARK AND OLIVER LEATHAM

After leaving the Army in 1978, Mark Leatham decided to shoot pigeons professionally and sell them to London restaurants. His brother Oliver, studying law at university, saw the feasibility of this and having completed his degree in 1979 joined Mark in his venture. The first problem came at the end of the game season – how to carry on the business until the start of the next. Sales of smoked salmon solved that one, with fresh lobster and salmon added to the range as the business grew. The enterprise has prospered to such an extent that in 1982 Leatham's Larder moved to their present premises in Camberwell where they now cure the salmon themselves, as well as the *gravad lax* – the Scandinavian method of curing salmon with salt and dill which has become as popular as smoked salmon. Every type of *fresh game* is processed here too, during the season, and can be supplied frozen out of season. There is a thriving export market too, including supplies to the Printemps stores in Paris. English retail outlets include Harrods, and Hobbs of South Audley Street, London W1, as well as hotels and restaurants – The Dorchester in Park Lane, The Waterside Inn in Bray. There is a small mail order service too. Personal callers are welcome, after prior notice, Monday to Friday, 5a.m. to 7p.m. Bethwin Road is situated just off Walworth Road, halfway between Elephant & Castle and Camberwell Green stations.

Lidgate's Kitchen

110 Holland Park Avenue,
London W11 4PZ
Tel. 01-727 8243

DAVID LIDGATE

We have one particular friend who rarely arrives at our Northern outpost without something delicious from 'lovely Mr Lidgate'. A large range of dishes is prepared on the premises, to take away, or to order for parties and buffets – *pâtés, home-cooked hams,* very good *chicken cutlets with herb and avocado mayonnaise, leek vinaigrette with carrot ribbons,* trays of *cold cooked meats* which include *shoulder of veal stuffed with green peppercorns,* are just some of the dishes this wonderful shop produces. Most of the fresh meat used and sold is now hormone and additive free, and the exceptions are moving in this direction too. The service is as good as the food – the present Mr Lidgate is the fourth generation in this family firm which began in 1850 – with free estimates for catering, and free delivery within central London; their motto is 'Whatever you want, we'll do'. Hours are useful – 7a.m.–6p.m. Monday to Friday, 7.30a.m.–5p.m. Saturdays.

La Maison des Sorbets

140 Battersea Park Road, London SW11 4NB Tel. 01-720 8983/4

JULIAN TOMKINS

La Maison des Sorbets began in 1982 as a business directed towards private customers, but the high quality of the products resulted in a large number of wholesalers approaching the company for supplies. Julian Tomkins himself has served a 2-year apprenticeship with one of Paris' top pâtissiers, which has led him to combine the two arts – *speciality sorbets* for dinner parties and *sorbet wedding cakes.* The *pâtisserie* side of the enterprise was developed to bridge the seasonal gap left by the sorbets which are essentially summer products – Julian Tomkins feels that London is still undersupplied with good quality pâtisserie. The best possible ingredients go into all the products. Fruit is bought from Covent Garden market, and the use of sugar is kept to a minimum to preserve the fresh taste of the fruit. Retail outlets include Justin de Blank, 42 Elizabeth Street, SW1; Partridges, 132 Sloane Street, SW1; Rosslyn Delicatessen, 56 Rosslyn Hill, NW5; With Relish, 1 Lacy Road, SW15. Julian Tomkins and his team are happy to receive telephone enquiries, and to make appointments for customers with special requests.

Neal's Yard Dairy

9 Neal's Yard, London WC2 9DP Tel. 01-379 7646

RANDOLPH HODGSON AND JANE SCOTTER

It was a visit to this tiny shop in Neal's Yard that made me realise what a wealth of good cheese was being made in the British Isles, undreamt of by those who, like myself, had had their knowledge limited to Dairy Crest's travesties of cheese. I have had many happy 'library' sessions at the dairy since, tasting my way through the *ever-changing collection of British farmhouse cheeses,* most of which are selected by Randolph and Jane on their regular visits to the farms. The dairy also make their own soft cheeses and yoghurts and ice creams on their farm in the Weald of Kent, using unpasteurised Friesian cows' milk and goats' milk. A wonderful, and peaceful, place to taste and browse and buy, but don't go too early, it only opens at 10.30a.m. and closes at 5.30p.m. Monday to Friday, 10a.m.–5p.m. on Saturdays. Neal's

Yard is tucked away, approached via alleyways from either Monmouth Street or Short's Gardens.

The Pasta Factory

261 King's Road, London SW3 5EL
Tel. 01-352 8573
JAMES TALBOT

The idea of The Pasta Factory was suggested to James Talbot by his sister, who had been impressed by the number of fresh pasta shops in Argentina, while she was living in Buenos Aires, and who decided that it would be a good plan to open one in London. So, in February 1983, The Pasta Factory was opened and has been proving James's sister right ever since. The fresh pasta boom is even ousting hamburger joints, which is all the better since pasta manages to combine a nutritious product with fast food qualities. You can watch the pasta being made here too, always fun, and further proof of its freshness; the range includes the *ribbon pastas* such as *linguine* and *fettucine*, and *filled pastas*. *Wholewheat and tomato* variations are available to order. Pasta sauces are very good – we loved the *wild mushroom*, the *quattro formaggii* and of course, the *pesto*. Sales are wholesale to restaurants, with deliveries made within a 3-mile radius. Shop hours are 10a.m.–8p.m. Tuesday to Saturday, 12–8p.m. on Monday. The shop is directly opposite Carlyle Square on the King's Road, very close to the junction with Old Church Street.

Proper Mayonnaise

The Proper Food Co. Ltd,
270 Earl's Court Road, London SW5 9AS
Tel. 01-370 1204
ROBERT FISH

Mayonnaise is the first product to be given the Proper Food treatment; that is, it's made exactly as one aims to make it at home, from egg yolks, white wine vinegar, olive and sunflower oil – no emulsifiers, no preservatives or colouring. This simple idea, so simple that few seemed to have thought of it, came to Robert Fish, who is by training a civil engineer. As he himself says, 'Inauguration of a food manufacturing company by a civil engineer with a wide interest in food shows a great diversity. Perhaps this would encourage other non-food industry people to "have a go".' There are also plans to produce a *Proper tomato ketchup* and *Proper fresh lemonade* too – a great step forward for the food industry. Currently distribution is within the London area, so please telephone Mr Fish for further details, as the company is new and growing. Shop hours are from 9a.m.–5.30p.m. Monday to Friday.

Rococo chocolates

321 King's Road, SW3 5EP
Tel. 01-352 5857
CHANTAL COADY

The idea of colour-coordinated confectionery is perhaps mystifying to those of us who eat it too quickly to allow it time to blend in with the decor, but it makes an irresistibly pretty shop. Chantal Coady studied textiles at Camberwell School of Art, and worked on the chocolate counter at Harrods on Saturdays. She felt that no one had yet combined design with confectionery, so she opened Rococo (a lovely pun) with the aid of a Manpower Services small business course and her bank manager. The interior of the shop is fin de siècle pink and white, and from a sky blue ceiling crowded with flying cherubs hangs a sugar crystal chandelier. *English and Swiss* chocolates are sold here, with seasonal specialities such as *Easter eggs* from *Mazet de Montargis, sugar 'diamond' rings in sugar boxes* for Valentine's Day. And of course, the *colour-coordinated range of chocolates* created by Chantal for one of Jasper Conran's Spring Collections. The shop is open from 10a.m.–6.30p.m. Monday to Saturday.

Whole Earth Natural Foods

Cumberland Avenue, London NW10 7RG
Tel. 01-965 1355
CRAIG SAMS

Craig Sams started his health food enterprise by opening a macrobiotic restaurant in 1967. This became so popular that he found he had to open a retail shop as well, in order to satisfy the demands of his customers. Now his new factory in Warrington, Lancs., produces a range of *natural sugar-free jams, pickles, sauces* and *peanut butter,* and there is a bakery which makes *breakfast cereals* and *biscuits* also *without added sugar* – avoiding the use of sugar has been part of Whole Earth's policy since the beginning. Now it is strengthening its links with the organic farmers of Britain and Europe, to advance the proportion of ingredients which are of certificated organically-grown provenance. Whole Earth prides itself on innovative convenience foods – their canned brown rice with vegetables, for instance, cuts down the 35-minute cooking time for raw brown rice to forty-five seconds for stir-frying or steaming the contents of the enamel-lined can. And what contents, too; 'organically grown Italian brown rice, hand weeded chemical free brown Basmati rice from the Punjab . . . aduki beans, burdock, wild sea lettuce from the Atlantic coast of Brittany, umeboshi plum vinegar . . . mirin sweet brown rice wine' – this must be one of the most romantic lists of ingredients on any product, and certainly makes a change from the dreary litany of E numbers. Most importantly, however, it also tastes as good as it sounds. Fortunately, Whole Earth products are very well distributed, and I can buy several of them in my local Sainsbury's. As Craig Sams told me, 'We are constantly gratified to see our products turning up in all sorts of retail outlets – on remote Mediterranean islands, Skye, the Shetlands and in grocers in remotest Wales.'

SURREY

The Curry Club

P O Box 7, Haslemere, Surrey GU7 1EP
Tel. Haslemere (0428) 2452
PAT CHAPMAN

The Curry Club provides an invaluable service for those for whom curry is not simply a passing fancy. It not only supplies a very wide range of *curry ingredients* by post (twenty-nine whole spices, twenty ground spices, spice mixes, pickles, poppadoms, and many more items), it also publishes a quarterly magazine full of recipes and recommendations of Indian restaurants, as well as other curry-related topics. It publishes *The Good Curry Guide* – now in its second edition – which gives over 700 of the best Indian restaurants in Britain and Eire; a very useful present for an impecunious student, since somehow Indian restaurants always manage to provide good food far more cheaply than any comparable ethnic cuisine. All this began in 1981 as a result of Pat Chapman's family returning to England from India, and finding how difficult it was to get the right ingredients for the Indian dishes to which they had become addicted. A retail shop is now open in Covent Garden – 37 The Market (first floor), London WC2; 01-240 5760. Open daily 10.30a.m.–8p.m.; walk down James Street from Covent Garden tube station. All Curry Club details (membership £10 for the first year, only £7 a year thereafter) from the Haslemere address.

Furzehill Farm ewes' dairy products

Furzehill Place, Pirbright, Surrey
GU24 0DN
Tel. Brookwood (048 67) 2165
R M STANLEY

The Stanleys have switched from producing pork and beef to the new venture of rearing sheep, adapting specialised buildings for their use, and making *soft cheeses*, and *yoghurt* from the milk. The cheeses are plain or flavoured, the yoghurt is plain only, and ewes' milk is also available – all products are additive-free and produced year round. Retail outlets include Holland & Barrett, Fleet, Hampshire; Farmers Fare, Shamley Green, Guildford; Naturally Yours, Banstead; Partridges, Sloane Street, London SW1; The Cheese Board, Twickenham; The Guildford Cheese Shop, Guildford.

Gordon's Mustard

*Charles Gordon Associates Ltd,
Hoe House, Peaslake, Guildford,
Surrey GU5 9SR
Tel. Dorking (0306) 730776*
CHARLES P GORDON

Charles and Jo Gordon's mustard began as the result of their hobby – an experimental vineyard. It produced more wine than they could drink one year, and made them consider the possibility of using the surplus to flavour a food product. So their *English Vineyard Mustard* was born, in 1975; since then they have gone on to develop the range to include *chutneys* and *horseradish* as well – I liked their *Mustard and Horseradish* combination very much indeed, as it offers a good solution to the problem of which to serve with beef, and their *Apricot with Walnut Chutney* which cheered up some cold duck nicely. There are two *dry mustard powders* – the smooth mix is recommended for mustard baths as well. All their mustards are gluten-free (some mustards on the market contain wheat flour, which of course makes them unsuitable for coeliacs). Sales are wholesale only, but mail order can be arranged if there are difficulties in obtaining supplies.

R & G Stevens fresh culinary herbs

*Lucas Green Nurseries, Lucas Green Road,
West End, Woking, Surrey GU24 9LY
Tel. Brookwood (048 67) 4041 or 88011*
MR AND MRS R STEVENS

Mr and Mrs Stevens began their business in a very small way some twenty years ago while Mr Stevens was working as a salesman in Covent Garden. They now employ over sixty people, as well as a small army of housewives and school children (who do a few hours a week), in order to supply *fresh herbs* on a national basis. They have built up a formidable reputation for supplying the freshest of herbs throughout the whole year (no easy task in cold springs) to the catering and hotel trades, and prepacked to large supermarket chains. They are currently developing a postal service for the smaller retailers who cannot reach Covent Garden or regional markets. Their stand at New Covent Garden Market is open from 4a.m.–8a.m. every weekday.

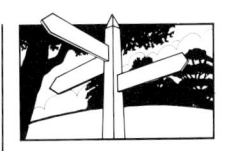

KENT

Cottage Farm turkeys

*Cottage Farm, Cacketts Lane,
Cudham, Sevenoaks, Kent
Tel. Knockholt (0959) 32506*

PHILIP AND FELICITY BAXTER

If you have become bored with mass-produced turkey, then try a *farm fresh* bird, such as those produced by the Baxters. Their birds are raised either in pole barns, or free range, are hand-plucked, and hung for at least seven days; no water, chemicals or fat are added. The flavour is incomparably better than the average supermarket turkey. The Baxters also rear *hormone-free beef*, keeping the cattle on grass until they are at least two years old, and hanging for at least fourteen days after killing. The *turkeys* are sold *oven-ready, jointed,* or *smoked*. The *beef* is never frozen, but is butchered ready for the freezer. Their products are available from: K Alkins, 11 Bramley Road, Beckenham; J Manson, Manson House, 4 Lyon Road, Merton, and from the farm, Monday–Saturday, 9a.m.–6p.m. Cudham is to the east of the A233, about 2 miles from Biggin Hill.

Duskin Farm apple juice

*Duskin Farm, Covet Lane, Kingston,
Canterbury, Kent CT4 6JS
Tel. Canterbury (0227) 830194*

ANDREW HELBLING

Andrew Helbling is one of the very few people making *apple juice* 'by variety'. He feels that standard blends lack character, and has discovered that he can retain the flavours of individual apple varieties in the juice by careful pasteurisation, which also improves the keeping qualities. Duskin (the name is Anglo-Saxon for 'Thrushes') Farm is a small family farm midway between Canterbury and Dover. Andrew Helbling began making apple juice in 1980 to make use of small outgraded apples, using a home-made traditional type cider press. He uses wine language to describe the characteristics of each juice quite unapologetically – 'The comparison with wine snobbery is quite deliberate and, I believe, well justified. I go further and maintain that East Kent Cox's are the best flavoured in the world.' He describes the various juices thus:

Cox's Orange Pippin (clear or cloudy)	'The Favourite'
Worcester Pearmain	Fruity, naturally sweet
Discovery	An amusing light rosé
James Grieve	For the discerning palate

81

Bramley	Dry but not too dry
Pear (Conference) & Apple (Bramley)	Sweet and delicate

The juices are comfortably priced, owing to the fact that a large number of the empty litre bottles are returned, and the delivery area is small. 'Besides, I want the juice drunk and enjoyed.' He will happily sell from the farm gate, although a telephone call helps to avoid disappointment. Duskin Apple Juice is on sale in a large number of shops in the area – please telephone for details. Kingston lies near the junction of the B2065 with the A2.

Mockbeggar Farm fruit, jams and chutneys

Mockbeggar Farm, Higham, Rochester, Kent ME3 8EU
Tel. Medway (0634) 717425
P S L BRICE

The Brice family have been growing fruit at Mockbeggar Farm for the last sixty years, during which time they have won many awards – since 1980 they have won the top awards for all the soft fruit classes in the Cherry and Soft Fruit Show at the Kent County Show. Their range of fruit is huge – seven varieties of *plums*, twelve varieties of *apples*, as well as *soft fruit*, *cooking cherries* and *pears*. Their fruit is sold wholesale to top-quality supermarkets, hotels and restaurants, and is available on a pick-your-own basis too. They also produce and sell *Mrs Twitchett's home-made jams and chutneys* from the farm shop (Peggy Twitchett is the farm shop manageress). Customers are advised to ring before coming to check availability, particularly if the weather has been bad. There is a pick-your-own 24-hour answering service on Medway (0634) 727136; the farm shop telephone number is 0634 725664. Farm shop hours are Monday to Friday, 10a.m.–6p.m., Saturday, 9a.m.–5p.m., Sunday, 10a.m.–1p.m. (5p.m. in summer). Pick-your-own hours are June and July, 9a.m.–8p.m.; August, 10a.m.–7p.m.; September, 10a.m.–6p.m. (weather permitting). Mockbeggar is on the B2000 to Cliffe, due north of Rochester.

Penshurst Vineyards apple wine, apple juice and English wines

Penshurst Vineyards, Grove Road, Penshurst, Kent TN11 8DU
Tel. Penshurst (0892) 870255
DAVID WESTPHAL

David Westphal's great-grandfather was a German winemaker who emigrated to Australia at the turn of the century; his grandfather turned from wine-making to wine retailing, and his father, now finally settled in England, has brought the wheel full circle by joining his son in producing wine again, this time in Kent. Five main varieties of grape are grown, and the wines are light and fruity, ranging in sweetness from dry to medium; they have won many awards since the vineyard went commercial in 1981 (ten years after their first experimental two acres of vines were planted). The *apple wine* and *apple juice* are both made from apples grown in the orchards on the estate, and *whole grain mustard* is made using the wine. Although I try not to let labelling and packaging sway my judgement, the Penshurst labels are particularly charming, showing an old print of Penshurst village. Apparently there is a wallaby incorporated into these labels, which I had failed to notice until told where to look. David Westphal admits that man cannot live by wine-making alone in England, and must attract visitors to the estate to supplement income; he has done this by keeping wallabies, black swans and rare breeds of sheep in the grounds. The wines are distributed via agents round the country, and are stocked widely in their own area. Stockists include: Stapylton Fletcher, North View Oast, Forge Lane, East Farleigh, Maidstone; Todd Vintners, The Pantiles, Tunbridge Wells; Priory Wine Cellars, 64 Priory Street, Tonbridge; Irvine Robertson Wines Ltd, 10/11 North Leith Sands, Edinburgh; South Manchester Wine Co., 40 Barkers Lane, Sale, Cheshire. Visitors are welcome at the winery (one of the most modern in the country) daily throughout the year between 10a.m.–4p.m. Penshurst is between Tonbridge and Tunbridge Wells. Take the B2188 out of Penshurst, cross the river and take the first major turning on the right, signposted to the Vineyard.

Pippins Kentish cider

*Pippins Cider Co.,
Pippins Farm, Stonecourt Lane, Pembury,
Tunbridge Wells, Kent TN2 4AB
Tel. Pembury (089 282) 4624, or
Tunbridge Wells (0892) 30879*

DAVID KNIGHT

Pippins is a fruit farm, whose owners decided to use up its surplus apples by making *cider* on the premises rather than sending the apples to the large cider makers in Sussex and Somerset. Made from Cox's, Worcesters and Bramleys, it is still and strong with a wine character – David Knight recommends mixing it with lemonade to make a long drink. No artificial additives are used. There are several retail outlets in the area which stock it, or you can buy it from the farm shop in Maidstone Road, Pembury, open in the *soft fruit season* from 9a.m.–6p.m. daily, and in *the apple and plum season* 2–5p.m. daily. Pembury is about 4 miles south-east of Tonbridge on the A21. Turn left at the Camden Arms in Pembury on the B2015, Stonecourt Lane is the second right turn.

St Nicholas Mill and wholefoods

*St Nicholas Court Farms Ltd,
St Nicholas-at-Wade, Nr Birchington,
Kent CT7 0PT
Tel. Thanet (0843) 81444*

RICHARD AND MARTIN TAPP

In 1984 St Nicholas Mill earned itself a place in the Guinness Book of Records for the fastest time to transform growing wheat into bread. Within 41 minutes 13 seconds of the combine roaring into a field of wheat near the mill, two dozen loaves emerged from the ovens of the village bakery, the grain having gone straight to the mill for grinding into flour for the bread. In 1980, Richard and Martin Tapp, seeing the demand for stoneground wholewheat flour was growing, decided to produce flour from their own wheat lands. They brought four millstones from an old mill in the West of England and incorporated them into a simple cleaning and milling plant. This now produces 100% *wholewheat flour* which, apart from being sold wholesale nationally to wholefood shops and supermarkets, is also used in the *St Nicholas range of frozen wholefoods* – five vegetable dishes: Leek and Lentil Cobbler, Courgette Soufflé Flan, Potato and Sweetcorn Cakes, Nutty Vegetable Pie, and Vegetable Samosas. Their products are also available from the farm from 9a.m.–12p.m., 1–5p.m. every weekday. St Nicholas-at-Wade lies just south of the A299, about 6 miles east of Herne Bay.

SUSSEX

Adsdean Farm hormone-free meat

Adsdean Farm, Funtington, Chichester, West Sussex PO18 9DN
Tel. Chichester (0243) 575212
DENNIS HOARE

Dennis Hoare became a farmer when he retired from the army in 1946, and has farmed at Adsdean since 1952, growing cereals on 300 acres of Sussex downland, as well as raising a herd of 100 sows, and 200 beef cattle. The animals are reared on homegrown feeds with no antibiotics or growth promoters, and have been since 1968. The products are all sold in the farm shop to personal callers, although there is now a Datapost mail order service for vacuum packed meat – telephone for details. The shop also sells *sausages, beefburgers* etc., all produced on the farm using the Adsdean meats. There is also a range of frozen fish and vegetables, and good quality ice cream. Shop opening times are: Wednesday, 2–5.30p.m.; Thursday, 10a.m.–4p.m.; Friday, 2–7p.m.; Saturday, 9a.m.–4p.m. Funtington is on the B 2178, about 6 miles north-west of Chichester.

The Ark seafood shop

51–2 Cliffe High Street, Lewes, East Sussex BN7 2AN
Tel. Lewes (0273) 476912
NICHOLAS ROE

The range of fish on sale at The Ark is so large that school children are taken there on piscatorial identifying trips to learn that fish isn't always covered in orange breadcrumbs and that there are kinds other than cod, haddock and kippers. The home-made products include *crab*, and *smoked salmon pâtés* (made with butter, and fresh lemon juice), delicious *fish-cakes*, with *salmon fish-cakes* in season. No artificial additives are used in any of the products made on the premises, and Nicholas Roe goes to considerable trouble to avoid suppliers who use

artificial colours in their smoked fish.
Open 8.30a.m.–1p.m. on Mondays,
Tuesday to Saturday 8.30a.m.–5p.m.

Battle Abbey goats' milk cheese

*Battle Abbey Farm, Powdermill Lane,
Battle, East Sussex TN33 0SP
Tel. Battle (042 46) 3972*
LESLEY BIRD

I found the *soft cheese* from Battle
Abbey Farm one of those I liked best
amongst the many I tried. Lesley Bird
has studied goats' cheese making in
France, and is experimenting with
small moulded cheeses. She also makes
a *hard cheese* based on a Caerphilly
recipe – called *Senlac*, it is matured for
about ten days, during which time it
develops a blue mould. All the milk is
used in the cheese production, so
there is rarely any for sale. Buy the
cheese at: Battle Wholefoods, 16
Upper Lake, Battle; Trinity
Wholefoods, 3 Trinity Street,
Hastings. Callers at the farm only by
appointment, please.

Bishop's bangers

*J F Bishop Ltd,
214 High Street, Uckfield, East Sussex
Tel. Uckfield (0825) 2820*
MR REGINALD BURCHETT

The recommendation for Mr
Burchett's sausages was so glowing that
I felt there must be a magic formula
involved. But no – Mr Burchett
describes the ingredients simply as
'pork meat and our special seasoning',
but they are also hand-made and
additive-free, and the recipe dates back
to Mr Burchett's grandfather, who was
a previous proprietor, as was his uncle.
Mr Reginald Burchett has owned the
business for the last twenty-five years.
Admirers of the shop praise not only
the sausages, but the salt pork and beef
(there is a brine tub on the premises),
and the personal and friendly service.
Game and good cheese are also sold.
This is an old-established family
butcher of the best sort. Open on
Mondays and Wednesdays,
8a.m.–1p.m.; Tuesdays, Thursdays
and Fridays, 8a.m.–5p.m., Saturdays,
8a.m.–2p.m., at the northern end of
Uckfield High Street (on the A22 East
Grinstead to Eastbourne road).

Bowyers Court Farm goats' dairy produce and meat

*Bowyers Court Farm, Wisborough Green,
West Sussex
Tel. Wisborough Green (0403) 700494*
KEITH WATSON

Bowyers Court Farm is the largest
wholesaler of *fresh goats' milk* in the
UK, supplying Safeways and
Waitrose. This is good news for allergy
sufferers who live far away from any
other source of goats' milk. The milk is
pasteurised; the *yoghurt* is either *plain*
or *flavoured*, without additives or
colouring, and is stocked by Waitrose
branches, with Sainsbury's taking
supplies in the next year. Kid meat is
available to order for wholesale
customers. Visitors are welcome by
appointment, and on telephoning will
be given directions to the farm.
Wisborough Green is on the A272
between Petworth and Billingshurst.

Dorothy Carter preserves

Oxenbridge Cottage, Readers Lane, Iden, Rye, East Sussex
Tel. Iden (079 78) 212
ALEX MORRISON

Dorothy Carter started her jam making in 1905, and in 1935 her jams were approved by Royalty, who actually visited the cottage at Iden. The *jams, marmalades* and *chutneys* are made in the same place to the same standards today, and use local garden and orchard produce (I can vouch for this, as I first traced the products by talking to someone who supplies strawberries from her garden in Beckley, nearby). Distribution is to high class grocers and delicatessens in the area, and to the David Mellor shops in London and Manchester; The General Trading Co., Sloane Street; Justin de Blank, 42 Elizabeth Street, both in London SW1. Personal callers are welcome at Oxenbridge Cottage at any time between 9a.m.–5p.m. Monday to Friday; on Saturdays only by prior arrangement. Iden is in beautiful countryside on the B2082, about 5 miles north of Rye, on the Sussex/Kent border.

Cedaridge Farm ewes' milk dairy products

Woods Mill, Henfield, West Sussex BN5 9SD
Tel. Henfield (0273) 494139
MRS CINDY BRIERLEY, DAVID SMITH

Cedaridge Farm *yoghurt* comes in two varieties, depending on the culture used. One is made with a Lactobacillus bulgaricus + Streptococcus thermophilus culture, the other, which has been perfected after many requests from those suffering from digestive problems, makes use of a Lactobacillus acidophilus culture and is sold mainly to clinics and health food stores. The *fruit yoghurt* is delicious, with the whole fruit and honey put into the tubs first, and the yoghurt on top, rather like a sundae. The *cheese* is *Labna*, a drained yoghurt curd. It comes in six flavours (including walnut, and apricot), and plain, and is also available in corn oil with peppercorns and bayleaves. There is a long list of suppliers in the area, so it is best to telephone for your nearest stockist, and for an appointment if you would like to visit the farm. Henfield is on the A281 about 7 miles west of Hassocks.

Flintan Farm Enterprises – hormone-free meat and veal

Clayton Farmhouse, Newick Lane, Mayfield, East Sussex TN20 6RE
Tel. Mayfield (0435) 873476
MRS JEAN FLINTAN

After the early death of her husband from cancer, for which she blamed chemicals in general and food additives in particular, Mrs Flintan decided to combine her love of the land with her love of good food and farm organically. The farm has the Soil Association Symbol of Approval and all her *meat* and *untreated dairy produce* is from humanely-reared animals. *Pigs* and *poultry* are all free-range, and are fed on skimmed milk and corn only. Mrs Flintan rears free-range *veal*, on the cow for five months – this produces a much darker meat than the pale pink of intensively-reared veal, but it is superlatively tender and full of flavour. The accent is on good husbandry and preventative medicine, using mainly herbal and homeopathic remedies, so no antibiotics are fed. All the produce – which includes *soft fruit*, *herbs* and *vegetables* in season as well as meat, poultry and dairy produce – is for sale from the house. It's best to ring before calling to check on availability, but the farm is open all day Monday to Saturday, and on Sundays by arrangement. Newick Lane runs from north to south between the Crown Inn on the A265 at Heathfield and the Railway Inn on the A267 ½ mile south of Mayfield.

Lurgashall Mill wholemeal flour

Lurgashall Mill, Weald & Downland Open Air Museum, Singleton, Chichester, West Sussex
Tel. Singleton (024 363) 348
ROBERT DEMAUS

The mill was moved from Lurgashall (about twelve miles north of Singleton) to the Weald & Downland Museum in the mid-1970s, and restored to working order so that milling could begin in 1980. Robert Demaus feels strongly that restored mills must be seen working to have any real merit – to this end, the mill grinds specially grown local wheat for the benefit of visitors to the museum, who can buy the flour as well as watch its production. Local bakeries, seventeen local shops, and regular customers are also supplied. Mr Demaus is delighted that the demand for stoneground flour is growing, but thinks that now the large milling companies have moved into the market it is becoming progressively more difficult for the very small mills to compete on prices. However, there will always be those who appreciate the very special flavour which comes from freshly milled flour, and who are happy to pay a little more for it. The mill is open from 11a.m.–6p.m. every day from April to October. Between November and March, it is open on *Sundays only*. The Weald and Downland Museum is very well worth a visit in itself, and lies just off the A286 about 8 miles north of Chichester.

Martlet vinegars and apple juice

Merrydown Wine plc,
Horam Manor, Horam, Heathfield,
East Sussex TN21 0JA
Tel. Horam Road (043 53) 2254
ROBERT A HOWIE

Merrydown was founded in 1946 by two friends, Ian Howie and Jack

Ward, to develop English country wines and vintage cider. Jack Ward has since retired, but Ian Howie and his family are still engaged in the running of this very successful company. The *Martlet health food products* started in 1955 when cider vinegar was launched, followed a year later by *Honegar*, a delicious mixture of honey and cider vinegar and made to a recipe described by Dr D C Jarvis in his bestselling book *Folk Medicine*. Whatever the claims for this, it tastes very good topped up with cold sparkling mineral water. *Merrydown's cider* is well-known – their *Vintage Dry*, which is very strong, is as good for cooking as for drinking. The *fruit wines* are rather too sweet for me, although the *redcurrant wine* topped up with vintage cider produces a very good English version of *Kir*; Merrydown's own recipe for Red Bullet adds gin to this. Distribution is nationwide, of course; the Martlet products are available in health food shops. Tours of the winery take place on Tuesdays, Wednesdays, Thursdays and Fridays at 10a.m., 11.15a.m., 2p.m. and 3.15p.m., and on Saturdays (by prior arrangement) at 10a.m., 11.15a.m. and 2p.m. – mid-April to mid-October. Horam is on the A267 about 5 miles south of Heathfield.

The Mill Oven bakery and pâtisserie

*Cutress & Charman Ltd,
Old Mill Square, Storrington, West Sussex
Tel. Storrington (090 66) 2459*
GEORGE AND BARBARA CHARMAN

George Charman trained on the Continent as well as in this country before starting his own business fourteen years ago. Although both his father and grandfather were bakers, The Mill Oven is entirely his own venture, and one in which his son has joined him. Continental influence is obvious in the range of *pâtisserie*, but there are plainer items such as *Wholemeal Cake* and *Cherry and Walnut Loaves*. There is a wide range of breads, and their Gold Medal winning wedding cakes are famous, as are their Christmas puddings. Retail sales are through their two shops – at the above address and in Petworth: 1–2 Petworth Food Arcade, Swan House, Petworth. Opening times: Tuesday, Thursday and Friday, 8a.m.–5p.m.; Monday, 8a.m.–4.30p.m.; Wednesday, 8a.m.–1.30p.m.; Saturday, 7.30a.m.–4.30p.m.

Miracle Herd dairy produce

*Redlays Farm, Cottage Lane, Westfield,
Hastings, East Sussex TN35 4RR
Tel. Sedlescombe (042 487) 696*
THE DOUGLAS FAMILY

Fifteen years ago on the small family farm of eighty-two acres Mrs Douglas started in business. She kept a small herd of goats and with their milk, she made and sold yoghurt and cheese. Eight years ago she was joined by her son, fresh from a food technology course and full of ideas on how to add modern knowledge to traditional recipes (passed down through the family from a Hungarian great-grandmother). He raised the pedigree Ayrshire herd from young calves and in turn was joined by his father who had just retired. Milk quotas have limited their output, but the Douglas family are content to stay small and keep their quality high. Their *unpasteurised Ayrshire double cream*, *live yoghurt* (natural, or flavoured with fruit and raw cane sugar), *low fat curd cheese*, *goats' milk yoghurt* and *soft cheese* are sold via the farm, and to a large number of local shops, as well as to a lesser number of small shops in the London area. The farm shop is open all year round, seven days a week, 8a.m.–9p.m. Westfield is on the A28 about 8 miles due north of Hastings.

St George's English wines

Waldron Vineyards, Waldron, Heathfield, East Sussex
Tel. Horam (043 53) 2156
MRS GAY BIDDLECOMBE

Mrs Biddlecombe's energy and marketing flair, together with her ability to grow and produce good wine, have won her orders from all over the world. Perhaps her most valued order is that from the Houses of Parliament, where *St George's Müller-Thurgau* is the House of Commons house wine. Mrs Biddlecombe started in 1979 with four acres, on a whim, after tasting a glass of English wine, and her vineyards now extend over twenty acres. The estate produces other things too – *mustard* made with the wine, *vineyard honey*, *preserves*, *fudge*, *free-range eggs*, *organically grown vegetables and herbs*, and even *pot-pourri* and *dried flowers*; all home-grown or home-produced by Gay Biddlecombe, her sister-in-law Ruth Robertson, and Gay's mother, who does the dried flower arrangements. Added to all this bounty, the beautiful eleventh-century tithe barn is used to hold functions and concerts, with a local farmer's wife doing the catering. Meanwhile, Mr Biddlecombe and Mr Robertson continue to earn their living in London, enjoying the fruits of their wives' labours, and proud of their considerable achievements. This is a beautiful place to spend a summer's afternoon – it is open from St George's Day (23 April) to 31 October between 11a.m.–5p.m. every day; from 1 November to 22 April, Thursday, Friday, Saturday and Sunday, 1–4p.m. The vineyards are 3 miles from the A22 London/Eastbourne road at the turn-off in the village of East Hoathly signposted 'Waldron Vineyards'.

The Sussex Smokehouse

Sussex Smoked Foods Ltd, Colehook Estate, Northchapel, Nr Petworth, West Sussex
Tel. Northchapel (042 878) 545 or 622
SIMON AND PATRICK FRIEND

Patrick Friend had been a restaurateur in Chichester for five years, and his brother Simon had been in personnel recruitment in London for seven years, when they both decided that they needed a new challenge. The

LONDON AND THE SOUTH-EAST

Sussex Smokehouse makes use of their respective skills in food production and marketing. The principle is to buy only the best local raw materials – *venison sausage* from Arundel, *quail* from Chichester, *trout* from Surrey – and smoke them on the premises. Patrick uses many of his own recipes, such as his *sherry marinaded herrings* and *smoked trout pâté*. The *kippers* are excellent, without artificial colouring, and the *smoked salmon* is good too. They supply mainly to wholesalers, but do a mail order service at Christmas for their luxury items such as smoked salmon. Personal callers are welcome at the smokehouse on Saturday mornings – on the Petworth to Northchapel road (A283), behind the Flower Bowl Garage.

Woodnutts Ltd – Sugarcraft specialists

97 Church Road, Hove, Sussex BN3 2BA
Tel. Brighton (0273) 205353/4
STUART MACGREGOR

Woodnutts provide an invaluable service for cake decorators and confectioners alike, by supplying hard-to-find items of equipment, and ingredients by post. They are one of the few suppliers of *chocolate couverture* – milk, dark and white – and also supply other items for chocolate makers, such as moulds and dipping forks. They teach chocolate-making techniques, and hold as many as fifty cake decorating courses a year. Their mail order service is very efficient, but a visit to their retail shop is a must for the enthusiast, where advice is on offer as well as an enormous range of equipment. Open 9a.m.–5p.m. Monday to Saturday, the shop is only a few yards from Hove Town Hall, with plenty of parking nearby.

WALES

One of the best ways to enjoy the good food being produced in Wales is to stay at the source. Leon Downay, ex-principal viola player with the Hallé and now maker of Llangloffan*, one of the best of the new farmhouse cheeses, has self-catering accommodation to let on his farm at Castle Morris. As he also keeps Gloucester Old Spot pigs, a good supply of pork is ensured. Add to that the Downays' reasonable proximity to one of the best smokeries in the country, run by the Kelseys at Cenarth*, near Newcastle Emlyn, and you have a good base for at least a week of good eating. The Kelseys specialise in smoked Welsh mutton hams, and sewin (sea-trout) from the Teifi. Or you can stay in a caravan on the Griffins' farm*, also near Newcastle Emlyn, and help them with their garlic growing venture. At the Kettles' farm* in Caernarfon, the use of their own dairy products in the kitchen and the comfort offered by their farmhouse rooms has won them awards.

Giraldus Cambrensis summed up Welsh food in the twelfth century succinctly: 'Almost all the population lives on its flocks and on oats, milk, cheese and butter.' Later, in the fourteenth century, Welsh wealth was measured in cattle. Wales is now a wonderful place for good 'revivalist' cheeses; the practice of taking cattle up to higher pastures during the summer lasted long here, and Dougal Campbell is applying similar techniques, learnt in the Swiss Alps, to his Ty'n Grug cheese*. Equally importantly, he is the only maker of farmhouse Caerphilly in Wales. Mrs Rickford makes a lovely rich goats' cheese called Marianglas* at Llanllyfni, and at Login, in Dyfed, Mrs Sue Jones* and her sister Alison Wells are drawing on the local cheesemaking traditions to produce Llanboidy cheese, made from the milk of their herd of rare Red Poll cows.

Although Swansea has declined as a fishing port, the range of fish and shellfish to be bought in the market is enormous. It is also the home of that wonderful Welsh dish, laver. Laver is a seaweed (Porphyra umbilicalis) found on the beaches of south and west Wales, and on some other western coasts of England and Scotland too. It takes many rinsings to rid it of sand and limpet shell, and long boiling to make it tender enough to serve as a sauce for fish or lamb, or to be dipped in oatmeal and fried with bacon for breakfast, but it is so good that even if you have to prepare it yourself it's worth the trouble. However, it can be found in neatly wrapped packages, ready prepared, in markets throughout south and west Wales – I have even found it as far north as Shrewsbury market. Warm the contents of a packet through in the juice of an orange and serve it with the first of the season's Welsh lamb – in May and June – it is a perfect combination.

Further round the coast, at Lawrenny, near Pembroke, Tim Holland* is farming oysters and turning them into high quality frozen dishes; he uses other local shellfish, too, for his *moules marinières* and *bouillabaisse*. To the north on Anglesey, Chris Neill* is farming Pacific oysters, and distributes them to fishmongers around the country. He is hoping to farm clams and lobster, too.

Again, good restaurants need good raw materials; The Walnut Tree Inn, at Llandewi Skirrid, where the Taruschios apply Italianate methods to Welsh produce, is largely supplied by energetic and imaginative Vin Sullivan, in nearby Abergavenny, where he stocks food from most of the food producers in this chapter. Much further north, in Corwen, at Valentine's, the Joneses make much use of local foodstuffs, and add sophistication to good simple ingredients.

Anglesey Oysters

Neilldu, Trearddur Bay, Anglesey
Tel. Trearddur Bay (0407) 860312
CHRIS NEILL

Chris Neill decided to try his hand at oyster farming six years ago when he settled in North Wales on a smallholding which looked out over the Irish Sea. The Ministry of Agriculture, Fisheries and Food already had an experimental oyster farm there, and they encouraged Chris to continue with this on a larger scale. He decided that the future for oyster farming looked brighter than for almost any other sort, and his decision has proved sound. He farms the *Pacific (gigas) oyster*, since it is not restricted to the 'R-in-the-month' seasons as the British native oyster is, and plans to farm clams and lobsters in the near future. He distributes to fishmongers, hotels and markets, both wholesale and retail. Please telephone him for further details.

Bryn Saron garlic

Bryn Saron Farm, Saron, Llandysul, Dyfed SA44 5HB
Tel. Velindre (0559) 370405
ANNE AND CHAS GRIFFIN

The Griffins grow organic vegetables, and specialise in *garlic* and *comfrey*. They manufacture a *dried garlic powder* which is 100% pure, and sold mainly through the Henry Doubleday Research Organisation (see page 161), and produce *garlic strings* for several local outlets, such as Felin Geri Mill, Cwm Con, Newcastle Emlyn. Despite the vagaries of the weather, they are optimistic about the future of Welsh-grown garlic, but augment their income by having two fully serviced and equipped caravans to let, as well as camping facilities. 'Anyone who picks up a hoe once in a while is positively encouraged,' Chas Griffin told me. Bryn Saron Farm is just off the A484 (Newcastle Emlyn to Carmarthen). Turn left at the school between Saron and Rhos and the farm is the second drive on the left.

Cenarth Smokery

Ffynnonddewi, Cenarth, Newcastle Emlyn, Dyfed
Tel. Llechryd (023 987) 579
MR AND MRS J KELSEY

Mr and Mrs Kelsey started the now famous Cenarth Smokery in 1974, at a time when no one else in the area was smoking the local *salmon* and *sewin* (sea trout). Their river, the lovely Teifi, is a natural breeding ground for these fish, and the Kelseys buy most of their produce from local seine netsmen and the few remaining coracle fishermen, now a rare sight. Coracle building is a fast disappearing skill as is the art of fishing from these cockle-shell canvas boats. The Kelseys have deliberately kept themselves as a small rural business, operated by themselves with occasional help in the season, in order to maintain the centuries-old method of smoking small batches of salmon over an oak fire. Their range includes W*elsh mutton hams, loins of lamb* and *pork, topside of beef, hams, bacon* and *sausages*, all subtly flavoured with herbs, which vary to suit various meats. There is a mail order service – please write or telephone for details. Retail outlets in the area include: BB's Deli, Mumbles, Swansea (0792) 66006; Julia's Cook Shop, Cathedral Road, Cardiff (0222) 371929; Captain Cook, Pembroke Dock (0646) 682652; Tivy Kitchen, Cardigan (0239) 612659. The smokery shop is open during the summer season – April to October, and is also open occasionally until January, but please telephone before coming as it is not manned at all times. The smokery is just off the A484 about 7 miles from Cardigan. Turn left to Llandygwydd, before rejoining the main road, the Smokery is on your left (before the village of Cenarth itself).

Decantae Welsh spring water

Trofarth Industries Ltd,
Trofarth Farm, Trofarth, Clwyd LL22 9PF
Tel. Llangernyw (074 576) 340
MRS ANNETTE HOSKING

When the Hoskings came as newly-weds to Trofarth Farm ten years ago, the spring was their only source of water. It was analysed and was found to be of such exceptional purity that the Hoskings felt it was worth investing in the installation of an expensive plant to enable them to bottle the water at source. They called it *Decantae* after the ancient Celtic tribe which once inhabited the area. It is now available from quality wine merchants, grocers and health food shops – please telephone Mrs Hosking for further details of retail outlets.

Denbigh Farmhouse ices

Gwaenynog, Denbigh, Clwyd LL16 5NU
Tel. Denbigh (074 571) 4053 (ansaphone)
TOM AND JANIE SMITH

Six years ago the Smiths decided that the current demand for real ice cream was worth investigating as a possible outlet for some of the milk from their Friesian herd. They have built up the business slowly since then, and now make a wide range of flavours – using natural Italian flavourings, double cream and whole milk. The house itself was visited by Dr Johnson during his 'tour of Wales', and was where Beatrix Potter conceived *The Story of the Flopsy Bunnies* when she stayed here with relations in 1903. *Denbigh Ices and Sorbets* are available wholesale and retail, through a number of shops in Clwyd, the Wirral and the Cheshire borders, as well as from the farm shop at nearby Broadleys Farm. This is open 8.30a.m.–5p.m. Monday to Friday (*except Tuesday mornings*), Saturday and Sunday, 9a.m.–5p.m. It is 1 mile out of Denbigh on the A543, on the left towards Pentrefoelas.

Fieldfare mustards

Fieldfare, East Street, Newport,
Dyfed SA42 0SY
Tel. Newport (0239) 820602
JANE HAWKINS

Jane's mustard business is still in its infancy, but despite the fact that she never meant it to be more than a sideline which would be small enough to run from home in order to support herself and her daughter, she has already added another couple of flavours to the range, and is thinking of expanding and developing a range of conserves and condiments. In the meantime, the three flavours of mustard are: *Spiced Honey*, *Chive*, (very good with mackerel and herring, I found), and *Chili & Ginger*. Ms Hawkins distributes the mustard to wholesalers in Wales and London – look for it in retail food and gift shops throughout Wales in the tourist season (March to October). Some is sold via mail order to personal customers. Telephone enquiries are always welcomed.

Garron Foods shellfish dishes

Garron Foods Ltd,
Lawrenny, Dyfed SA68 0PX
Tel. Martletwy (083 485) 394
T M R HOLLAND

Tim Holland and a partner, both farmers, began oyster farming in the fertile waters of Milford Haven in 1979. To reach a wider public they formed Garron Foods, to prepare *frozen oyster dishes*, and other *shellfish specialities* such as *bouillabaisse*, *moules marinières* and *scallop dishes*.

The emphasis is on flavour and quality without additives. Sales are wholesale only at present, with plans to go retail later. Personal callers for wholesale supplies are welcome, but by appointment first, between 9a.m.–5p.m. Monday to Friday. Lawrenny is to the west of the B4075 which runs between the A477 and the A40.

Gwent Vale Apiaries

Bryn-y-Pant Cottage, Upper Llanover,
Abergavenny, Gwent NP7 9ES
Tel. Nantyderry (0873) 880625
L CHIRNSIDE

MÊL PUR CYMREIG
PURE WELSH HONEY
GWENT VALES APIARIES
(L. & G. R. Chirnside)
BRYN-Y-PANT COTTAGE
UPPER LLANOVER
ABERGAVENNY
Tel: Nantyderry 880625

1 PWYS
1 POUND
453 GRM

This is lovely Welsh honey straight from the producer, and infinitely superior to any of the factory blends. The Chirnsides also make beeswax candles, which burn with a wonderful smell, and polish. Distribution is wholesale to local shops in Gwent, and to personal callers to the cottage, from 9a.m.–9p.m. daily. Take the road signposted to Upper Llanover, off the A4042 Abergavenny to Pontypool road.

Hadari goats' cheese

Hadari Cheese Ltd,
Unit 1, Canalwood Industrial Estate,
Chirk, Clwyd
Tel. Chirk (0691) 773100

MR AND MRS D KING, MRS H McCRYSTAL

Hadari (the name is an anagram of the first letters of the Christian names of David and Rita King and their daughter Hazel) is a *soft goats' cheese*, which comes in various flavours with various coatings – *chive with toasted sesame seeds*, for example. There is also a *semi-hard cheese*, which comes in nine flavours which include a *blue cheese*, and *celery*. Hadari Cheese started as a cottage industry, but has recently moved to a 15,000 square foot dairy unit to cope with the demand.

CLWYD
Goat Cheese
TY'N RHYD MAERDY CLWYD N.WALES

The products are available by mail order, wholesale and retail, and visitors are welcome, by appointment, during office hours. From the A5 through Chirk, turn off by the monument, go over the railway bridge and take the first right.

Kettle's Farm dairy products

Ty'n Rhos Farm, Seion, Llanddeiniolen,
Caernarfon LL55 3AE
Tel. Portdinorwic (0248) 670489

LYNDA AND NIGEL KETTLE

The Kettles make *cream* and *yoghurt* and some *soft cheese* from the milk of their mixed Jersey/Friesian herd, which grazes on traditional pastures. The excellence of these products no doubt contributed to their winning a Wales Farmhouse Award for their farmhouse accommodation, since the Kettles use the products in the kitchen. 'Weight watchers beware, although special diets can be catered for.' They distribute the products to: Bates and Hunt, Upper Bangor, Gwynedd; Caernarfon Cottage Kitchen, Market Mall, Caernarfon, Gwynedd; Garnedd, Bethesda, Gwynedd. Sales from the farm are possible between 9a.m.–5p.m. Monday to Saturday. Turn off the A5, just before its junction with the A55, on to the B4366 (signposted Llanberis). After 4 miles, cross the roundabout and take the Seion road. Ty'n Rhos is the first farm on the left.

Little Acorn ewes' dairy produce

Mesen Fach Farm, Bethania, Llanon,
Dyfed SY23 5NL
Tel. Llangeitho (097 423) 348

DON AND KAREN ROSS

The Ross's decided to revive the old Welsh tradition of sheep dairying as a way of getting back to the land themselves, at the same time avoiding the intensive systems involved in most modern farming. At Mesen Fach Farm, the flock of Friesland sheep grazes pastures estimated to be at least 300 years old, and totally untainted by artificial sprays or fertilisers. The flavour that the wild plants and grasses give to the cheese is distinctive, and Little Acorn cheese is inclined to blue on maturity. The range consists of a *hard full fat cheese, yoghurt, ricotta* and *milk*. The Rosses sell direct to retailers, high class delicatessens, restaurants, hotels, health food shops and 'discerning wholesalers'. They also operate a mail order service, and personal callers are most welcome by prior appointment. Bethania is on the B4577, about 10 miles inland from Aberaeron.

Llanboidy farmhouse cheese

Cilawen Uchaf, Login, Whitland, Dyfed SA34 0TJ
Tel. Llanboidy (099 46) 303
MRS S W JONES

The herd of rare Red Poll cows which graze the traditional herb and grass pastures here gives milk of superlative quality, with a well-balanced ratio of fat to protein – ideal cheesemaking milk. In formulating the recipe for *Llanboidy cheese*, Sue Jones, her son Darren and her sister Alison Wells (who makes the cheese), were in touch with people who could remember the old cheese of west Wales, and their recommendations have been incorporated. This family business only began in the summer of 1984 and already the retail outlets are too numerous to mention; Sue Jones recommends ringing or writing for a list of stockists near you. Certainly Hugh Rance stocks it at Wells Stores, Streatley, Berkshire, and Randolph Hodgson at Neal's Yard Dairy, Neal's Yard, Covent Garden, London WC2. Visitors are welcome to watch the cheesemaking, and should telephone first to ascertain times and exact location. Login is about 3 miles east of Efailwen on the A478 between Cardigan and Narberth.

Llangloffan farmhouse cheese

Llangloffan Farmhouse Cheese Centre, Castle Morris, Haverfordwest, Dyfed SA62 5ET
Tel. St Nicholas (034 85) 241
LEON AND JOAN DOWNEY

Leon Downey was, for fifteen years, principal viola player with the Hallé Orchestra, before he and his wife Joan decided to opt for a quieter life in beautiful Pembrokeshire. They began with one Jersey cow, which has now

WALES

A REAL TASTE OF WALES · LLANGLOFFAN FARM · TEL. ST. NICHOLAS 241 · PEMBROKESHIRE

Llangloffan FARMHOUSE CHEESE

FULL FAT HARD CHEESE FROM JERSEY MILK

grown into a herd of fifteen to meet demand for *Llangloffan cheese*, a delicious rich cheese with a natural crust. There is also a *chive* version, which is seasonal, as it is made with fresh chives. Unpasteurised milk is used, and no artificial sprays or fertilisers are used on the pastures. The Downeys also have a herd of *Gloucester Old Spot* pigs, chosen for their hardiness, and for the flavour of the pork; the *meat* from these pigs will be on sale shortly. The Downeys also offer self-catering accommodation for holiday visitors, and not surprisingly won a special Judges' Award for the most outstanding Individual Farm Enterprise in the 1984 National Farmers' Union Mutual Marketing Award. Visitors are naturally very welcome, both to buy the cheese, and to see it being made. The shop is open every day except Sunday. Cheesemaking can be seen on Monday, Wednesday, Thursday and Saturday mornings from 10a.m.–12.30p.m., April to November. There is a mail order service for the cheese, and it can be bought from the following retail outlets: Neal's Yard Dairy, Covent Garden, London WC2; Wells Stores, Streatley, Berkshire; Gloucesters Cheese and Wholefoods, 5 New Market, Otley, West Yorkshire; Humble Pie, Burnham Market, Norfolk; Cookery Nook, Church Street, Pershore, Worcestershire; Gibbs Food & Wine Shop, St. David's, Pembrokeshire; Gibson's Restaurant and Shop, 8 Romilly Crescent, Canton, Cardiff. Llangloffan is just north of Castle Morris on the B4331, about 8 miles south-west of Fishguard.

Marianglas goats' cheese

Maes Mawr, Llanllyfni, Caernarfon, Gwynedd LL54 6DG
Tel. Penygroes (0286) 881809
MRS J RICKFORD

The unique flavour of this goats' cheese is attributed both to the breed of goat – British Alpine and Anglo-Nubian – and to the pastures – rough grazing on acid soil. These two

MARIANGLAS GOAT'S CHEESE

MAES MAWR, LLANLLYFNI,
CAERNARFON, GWYNEDD.
Tel. Penygroes **881809**

factors combine to produce a *rich creamy cheese with a natural crust*, matured for a month or two. Mrs Rickford does not class her cheesemaking as a business, but rather 'a useful sideline to the keeping of goats, in which I take great pleasure, as well as in providing people with something they want'. Some of this lovely cheese can be supplied by mail order, and retail outlets include: Wells Stores, Streatley, Berkshire; Mike's Fresh Foods, High Street, Portmadoc; Just Natural, Little Pool Street, Caernarfon, Gwynedd, and at local agricultural shows. Visitors can also buy it at the farm, but they should telephone for directions first, as it is off the beaten track. Llanllyfni itself is on the A487 about 10 miles south of Caernarfon.

Thorncliff goats' yoghurt

Pant Erwyn, Pant Erwyn Road, Dyserth, Clwyd
Tel. Dyserth (0745) 570670
MRS DIANE HARPER

Mrs Harper began making yoghurt from her small herd of goats after reading the list of ingredients on the tub of commercial yoghurt she was feeding to her baby son. Her family and friends enjoyed her goats' yoghurt so much that she became self-employed and with the help of a grant bought more goats and set up a small dairy in a converted outhouse. The *yoghurt* comes in four fruit flavours (sweetened with a little raw brown sugar), and an unflavoured version. Retail outlets are increasing all the time, but at the moment they include, in Clwyd, Kays Delicatessen, High Street, Prestatyn; Meliden Fresh Fish Shop, Meliden; Jennie's Good Food Shop, Abergele; Scott's Pantry, St Asaph; Holywell Wholefoods, off High Street, Holywell. Personal callers are welcome, but Mrs Harper would appreciate a telephone call first. Pant Erwyn is situated between Dyserth and Trelawnyd on the B5151; take the Mia Hall turn off, and it's 200 yards on the right.

Ty'n Grug farmhouse cheese

Ty'n Grug, Esgerdawe, Llandeilo, Dyfed SA19 7SE
Tel. Pumpsaint (055 85) 400
DOUGAL CAMPBELL

Dougal Campbell learnt a great deal about cheesemaking in the Swiss Alps, before trying his hand at making it on his own forty-six acres of land in Dyfed, 1000 feet above sea level. His *Ty'n Grug farmhouse*, and *farmhouse Caerphilly* (the last is something of a revival), have both won golden opinions. The milk is unpasteurised, and the pastures unsprayed. The cheeses are stocked by the good cheese shops, and local outlets include: Curds & Whey, Swansea Market, Swansea; Dianne's Delicatessen, The High Street, Lampeter; Teify Kitchen, Cardigan, Dyfed. Humble Pie Foods, Burnham Market, Norfolk, and Cookery Nook, Pershore, Worcestershire both stock the cheeses in the winter only. There is some mail order during the winter, although Dougal Campbell does not encourage this due to the expense to the customer. During the summer Leon Downey (see page 98) sells it through his farm shop. Farm gate sales are between 10a.m.–5p.m. on weekdays from April to October, closed on Sundays and Mondays. Esgerdawe lies between the A48 and the B4337, about 7 miles due south of Lampeter.

THE WEST MIDLANDS

HEREFORD AND WORCESTER
WARWICKSHIRE
SHROPSHIRE
STAFFORDSHIRE

Hereford, Worcester and Warwickshire are the counties for fruit, vegetables and fine beef – and much of the fruit and many of the vegetables are now being grown organically, to satisfy our demands for purer food. I list a group of the organic growers, all recommended by Pete Blench, who runs an organic greengrocery in Hereford. The number of organic growers is increasing rapidly, especially since some of the better supermarkets have begun to stock organically grown vegetables. Expect to see slightly smaller fruit and vegetables, with some imperfections – proof that the produce has not suffered the far greater blight of treatment with chemical fertilisers and pesticides. The range of vegetables being grown is interesting, as well as safe – the Jenkins*, at Dinmore, grow kohl rabi and fennel, Muttons Organic Growers* specialise in unusual winter salad vegetables.

Herb growers also flourish here, including Madge Hooper*, who has been growing her herbs for almost fifty years, and whose herb garden at Stoke Lacy, near Bromyard, is a beautiful encyclopaedia of almost every known variety. Markets in this part of the country, in the growing seasons of the year, overflow with the bounty of orchards and gardens, and there are numerous places where you can go to pick your own produce, too.

For fine Hereford beef, properly hung and raised without added hormones, go to Callwoods* (once Churchills) in Ledbury High Street, or to their other branch in Ross-on-Wye.

Shropshire was the county which surprised me, so stuffed full of good hams and bacon is it. We found three good producers of dry-salted hams and bacon in one day, as we travelled no great distance down the A49 south of Shrewsbury, and bore delicious bacon back for Sunday breakfast.

Another Shropshire wonder is the Cheshire cheese – not quite such a contradiction as it sounds, since both cheesemakers listed are only just this side of the Shropshire/Cheshire border, and still on the salt-rich pastures which are always thought to have given Cheshire cheeses their particular quality. The Applebys' Hawkstone Cheshire* is a good example of a battle fought, and won, against the Milk Marketing Board, another blow against *banalisation*; the Hutchinson Smiths' Blue Cheshire* is a triumph of investigation – how to capture the elusive blueing capabilities of Cheshire cheese. Ten years' experimentation has resulted in this festive-looking and splendid-tasting cheese.

Also in Shropshire can be found a determined dairy farmer, bent on creating a happy relationship between farmer and consumer via excellent products. Edward Dorrell* has researched ice cream thoroughly in America, and now offers his Hadley Park ice cream to appreciative customers who can also watch the cows that produce the real milk and cream which go into it – and who can therefore learn to put a little more faith in what goes into a quality product. It's an excellent idea, and one which many dairy farmers are copying.

By the time Staffordshire is reached, the gradual change of diet, from fresh fruit and vegetables to more substantial fare born of industry and bleaker weather becomes apparent. Staffordshire oatcakes are no longer produced in the quantities they once were, by hundreds of small oatcake makers throughout the Potteries and their satellite towns, but they are still made, and can even be found in the sophisticated towns south of Manchester. And in Longton, southernmost of the six (not five, as Arnold Bennett recorded erroneously in his books) towns which make up the Potteries, Sam Gosling* sells tripe, cowheel, udder and hodge – sure signs that the North has begun.

Hereford and Worcester

Callwood & Son – Hereford beef

12 High Street, Ledbury, Herefordshire
Tel. Ledbury (0531) 2526
ANDY CALLWOOD

The Callwoods, father and son, took over this shop in 1985 from Mary and Charlie Churchill who, over two generations, had built up a reputation for selling the best *Hereford beef*. The Callwoods aim to carry on this tradition of supplying the finest of this fine beef – hormone-free, home-killed and properly hung. They also make their own *pies, sausages and cooked meats*, and supply *game* – venison, ducks, pheasant – all to the same high standard. Their other shop is 11 High Street, Ross-on-Wye (Ross-on-Wye (0989) 62577). Shop hours are 7.30a.m.–5p.m. daily, except Monday and Wednesday.

CIDER

I only list three of the good cider makers in this area. If you live here, or are here for any length of time in the cider-making season, then you might try tasting your way through the cider makers in the local Yellow Pages.

Dunkerton's Cider Co

Hays Head, Luntley, Pembridge, Leominster, Herefordshire HR6 9ED
Tel. Pembridge (054 47) 653
SUSIE AND IVOR DUNKERTON

Five ciders are made here – Traditional Dry, Medium Dry, Medium Sweet, Sweet, Old Adam (medium dry and slightly sparkling). Traditional cider apples are used, such as Binet Rouge and Cider Ladies' Finger. Dunkerton's also specialise in *Perry*, made from perry pears. There are many retail outlets, so please telephone for those nearest you. There is an off-licence here in a timbered barn where tastings are offered. Real ale festivals are supplied; a mail order service is available for packs of 3 × 1 litre bottles. Open hours are as follows: 1 April–30 September, weekdays,

10a.m.–7p.m., Sundays, 12–2p.m.; 1 October–31 March, weekdays, 4–6p.m., Saturdays, 10a.m.–7p.m. Take the A44 from Leominster to Pembridge. Turn left at the New Inn and follow this road for just over 1 mile – Dunkerton's Cider is on the left.

Knight's Cider

Crumpton Oaks Farm, Storridge, Nr Malvern, Worcester
Tel. Malvern (068 45) 4594

K AND S C KNIGHT

The Knights make *dry, medium and sweet cider* from old cider varieties of apples grown locally, without using any artificial sweeteners or colourings. They also have a full range of pick-your-own soft fruit. They used to grow cider apples for the larger cider makers, before taking a family decision to revive the farm cider-making tradition of the area. The farm is open seven days a week throughout the year from 10a.m.–6p.m., but is open later during the soft-fruit season when you can pick your own fruit. Crumpton Oaks Farm is located 200 yards along the B4219, after you turn off the main Worcester–Hereford road (A4103) at Storridge Village Hall. Look for the signs.

Norbury's Cider Co.

Crowcroft, Leigh Sinton, Nr Malvern, Worcester WR13 5ED
Tel. Leigh Sinton (0886) 32206/33391

T P NORBURY

Norbury's Cider Company

The Norburys make *Black Bull cider, perry*, and *cherry*, and *apple wine*, none of which contains any artificial additives. The name 'Norbury' is a corruption of *Noir boeuf* – a black bull being their family crest, and therefore the proud trademark of their products. They do aim at the top end of the market, producing cider for the connoisseur. Their sales are two-thirds wholesale, one-third direct to the public from the off-licence at Crowcroft, and from the pick-your-own shop. Hours are Monday–Friday, 9a.m.–5.30p.m., Saturday, 9a.m.–6p.m., Sunday, 12–2p.m. Location is 6½ miles from Worcester on the A4103 Worcester–Hereford road, ½ mile from Leigh Sinton.

Collins' sausages and hams

H H Collins (Broadway) Ltd, 28 North Street, Broadway, Worcester WR12 7DT
Tel. Broadway (0386) 852374

R COLLINS

This family firm was started in 1900 by the father of the present chairman. They pride themselves on their *dry cured York hams*, on their *bacon*, and on their *hand-raised pork pies*,

Cotswold and Gloucester sausages, and Broadway Special sausage in natural casings. They supply many retail outlets in the area, and in London (Harrods, Paxton & Whitfield, Fortnums). Their own retail shop in Broadway is open daily from 8a.m.–5p.m., with early closing on Mondays and Saturdays.

Country Cooks classic country cooking

The Old Rectory, Tretire, St Owen's Cross, Herefordshire HR2 8NB
Tel. St Weonards (098 18) 316
JENNY ALLDAY

The damson parfait we were given at dinner one evening was unsurprisingly excellent – our hostess was a wonderful cook. What did surprise us was that the parfait came from a shop, in a box. We were in London, the dessert came from Herefordshire, and yet tasted as though it had been made that afternoon with damsons fresh from the tree. If all this sounds eulogistic, it is no less than the truth. The product was one of Jenny Allday's range from Country Cooks, a truly rural company buried deep in the Herefordshire countryside. It specialises in good country food, using top quality ingredients, and with additives of any sort banned from the kitchen. The range consists of nine *main courses*, including a *navarin of lamb, boeuf bourguignon, seafood crumble*; three wholefood vegetarian *dishes* and *eleven ice creams* and *sorbets* in interesting flavours – apart from the *damson* ice cream already mentioned, there is *Marron* (with layers of chestnut puree), *Loganberry*, and

Brown Bread. The products are well distributed throughout a wide area, with several outlets in London – branches of Europa Foods, London Superstores, Cornucopia, Partridges, Harrods. Personal callers are welcome to come and collect their orders. Directions for the last 5 miles to The Old Rectory are lengthy; Tretire is to the west of the A491 between Ross-on-Wye and Hereford; take the B4521 signposted Skenfrith and Abergavenny. After 1 mile, at the bottom of the hill, take the lane to the right by a hump-back bridge. Pass a farmhouse on the right, a new bungalow on the right. The road then swings to the right and Country Cooks is immediately on the left.

Cromwell's Chocolates

20 Church Street, Upton-upon-Severn, Worcestershire WR8 0HT
Tel. Upton-upon-Severn (068 46) 3926
ALAN CROWE

See main entry on page 162, also on page 41 for the Bath branch.

The Dairy House fresh dairy foods

The Dairy House, Weobley, Hereford HR3 8RD
Tel. Weobley (054 45) 8815 or 349
PRUDENCE M LLOYD

Miss Lloyd studied dairying at Seale Hayne Agricultural College in Devon before starting her venture on her family dairy farm in 1977. The Dairy House aims to produce a variety of fresh dairy foods which are locally made and sold mainly in the area. All the products are free from artificial flavours, colourings and preservatives. The *yoghurt* is live, and is either plain, or flavoured with locally grown fruit and a little sugar. A new *whole milk natural set yoghurt* is planned. The *skimmed milk soft cheese* contains less than 2% fat, the *curd cheese* is medium fat (11–12%) and is ideal for *cheesecakes*, which The Dairy House also makes, in five flavours. *Cultured soured cream* is also available. Prudence Lloyd is always interested to have new ideas and suggestions for additions to the range, and is pleased to deal with special requests and problems. Contact her at the above address, and also for your nearest stockist.

ORGANIC VEGETABLE GROWERS

Pete Blench, who with his partner Charles Williams runs a 100% organic greengrocery – Green Door, 89 East Street, Hereford (within Gaffers Wholefood Café) – has been immensely helpful in introducing me to his list of organic vegetable growers, of which there are a number in the area.

Frome Organic Growers

Canon Frome Court, Canon Frome, Ledbury, Herefordshire HR8 2TD
Tel. Trumpet (053 183) 534
DAVID AND JANE STRAKER

The Strakers provide organically grown vegetables to Soil Association Symbol standards. Retail outlets: Green Door, Hereford; Friday market stall, Malvern market, Malvern; Ledbury Wholefoods, Ledbury.

Jack's Produce

Upper Bache Farm, Kimbolton, Leominster
Tel. Leominster (0568) 4409
GEOFF AND PAT KAY

The Kays specialise in brussels sprouts, leeks, red cabbage, cauliflower and calabrese to Soil Association standards. Routine tasks at the farm are carried out by a working horse. Sales are mainly wholesale to: Clean Foods Ltd, Units B N E W N, Mount Street, Nechells, Birmingham (021 327 0386); John Redfern, Peppers, Cheltenham, Gloucestershire; A Pickles, Yorkshire Organics, Bradford, Yorkshire. Visitors are welcome at any time, but telephone first for directions as access is difficult.

D R & S M Jenkins

Green Acres, Dinmore, Herefordshire
Tel. Bodenham (056 884) 7045
DAVID AND SHEILA JENKINS

A wide range of vegetables and fruit are grown organically here, including fennel, kohl rabi, and spinach. Some vegetables go to wholesalers, but most sales are through their own farm shop – open daily 9a.m.–5.30p.m. in winter, and 9a.m.–dusk in summer. Green Acres is on the A49, equidistant between Hereford and Leominster, on the south side of Dinmore Hill.

Muttons Organic Growers – Thornbury Herbs

Elm Grove, Thornbury, Bromyard, Herefordshire HR7 4NJ
Tel. Kyre (088 54) 204
GEOFF MUTTON

A wide range of vegetables, herb plants and fresh-cut herbs are grown here to Soil Association standards on twenty-seven acres. Unusual winter salad vegetables are a speciality. Sales are wholesale only. Retail outlets include Green Door, Hereford, and Jane Straker's market stall on Malvern market (see Frome Organic Growers).

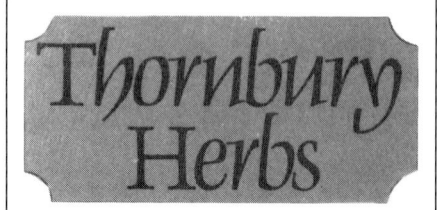

Revells Fruit Juices

Wye Valley Fruit Farm Ltd,
Revells Farm, Linton, Ross-on-Wye,
Herefordshire HR9 7SD
Tel. Gorsley (098 982) 626
MR R J M BURTON

Revells fruit juices come in six varieties, and their *Apple & Blackberry* and *Golden Russet* are particularly delicious. They contain no preservatives nor (most importantly) any added sugar, so the flavours are those of the fruit alone. The Barters travel the world looking for new ideas in equipment, so that traditional techniques are used in super-hygienic surroundings and with the best modern technology. A Nuffield Farming Scholarship enabled them to study in the Far East, which gave them even more ideas. They do not encourage personal callers as they have no retail outlet open on the farm, however, as Mrs Barter says, 'We *never* turn people away. If they can be bothered to find us, we will always serve them.' You can meet the Barters, and taste their fruit juices at the following shows during the summer: May, Devon County Show, Exeter; June, Royal Bath & West Show, Shepton Mallet; June, South of England Show, Ardingly; June, Three Counties Show, Malvern; July, Royal Agricultural Show, Stoneleigh; July, Royal Welsh Show, Builth Wells. Their products are widely available in health food shops round the country, and in farm shops too.

Stoke Lacy Herb Garden

*Stoke Lacy, Bromyard, Herefordshire
HR7 4JH
Tel. Burley Gate (0432) 820232*
MADGE HOOPER

Madge Hooper is the doyenne of herb growers. She began growing herbs in Stoke Lacy in 1939, when six acres were devoted to crops of medicinal and culinary herbs, which were harvested and dried for manufacturing chemists and food firms. Flowers, lavender and other fragrant plants were grown to provide material for pot pourri which was largely exported to America. Later, a herb nursery was developed to cater for the growing demand from the public for plants for their own gardens, and plants and seeds were sent to many parts of the world. Stoke Lacy is now designed to help visitors identify and enjoy a very wide range of plants grown in a garden setting, and enquiries are invited for any variety not shown in the catalogue. Half-day herb schools are held in June, July and August – please telephone for details. The herb garden is a single-handed enterprise, open to visitors on Saturdays only from 10 to 12a.m. and 2 to 4.30p.m. from mid-April to mid-September, but it has no facilities for parties. Plants and seeds are also available by mail order. Please send a stamped addressed envelope for the catalogue. Stoke Lacy is on the A465, 4 miles south-west of Bromyard and 10 miles north-east of Hereford. The Herb Garden is signposted, approached by a short lane nearly opposite the church.

Zorapore goats' dairy produce

*Wern-Hir, Long Lane, Peterchurch, Herefordshire HR2 0TE
Tel. Peterchurch (098 16) 310*
MRS SUSAN WRIGHT

Mrs Wright's goats are tuberculosis and brucellosis tested, and she always has *skimmed milk* available, as well as *fresh* or *frozen whole milk*, something which is not always offered by other producers. Currently *yoghurt*, *cheese*, *butter* and *kid meat* are only available to order, but as the herd is expanding all the time, it is hoped to be able to produce all these products on a permanent basis. Mrs Wright experiments with recipes and techniques passed down by her French grandmother. 'The French have always given the goat the respect it deserves and I like to feel I am providing a small, interesting blend of French and English traditions,' she told me. Sales are from the farm gate, with deliveries to some customers. Visitors are encouraged to telephone first to make sure they and farm routines don't clash. If there's no reply, then after 11a.m. and before 3p.m. is the best time, except on Sundays. Location: take the Hay-on-Wye road from Hereford. At Peterchurch turn left at the Nags Head – Wern-Hir is 1½ miles up this lane.

WARWICKSHIRE

Charlecote Mill wholemeal flour

Charlecote Mill, Hampton Lucy, Warwickshire SV35 8BB
Tel. Stratford-on-Avon (0789) 842072
JOHN BEDINGTON

John Bedington and friends spent five years restoring Charlecote Mill, and corn grinding restarted there in 1983. Using 'All English' locally grown wheat, the mill now produces several grades – AEC is *wholemeal flour* suitable for wholemeal pastry, cakes and chapattis. AEB is for home bread baking, and *Baker's Blend* is a stronger flour milled from English wheat with some Canadian wheat added and is used mainly for commercial baking. In addition there is *wholemeal flour* milled from *organically grown wheat*, and a range of *animal and poultry feeds*. Distribution is via delivery to

Charlecote Mill

Wholemeal Flour
Stone ground at our watermill in rural Warwickshire

Weight
1·5Kg.

Best before:
Keep Dry and Cool

Charlecote Mill, Hampton Lucy, near Warwick.
Telephone Stratford-on-Avon 842072.

bakers or individuals in Leamington, Warwick, Coventry, Redditch, South Birmingham. For retail outlets near you, please telephone the mill.

Visitors who wish to buy from the mill should ring first as the mill is not always attended, and access is shared with a private house. The mill is open to the public several times a year, as advertised in the local press, and parties from schools, clubs and societies are also welcome by arrangement. The Mill is situated at Hampton Lucy, not Charlecote. Take the B4088, signposted Charlecote and Stratford, from the A429 3 miles from Wellesbourne, and in Charlecote turn right to Hampton Lucy.

Lighthorne Associates – fresh herbs

Lighthorne Associates Ltd, Moreton Morrell, Warwickshire CV35 9DB
Tel. Warwick (0926) 651426
PETER AND ANNE TURNER

Anyone who has been able to buy fresh basil in a supermarket to cheer up a tasteless salad of commercially grown tomatoes probably has the Turners to thank. They had produced herb plants for garden centres for fifteen years before deciding, as a result of a number of requests, to grow field crops of fresh herbs. Since then, they have built up a network of retail distribution via supermarkets such as Sainsbury's, Safeway's and Asda, as well as various wholesale markets. A mail order service is available for restaurants. Peter has many years' experience as a horticulturist and herb grower, Anne is responsible for the sales side and for the recipe ideas on the labels. The herb mixtures for various dishes are especially useful, and the blends original – I liked the inclusion of burnet in the salad blend.

Lyneve goats' dairy produce

2 Ascote Cottages, Chapel Ascote,
Ladbroke, Leamington, Warwickshire
CV33 0DB
Tel. Southam (092 681) 4214
LINDA DOYLE

The Doyles are building up a small herd of dairy goats in order to produce a *year round* supply of *milk* for those who suffer from bovine allergies. The milk is usually seasonal, but by careful breeding this problem can be eliminated. A *soft cheese* is also produced, and an ice cream is made by a commercial ice cream dairy which replaces cows' milk with goats' milk from the Lyneve herd. Goat meat is available to order. Retail outlets are: Goodness Foods, London Road, Daventry, Northamptonshire; Goodness Foods shops in Leamington Spa, Warwickshire, Braunston, Rugby and Towcester, all in Northamptonshire; Drop in the Ocean, The Arcade, Coventry, West Midlands; Country Kitchen, Earlsdon, Coventry, West Midlands; Meadows, Smith Street, Warwick. Personal callers are welcome, but please telephone first. Chapel Ascote is situated on the A423 3 miles south of Southam, almost equidistant between Rugby, Banbury and Leamington Spa.

Snitterfield Fruit Farm

Kings Lane, Stratford-on-Avon,
Warwickshire CV37 0QB
Tel. Stratford (0789) 731711 (24 hours)
R A CORSER

Snitterfield is a pick-your-own fruit farm with a farm shop, and the Corser family specialise in *apple and pear* varieties not usually found at the greengrocer's – James Grieve, Laxton's Superb, Blenheim Orange, Codling. They also have a wide range of cane and bush fruit and vegetables (*asparagus, brussels sprouts sold on the stem*). Their pick-your-own venture started eighteen years ago, when they found they had a shortage of pickers for the strawberry crop. Customers were told they could have the fruit if they were prepared to pick it themselves. This was so successful that now pick-your-own customers clear 100 acres every season. Open seven days a week. Mid-June to mid-July, 10a.m.–8p.m. (weekends 10a.m.–6p.m.). Mid-July to end October, 10a.m.–6p.m. November and December, 10a.m.–4p.m. Snitterfield is just north of Stratford, between the A34 and the A46.

Wholewheat Crisps

Protein Foods (Health Foods) Ltd,
Barnfield Trading Estate, Tipton, West
Midlands
Tel. Birmingham (021) 557 7655
MARK WHITTLE

Mark Whittle invented these crisps after his father had a major heart operation and was put on a stringent diet. 'I became fascinated with diet foods and invented the formula for *Wholewheat Crisps* – they are a tasty way to take fibre.' The process is secret, but the ingredients are solely stoneground wholewheat flour, vegetable oil and sea-salt. They are also popular with diabetics, since each packet contains only 10g of available carbohydrate. Perhaps the most important thing is that they also taste good, and come in four flavours – *ready salted, cheese, cheese and onion,* and *smoky bacon* – all free from artificial colourings, preservatives, monosodium glutamate and E numbers generally. They are sold through good health food shops, such as the Holland & Barrett chain, and through better supermarkets – Boots, Safeway, major branches of Sainsbury's and Waitrose.

SHROPSHIRE

Appleby's Hawkstone Cheese

Broadhay, Lower Heath, Prees, Whitchurch, Shropshire SY13 2BJ
Tel. Whitchurch (0948) 840387/840221/840445

THE APPLEBY FAMILY

The Appleby family have been making the finest *Cheshire cheese* just inside the Shropshire/Cheshire border for more than forty years, from the unpasteurised milk from their herd of Friesians. They still use the same labour-intensive methods, which include the cloth binding of the cheeses, some of which weigh as much as fifty pounds. They have kept loyally to these methods in the face of rising costs in order to protect the superlative quality of their cheese, while other Cheshire cheese manufacturers have succumbed to cheaper production methods, and a price which satisfies the supermarket chains. This loyalty left the Hawkstone cheese out on a limb, as far as the Milk Marketing Board were concerned; they found this traditional farmhouse cheese 'difficult to market', and tried to persuade the Applebys that tastes were changing in favour of the mass-produced block Cheshires. Fortunately for us all, the Applebys decided that they could market their own cheese far more successfully than the Milk Marketing Board, certain that there was enough of a discerning public who still wanted the real thing. Over the last three years they have

SHROPSHIRE

CHOICE FARMHOUSE CHESHIRE CHEESE
Produce of
HAWKSTONE ABBEY FARM
WESTON-U-REDCASTLE   SHROPSHIRE

Hutchinsons over some ten years. They are now the sole manufacturers of this splendid cheese, only a few miles north of the Applebys' farm (see above). This area of Shropshire and Cheshire has rich salt deposits, which contribute to the saline composition of the milk of cattle grazing on the pastures, and thus to the peculiarities of Cheshire cheese. Look for this colourful cheese (annatto is used) in the good cheese shops round the country – I have found it to be very widely distributed. Read all about its very interesting history in Patrick Rance's *The Great British Cheese Book*. Visitors are welcome by prior arrangement – the location is 1 mile north of Whitchurch on the west side of the A49.

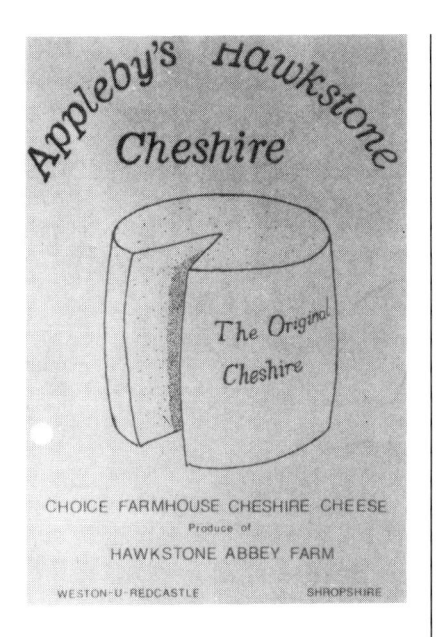

been proved right, and production is now up to capacity at certain times of the year. Their great strength lies in their *family* business; all members play a part in the marketing and distribution. They sell mainly through wholesalers to top cheese shops in London and round the country, and to local shops within a 15-mile radius of the farm. They do not sell from the farm; however, they are happy to give information by telephone about your nearest stockist of their *Cheshire*, *Smoked Cheshire*, and *goats' cheeses*.

Blue Cheshire cheese

Hinton Bank Farm, Whitchurch, Shropshire SY13 4HB
Tel. Whitchurch (0948) 2631

D W HUTCHINSON SMITH

The mystery of why some Cheshire cheeses 'blued' during the ripening period was finally solved by the

Hinton Bank Farm, Whitchurch, Shropshire, England

113

The Cressage Bakery

Shrewsbury Road, Cressage, Shropshire
Tel. Cressage (095 289) 239
LES HORLER

Despite its pleasantly small and cosy look, this bakery had *gross sales* of £120,000 in 1985. Nevertheless, the basic processes by which their range of bread, confectionery and pies are produced have remained unchanged for the last fifty years. The shop is alongside the bakery itself, so while you wait for your wholemeal loaf to be transformed on a Heath-Robinson machine, into slices acceptable to the average toaster, you can see the unbaked loaves being fed into ovens, and smell that best of all smells – freshly baked bread. You find yourself buying far more than you need as a result. The Bakery sells wholesale to a number of local shops, and has a door-to-door delivery service. Open 4.30a.m.–7p.m. Monday to Saturday, it is situated on the A458 in the village of Cressage, about 8 miles south-west of Shrewsbury.

Fordhall Organic Farm

Fordhall Farm, Market Drayton, Shropshire TF9 3PS
Tel. Tern Hill (063 083) 255
ARTHUR HOLLINS

Chicken, ducks, geese, pheasant, beef, lamb and *pork* – everything produced at Fordhall Farm, or served in its restaurant, is free from sprays, chemical fertilisers, growth promoters and hormones. Mr Hollins is a member of the Soil Association, and has written a book – *The Farmer, The Plough and The Devil* (published by Ashgrove Press, Bath), about the farm, and the growth of the Hollins' organic thinking, and the theory that the plough destroys the soil. He is working on another book, on the development of an agricultural machine which will do something to redress this balance 'and open up the secrets of natural soil energy'. A morning spent with Mr Hollins is fascinating, whether or not you are buying any of his products, but please ring for an appointment first.

Hadley Park Farm natural dairy produce

Hadley Park Farm, Leegomery, Telford, Shropshire TF1 4QJ
Tel. Telford (0952) 3677 (9a.m.–7p.m.); 86370 (evenings)
EDWARD AND ELIZABETH DORRELL

Edward and his sister Libby began researching into the ice cream business when farming seemed increasingly insecure. Edward travelled to America on a Nuffield Farming Scholarship to study the manufacture and marketing of dairy ice cream. He found American ice cream to be an infinitely superior product to that offered under the same name in this country – only 8% of British ice cream contains any milk fat at all; 'The American economy ice cream is equivalent to the British top-of-the-range.' Armed with all this information, and the desire to familiarise the British public with real ice cream, the Dorrells now produce a range of *additive-free ice creams in seasonal flavours,* from fresh fruit in the summer to liqueurs in the winter, using the milk from their pedigree Friesian herd. There is also a range of natural *fruit sorbets, ice cream gâteaux,* and *low fat live yoghurt, untreated cream* and *milk*, as well as *skimmed* and *pasteurised milk*. Added to these, free-range eggs, home-made cakes, jams and horseradish sauce are all available in the farm shop, together with cheeses, butter, organic cereals and home-produced hormone-free meat. All this is on offer on a farm where you are not only invited to see the milking take place on Saturday and Sunday afternoons (and help feed the calves), but also to explore the farm's nineteenth-century corn mill (which used both wind and water power), and the two rare guillotine locks on a branch of the Shropshire Union Canal which runs through the farm. The Dorrells' aim is to create a relationship between the farm, the product and the consumer – something which is bound to restore some of the trust lost through much-publicised intensive farming practices. There is wholesale distribution of their products to eleven shops and restaurants in the area. The farm shop is open daily from 10a.m.– 6p.m. (November to March), and 10a.m.–7p.m. (April to October). Milking can be seen every Saturday and Sunday between 3.30 and 4p.m. from April to October. Hadley Park Farm is on the edge of Telford between Hortonwood and Leegemery on the A518.

HAMS AND BACON

Dry-salted *hams* are a feature of Shropshire. Whether this is because of the long tradition of salt working just over the border in Cheshire, I don't know, but it seems easier to buy 'real' bacon and ham here than almost anywhere else in the country. I list only three places here, but an exhaustive search would reveal many more.

A H Griffiths

22 High Street, Leintwardine, Craven Arms, Shropshire SY7 0LB
Tel. Leintwardine (054 73) 231
D E GRIFFITHS

Griffiths sells *dry salted hams* and *bacon* made to a family recipe, and *black pudding* – also to an old recipe, but which can be adapted to suit customer requirements. Distribution is through limited wholesale sales, a stall on Ludlow Market; and D & A Mailes, 45 Eign Gate, Hereford. Shop hours are 8a.m.–1p.m., 2–5.30p.m. Monday to Saturday, with half-day closing on Mondays and Thursdays. Leintwardine is on the A4113 about 5 miles due south of Craven Arms.

Reg May

The Butcher's Shop, South Road, Ditton Priors, Bridgnorth, Shropshire WV16 6SJ
Tel. Ditton Priors (074 634) 628 or 527
REGINALD MAY

Hand-raised *pork pies*, *Virginia hams*, home-cured *dry-salted hams* and *bacon*, home-made *faggots* with home-grown onions and sage are available here. Open Monday–Friday, 8a.m.–6p.m.; Saturday, 8a.m.–1p.m. Ditton Priors is situated between the B4368 and the B4364 about 8 miles east of Bridgnorth.

Clive Sadd

The Butcher's Shop, Dorrington, nr Shrewsbury, Shropshire SY5 7JP
Tel. Dorrington (074 373) 215
CLIVE AND DARREN SADD

The window of the Sadds' shop is a joyful sight just before Christmas, hung with magnificent *dry salted hams* and *sides of bacon*. They do good *sausages*, *pork pies* and *cooked meats*, and combine the old with the new by offering *continental cuts of lamb*, stripped of skin and sinew. Shop hours are from 8.30a.m.–5.30p.m. Tuesday to Saturday. The shop is in the village of Dorrington on the A49 between Shrewsbury and Ludlow.

The Krusty Loaf

High Street, Market Drayton, Shropshire
Tel. Market Drayton (0630) 292
TERRY MCCARTHY AND GEORGE RHODES

This is another very good small bakery, which produces particularly delicious *bread*, and some of the best *white bread* that I've eaten for a long time. Customers come from miles around, especially on market day when the town lives up to its name. There are branches of The Krusty Loaf in Stone (Staffordshire), and in Shrewsbury, and they supply the following shops: Ken Garland, Audlem, Cheshire; P Davies, Ightfield Post Office, nr Whitchurch, Shropshire; D J Rhodes, Hodnet, Shropshire. Their own shop hours are 7.30a.m.–5p.m., Monday to Saturday, Thursday, 7.30a.m.–1.30p.m. Market Drayton is at the junction of the A529 with the A53 just inside the Shropshire/Staffordshire border.

Pimhill Organic flour

Lea Hall, Harmer Hill, Shrewsbury, Shropshire SY4 3DY
Tel. Bomere Heath (0939) 290342
R MAYALL AND FAMILY

Sam Mayall and his son Richard began their organic farming system as long ago as 1949, when their theories were considered simply 'all muck and magic'. Even then the growing amounts of chemicals being used on Britain's farmland made them concerned; it seems sad that it has taken the rest of us so long to come to the same conclusion. The farm is now run by Richard Mayall, and he in turn has just been joined by his daughter Ginny, who hopes to carry on the family business. The Pimhill range of *flour and cereals* is all grown organically, and milled on the farm using traditional millstones. *Organically grown vegetables* are available from September to February; the Mayalls hold the Soil Association Symbol for organically grown produce. The cereals range consists of *wholewheat flour, brown flour 85% extraction*, both *plain* and *self-raising*, *Shropshire Brown flour* (a delicious blend of 85% extraction flour, malt flour, toasted malt flour and malted wheat flakes), *muesli and muesli base, breakfast oats and groats, oatmeal* in three grades, *jumbo oats, wheatgrain, wheat flakes, cracked wheat* and *wheaten bran*. Wholesalers and local shops are supplied, and there is a mill shop. Personal callers are welcome Monday to Friday, 8a.m.–1p.m., and 2–5p.m. Harmer Hill is 6 miles north of Shrewsbury on the A528, and 5 miles south of Wem.

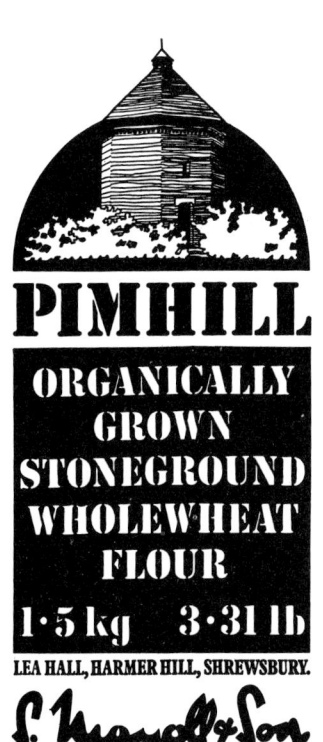

Rays Farm products

Rays Farm, Billingsley, Bridgnorth, Shropshire
Tel. Kinlet (029 924) 255
MRS R CARTWRIGHT

The whole Cartwright family help to run Rays Farm, which produces thick *untreated Jersey cream, salted and unsalted butter, flavoured butters* in season (i.e. *mint butter* in the new potato and pea season, *brandy butter* at Christmas, and so on), *buttermilk, fruit, scones* and *wholemeal brown bread*. Only organic based fertilisers and farmyard manures are used on the ten acres of permanent pasture. Visitors to the farm are able to see 'horses, Jersey cows and calves, geese, ducks, hens, bantams, gleenies, sheep, peacocks, turkeys, owls and Jasper the donkey, most of which free range together around the farmhouse and buildings'. Rays Farm Produce is available on various local market stalls in Shropshire market towns. The butter can be salted to personal requirements for orders of 2kg or more. The farm is open all hours, but baking days are Fridays and Saturdays. Billingsley is on the B4363 about 5 miles south of Bridgnorth – Ray's Farm is the first turning on the right after the Cape of Good Hope pub.

Tern Fisheries trout

Broomhall Grange, Peatswood, Market Drayton, Shropshire TF9 2PA
Tel. Market Drayton (0630) 3222
G R J SPARROW

Fresh pink-fleshed trout, and *smoked trout* are available here. The trout are smoked over hard woods such as oak and elm, and this side of the business is expanding all the time, to include *chicken, pheasant* and *sausage*. Local hotels, restaurants and pubs are all supplied, and personal callers are welcome from Monday to Friday, 9a.m.–4p.m., and at weekends by arrangement only. Tern Fisheries is situated ½ mile from Market Drayton town centre. Go down Great Hales Street towards the Grove School, turn into Berrisford Road which runs adjacent to the school, continue under the canal bridge and Tern Fisheries is immediately ahead. Go up the drive to the farmhouse at the top.

Wackley Farm ewes' dairy produce

Wackley Farm, Burlton, Shrewsbury, Shropshire SY4 5TD
Tel. Cockshutt (093 922) 660
JOHN AND ELIZABETH DAKIN

It took Elizabeth Dakin about eighteen months to persuade her husband John to switch from arable crops, with some beef cattle, to sheep dairying. 'It has taken a great deal of hard work to get this far,' says Elizabeth, but as that includes producing and marketing a *soft Coulommier-style cheese*, *yoghurt* and *frozen milk* to outlets such as Harrods in London, Rackhams and Lewis's in Manchester, Lewis's in Birmingham and good cheese shops as far afield as York, in a year, then it has obviously been worth it. 'The hardest part is trying to find the cheese shops and persuading them to try our products. Selling products direct to the public is something farmers do not usually have to do, and we find it very hard!' But personal callers are very welcome – any time, any day. Wackley Farm is situated on the A528, 10 miles from Shrewsbury and 6½ miles from Ellesmere, between the villages of Burlton and Cockshutt, right on the main road.

STAFFORDSHIRE

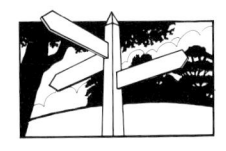

Farmhouse Fare home-made preserves

Common Farm, Pasture Fields, nr Great Haywood, Staffordshire ST18 0RB
Tel. Weston (0889) 270209
MRS J PICKARD

Mrs Pickard has adapted the dairy of the 30-acre small-holding to which she and her husband moved in 1984. In her first six months in business 10,000 pots of jam and marmalade were made. There is a range of *twelve jams*, *eight marmalades* and *eight sauces*, all made from local fruit without additives. Personal callers are able to buy from the Pickards' farm shop, and twenty-five shops in Staffordshire are supplied wholesale. The farm shop is open Tuesday to Sunday, 10a.m.–7p.m., and is on the main A51 midway between Stone and Rugeley.

Sam Gosling, Ltd, butcher

30 The Strand, Longton, Stoke-on-Trent, Staffordshire
Tel. Stoke-on-Trent (0782) 313715
SAM AND BARBARA GOSLING

Gosling's is an old-fashioned butcher's shop which still sells the traditional food of the Potteries – *tripe, cowheel, udder* and *hodge*, although these are now 'dressed' in Manchester, instead of on the premises. But the Goslings make their own *sausages* and *brawn*, by hand, cook their own *pork*, *beef* and *turkey, ham, pigs' feet* and *pork hocks* (these last two are brine-pickled before being soaked and cooked). Shop hours are the usual ones. Longton is the southernmost of the six towns which make up the Potteries – or the City of Stoke-on-Trent as it should now be called. The Strand is at the north end of the town, leading south-west from Longton station.

Linden Lea English Pâté

Linden Lea Fine Foods Ltd,
95 Trentham Road, Dresden,
Stoke-on-Trent ST3 4GG
Tel. Stoke-on-Trent (0782) 826448
DAVID WIGGINS

David Wiggins had been involved in the catering business for ten years before starting Linden Lea, and was sufficiently appalled by the quality of commercial products to try his hand at producing something better. His range of *pâtés* and *terrines* – *thirteen different types from a terrine of turkey to Hampshire Hog Pâté* – contains no colours, preservatives, cereals, dairy products, stabilisers or flavours (other than herbs and spices). They do, however, contain 90% meat, which is 'real' and not recycled. 'We cook with care, not chemicals,' is the motto. For this reason, he has turned down offers from supermarkets – as he told me, 'How can you expect to retain natural quality in our type of product at five tons plus weekly?' Although they are solely wholesale manufacturers, members of the public can buy small amounts direct from the kitchens.

Take the A34 from Newcastle-under-Lyme to Trentham, turn left on to the A5020 to Longton. After 2½ miles, the premises are on the right, immediately before the Uttoxeter turning.

North Staffordshire oatcakes

North Staffordshire Oatcake Bakers Ltd, Turner Crescent, Loomer Road, Chesterton, Newcastle-under-Lyme, Staffordshire
Tel. Newcastle (0782) 562804/513072
DEREK BOOTE

Staffordshire oatcakes are round and floppy, quite unlike Scottish ones, and are usually eaten wrapped round something else, such as bacon, ham, black pudding, or cheese. They have been made in the area for hundreds of years, and are usually to be bought from butchers, and cheese stalls in local markets. However, the present health food boom has caused supermarkets within a 20-mile radius of Mr Boote's bakery to stock them too. I was surprised to see them in Sainsbury's in Wilmslow. The local hospitals have them on the menu too, a nice touch of the vernacular. Mr Boote's oatcakes haven't changed their traditional construction, and there are no additives – oatmeal, water, yeast and salt being the ingredients which have always been, and continue to be, the stuff of life in the Potteries. Look for them in the local supermarkets (Sainsbury's, Tesco, International Stores, The Co-Op), market stalls, bakers and butchers shops. Personal callers are welcome to watch the baking process, expecially on Thursday and Friday mornings when oatcakes and pikelets (a sort of drop scone) are being made. Chesterton is just off the A34, north of Newcastle-under-Lyme.

Rowena's Fudge

The Farm Shop, Market Street, Penkridge, Staffordshire
Tel. Penkridge (078 571) 2182
C BOWERS

Mrs Bowers and her daughter have been making their very good *fudge* for ten years or more, and its appeal seems as strong as ever. It is sold in great quantities, in its six flavours (vanilla, cherry brandy, butterscotch, chocolate, coffee, and rum and raisin) in the area's National Trust shops, at Quarry Bank Mill, Styal, Cheshire, in Peters of Penkridge, Staffordshire, and on the farm shop premises. Other products are *rum truffles*, and *chocolate-covered peppermint creams*. Penkridge is on the A449, 8 miles south of Stafford.

Staffordshire organic cheese

New House Farm, Acton, Newcastle-under-Lyme, Staffordshire ST5 4EE
Tel. Stoke-on-Trent (0782) 680366
M J AND B G DEAVILLE

New House Farm has been run organically for the past ten years, but only started retailing cheese in 1984. It is made from unpasteurised milk, using vegetarian rennet, and has a pleasant texture and mild flavour. Some of the cheeses are flavoured with mixed herbs, garlic, or chives – all are traditionally muslin-bound. The farm shop also sells free-range eggs and seasonal vegetables. The cheese is sold in local shops, and sent to organic wholesalers in London, Wales and Scotland. Local outlets include: R Johnson, Baldwin's Gate, and Kermase, both in Newcastle-under-Lyme, Staffordshire; Good Food Store, and Health Care, Stafford; The Country Butcher, Eccleshall, Staffordshire; Natural Choice, Hanley, Stoke-on-Trent. The farm shop is open on Tuesdays, Thursdays, Fridays and Saturdays from 9a.m.–6p.m.

Staffordshire Organic Cheese

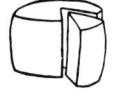

M & B DEAVILLE
NEW HOUSE FARM
ACTON
NEWCASTLE-UNDER-LYME

Symbol of Organic Quality

THE EAST MIDLANDS

NORTHAMPTONSHIRE
—
LEICESTERSHIRE
—
DERBYSHIRE
—
NOTTINGHAMSHIRE
—
LINCOLNSHIRE

The birthplace of one of the world's greatest cheeses, Stilton, is said to have been Quenby Hall, on the outskirts of Leicester. The cheese was supplied to the Bell Inn at Stilton, thirty miles over the border into what was then Huntingdonshire, and as the Bell at Stilton became known to travellers for its good cheese, the name of the place became the name of the cheese, and so it has remained. I have included four makers of Stilton in this section; Long Clawson* is the largest producer, and makes a widely distributed cheese of excellent quality once it is mature. The Colston Bassett Dairy*, in Nottinghamshire, and Webster's Dairy* at Melton Mowbray, are the only two independent dairies who make the cheese, and of these, Colston Bassett is the only one to use unpasteurised milk, although Somerset Creameries* – the most recent producer – are aiming to use both pasteurised and unpasteurised milk.

This region is the home, too, of the famous Melton Mowbray pork pie, but that has failed to survive with any of the honours which still attach to Stilton. However, in Nottinghamshire, Kenneth Parr*, a pupil of Melton Mowbray pie-makers fifty-six years ago, is still making pies, and winning prizes for them, including the coveted First Prize in the Melton Mowbray Pork Pie Exhibition. As his grandson is following in his footsteps, the tradition may yet survive.

Quite untraditionally, but with innovatory zeal, Jillian Woodford* is making some of the best of the New British goats' cheeses in her dairy at Castle Ashby, Northamptonshire. She and her partner, Didier Jaubert, saw the interest in goats' cheese in America, studied cheesemaking in the Charente region of France, and then came here to create some exceptional cheeses – all named after the villages surrounding Castle Ashby.

Derbyshire offers Bakewell Pudding*, Ashbourne Gingerbread*, and some superb bacon, as well as the famous chocolates from Thorntons*, about to celebrate their anniversary. Despite their new factory at Swanwick near Belper, and a £5 million production line, the truffles are still 'roughed-up' by lines of cheerful ladies, to give them just the right finish, and the ingredients are still of the very highest quality.

Everyone I talked to about sausages recommended those from Lincolnshire, without specifically mentioning any one butcher – perhaps they had all shopped at branches (there are eighteen) of Curtis & Sons*, purveyors of excellent sausages, and of the traditional Lincolnshire chine. Florence White, in *Good Things in England* (Cape, 1932), mentions a similar dish from Gloucestershire, called a Christening Chine since it was kept for those particular occasions. And in John Clare's 'The Shepherd's Calendar', mention is made of it as a Christmas dish:

> *And huswifes sage stuff'd seasoned chine*
> *Long hung in chimney nook to drye.*

Mrs White's Lincolnshire recipe includes raspberry and currant leaves, spring onions and lettuce, as well as the more usual parsley, thyme and marjoram, in the herb stuffing for the chine. It is the use of these fresh herbs that gives the dish its seasonal quality; Curtis & Sons prefer not to give exact details of the herbs they use, and they simmer the chine, rather than covering it in a puff paste and baking it, as the old recipes do. Either way, it is a wonderfully fresh flavoured dish, and lovely to look at too, striped pink, white and green. Verlaine much appreciated it while he was a school master for a short time in Boston in the 1870s, as Jane Grigson discovered. Praise indeed from a Frenchman, especially if he was familiar with that Burgundian Easter speciality – *jambon persillé* – ham and quantities of parsley set in a fragrant jelly.

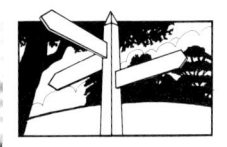

NORTHAMPTONSHIRE

Deaward farmhouse ice cream

Iron Hill Farm, Priors Marston Road, Byfield, Daventry, Northamptonshire NN11 6YJ
Tel. Byfield (0327) 60233
MR AND MRS B P DEACON

The Deacons' *goats' milk ice cream* contains no bovine ingredients at all – ideal for allergy sufferers – and has a good creamy texture and flavour. The *double dairy ice cream* contains both Jersey milk and double cream. The fruit used for these and their *sorbets* is all grown on the farm; the ice cream enterprise was started to complement their pick-your-own enterprise. They also produce a *special wholemeal loaf*, and very good *spicy sausages*. All the ice creams and sorbets are sold wholesale to health food and farm shops, hotels, pubs and restaurants, the other products through the Iron Hill Farm shop, which is open Tuesday to Sunday, 10a.m.–6p.m., situated 1 mile from the village of Byfield, on the Byfield–Priors Marston road, off the A361 Daventry to Banbury road.

Threeshires Dairy goats' cheese

The Woodyard, Castle Ashby, Northampton NN7 1LG
Tel. Wellingborough (060 129) 587
JILLIAN WOODFORD

Jillian Woodford and her partner, Didier Jaubert, met while working in the same goat cheese factory in California; they were astonished at the rapidly growing popularity of goats' cheese among 'the chic crowds of the West Coast', and found that they were quickly shipping cheese to all parts of the United States. Having learnt as much as they could, they decided it was worth trying the English market. Before starting they spent several weeks in France, visiting dairies in Didier's home region, the Charente; then, armed with considerable expertise, experience and enthusiasm, they set up their dairy in February 1984 with a Manpower Services Commission grant and very little equipment. Only eight months later they moved to the larger dairy at Castle Ashby, which they have renovated themselves. They are now producing some of the best goats' cheese currently being made in Britain: *Castle Ashby* is a semi-soft

THE EAST MIDLANDS

pyramid shaped cheese, ripened to form a natural rind; *Grendon* is a firm cutting cheese, ripened and then waxed, with a full flavour; *Easton Maudit* is small, firm and tangy, my own favourite and delicious in salads; *Ashed Cheese* is semi-soft and rolled in charcoal; *Yardley* is a fetta-type textured hand-pressed cutting cheese, mild and fresh flavoured; *Bozeat Curds* are fresh whipped curds, unseasoned, rather like a *fromage blanc*; *Bozeat Rounds* are soft creamy cheeses, mild flavoured and either plain, or rolled in mixed herbs or poppy seeds. All the cheeses are named after the surrounding villages. Wholesale distributors are Harvey & Brockless, 17–23 Linford Street, London SW8. Stockists include Harrods, Paxton and Whitfield, and Neal's Yard Dairy, all in London; Wells Stores, Streatley, Berkshire; Gluttons, Walton Street, Oxford; Castle Delicatessen, Kettering, Northamptonshire; Arjuna Wholefoods, Mill Road, Cambridge; Backs (health foods), George Row, Northampton. There is some mail order, and personal callers are encouraged to choose the freshest and best cheeses, between 2.30–5.30p.m., Monday to Friday and 10a.m.–1p.m. on Sundays – or by arrangement. The Dairy is in the grounds of Castle Ashby House, owned by the Marquis of Northampton, with grounds landscaped by Capability Brown. The Woodyard itself is being developed as a small industry site – at present there is a carpentry shop, a blacksmith and forge, and on Thursday the farrier shoes horses in the yard in front of the dairy. Castle Ashby is about 2 miles to the north of the A428 between Northampton and Bedford.

LEICESTERSHIRE

Manor Farm dairy products

Manor Farm, Thrussington, Leicestershire LE7 8UF
Tel. Rearsby (066 474) 245

MR AND MRS PETER HOLMES

Low fat yoghurt and *cream* are both produced on the farm. As the yoghurt is made within six hours of milking it has excellent keeping qualities without any added preservatives. There are *ten fruit flavours*, all with a low sugar content, and a sugar-free natural yoghurt. The Holmes now process 500 gallons of milk a week into yoghurt, and production is expanding all the time. Retail outlets are grocery shops and delicatessens in Leicester, Loughborough and Nottingham, with Coventry and Rugby supplied through a wholesaler. There is no farm shop as such, but cream and yoghurt is sold in quantity from the dairy, open 8a.m.–6p.m., Monday to Friday. Situated in the village of Thrussington, just north of the A607, approximately 8 miles from Loughborough, Leicester and Melton.

Long Clawson Dairy Stilton

Long Clawson, Nr Melton Mowbray, Leicestershire LE14 4PJ
Tel. Melton Mowbray (0664) 822332
MR R H READER, MR N BAILEY, JOINT MANAGING DIRECTORS

The Long Clawson Dairy was originally formed in 1911 by a group of local Stilton cheesemakers who joined forces to form a farmers' co-operative. It is now the largest producer of Stilton, which, when mature, is excellent; the Dairy also makes *Blue Shropshire*, a coloured cheese, which Patrick Rance feels should more properly be called a Stilton Cheshire. In 1968, Long Clawson acquired a third dairy, at Harby, and a range of specially flavoured cheeses was created, using natural ingredients, and combining them with territorial English cheese. The name of the dairy is *Tythby Farm*, at Bottesford, and here the following cheeses are made under the Long Clawson name; *Bellshire* – a semi-soft white cheese with chives and onion; *Charnwood* – a smoky Cheddar with added paprika; *Cheviot* – white Cheddar with chives; *Cotswold* – Double Gloucester with chives and onion; *Huntsman* – Double Gloucester banded with Stilton; *Nut-cracker* – Cheddar with walnuts; *Nutwood* – Cheddar with hazelnuts, cider and raisins; *Peppervale* – Double Gloucester with red and green peppers; *Rutland* – Cheddar with beer, garlic and parsley; *Sherwood* – Double Gloucester with pickle; *Walton* – Cheddar and Stilton with walnuts; *Windsor Red* – Cheddar with elderberry wine (made by Merrydown, see page 87). They are, of course, very well distributed, via supermarkets as well as specialist cheese shops. Special visits to the dairies can be arranged on application to the manager, at the Long Clawson address and telephone number.

Webster's Dairy Stilton

Saxelby, Melton Mowbray, Leicestershire
Tel. Melton Mowbray (0664) 812223
MR D W CALLOW

If Long Clawson is the largest manufacturer of Stilton, Webster's Dairy is the smallest, and one of only two who are still totally independent. The cheese is hand-made to traditional methods, and Patrick Rance attributes the creamy colour and texture, and uneven blueing to those methods (see *The Great British Cheese Book*). The *White Stilton* which this dairy also produces, is young Stilton before the blueing process starts. It is a lovely fresh cheese, and one which I prefer to its senior partner. Distribution is via Webster's Dairy's parent company House of Callow Ltd, Leicester Wholesale Fruit Market, Freemens Common, Leicester (Tel. 0533 541637 or 543415).

DERBYSHIRE

Ashbourne Gingerbread

*The Ashbourne Gingerbread Shop,
26–30 St John Street, Ashbourne,
Derbyshire
Tel. Ashbourne (0335) 43227*
MR J R PEARSON

The gingerbread from this lovely shop is a traditional regional recipe – a *ginger biscuit* with a *shortbread texture* and an unusual history. During the Napoleonic Wars, the captured French General Rochambau and his officers and staff spent several years on parole in Ashbourne. The story goes that the general's cook eventually settled in Ashbourne and was the creator of the gingerbread; he is thought to have given the recipe to Mr French, a baker in St John Street, who in turn passed it on to Mr Spencer who succeeded him in the business in 1887. Mr Spencer's descendants are still baking and selling *Ashbourne Gingerbread* from the same shop today. The shop is also well-known locally for its ten different *brown breads* (and a delicious *speckled white loaf*, with sunflower seeds, soya beans and malt), its *hand-made chocolates*, and *wedding* and *birthday cakes*, as well as a wide selection of *teas* and *coffees*. Sadly, the soup and rolls we had there for lunch came nowhere near the standard of the bakery products sold in the other half of the shop – a great pity, but don't be put off. The shop is open Monday and Tuesday, 8.30a.m.–5p.m., Wednesday, 8.30a.m.–2.30p.m. (but at Easter and Christmas until 5p.m.), Thursday and Friday, 8.30a.m.–5.30p.m., Saturday, 8a.m.–5.30p.m. Ashbourne is 12 miles from Derby on the A52 to Leek. St John Street is in the centre of the town.

Ashdale ewes' dairy products

*One Ash Grange, Monyash, Bakewell,
Derbyshire DE4 1JS
Tel. Youlgrave (062 986) 291*
MR AND MRS M J WELLS

Mr and Mrs Wells rent their farm from the Chatsworth Estate, and began sheep milking four years ago, at the suggestion of the student who was then working for them. They bought a ram and six Friesland lambs to cross with the sheep they already had, thus slowly building up the milking strain. They now milk over thirty-five ewes – 'a very mixed assortment', as Mrs Wells describes them – and produce *natural yoghurt, whole milk (fresh or frozen)*, and a *soft cheese*, which they distribute to farm shops, small wholesalers and restaurants: Chatsworth farm shop, Pilsley, Nr Bakewell, Derbyshire; Cheddar Gorge, Compton Street, Ashbourne, Derbyshire. Personal callers are welcome at the farm, but it is best to arrange a time by phone. The farm is just off the B5055, (running from the A515 to Bakewell) in Monyash.

The Old Original Bakewell Pudding Shop

The Square, Bakewell, Derbyshire DE4 1BT
Tel. Bakewell (062 981) 2193
GRAEME MCBAIN (MANAGER)

The classic story of Bakewell Pudding (*not* tart) is that it was a mistake made by the cook at a local inn in about 1860. The mistake was such a success that a Mrs Wilson began baking these puddings and selling them from her house, still the Bakewell Pudding Shop. In fact, Bakewell Pudding is very like the 'transparent' puddings popular at least a hundred years earlier – very rich, somewhat bland eggy confections made with puff pastry rather than the shortcrust pastry which we associate with such dishes today. But the story is a good one, and sells the pudding around the world. The recipe is a secret, but is quite unaltered from the original, and is still made by hand, as is obvious from the puddings' pleasant irregular appearance. To be eaten at their best, they should be served warm, with cream, as they are served in the small restaurant that is part of the shop. Bakewell Puddings can be sent by post all over the world; the shop is open seven days a week throughout the year (except Christmas and Boxing Day), 9a.m.–5p.m. Monday to Saturday, 10a.m.–6p.m. on Sundays (it closes an hour later from Easter to the end of October). The restaurant is open seven days a week too, from 10a.m.–5p.m., and 9a.m.–6p.m. Easter to September.

Caudwell's Mill wholemeal flour

Caudwell's Mill Trust Ltd,
Rowsley, Matlock, Derbyshire DE4 2EB
Tel. Matlock (0629) 734374
M J TILLEY, MILL MANAGER

Caudwell's Mill is one of the few mills still to possess a complete set of roller milling machinery driven by water turbines. For the last eight years a team of volunteers raised funds to preserve this remarkable survivor – forerunner of today's mass-production plant. The mill is now open again, and producing *wholemeal flour*, which is milled at a slow speed, thus avoiding the over-heating which destroys enzymes and vitamins. Plansifters extract the fine flour and the larger particles pass through the rolls again – nothing is removed from the flour, no chemicals are added, nor is it bleached. The proceeds from sales of the flour help to maintain the mill. Flour deliveries are made over a radius of about twenty-five miles, to commercial bakers and health food shops in Bakewell, Cromford, Belper, Derby, Sheffield and Ashbourne. And it is always available from the mill, which is open during normal shop hours during the week. For special open days, ring to enquire – there are several during the summer season. The mill is on the A6 in Rowsley village, 6 miles north of Matlock.

Green Dragon biscuits

Green Dragon Bakery Ltd,
Airfield Industrial Estate, Blenheim Road,
Ashbourne, Derbyshire DE6 1HA
Tel. Ashbourne (0335) 42373
ROY JOHNSON

The Green Dragon Shoppe, in St John Street, Ashbourne, is the place to buy the ratafias, butter biscuits, macaroons and other traditional biscuits baked by this small factory. There are no additives or preservatives used and the flavours are good and entirely natural – I find the flavour of their ratafias, made with apricot kernels and no other flavouring at all, delicate and subtle. Much of their production is made for 'own label' customers. The shop is open during normal shop hours, with early closing on Wednesdays.

Moorland farm bacon and hams

High Ash Farm, Barrow Moor, Nr Longnor, Buxton, Derbyshire SK17 0QY
Tel. Buxton (0298) 5727
MAYNARD AND PATRICIA DAVIES

Patricia Davies is managing director, while Maynard – who served an apprenticeship in the curing and manufacture of pork products – produces the best possible *hams*, *bacon* and *sausages* high up on the Derbyshire moors. They have for a long time taken an interest in the production of purer foods, and no area in the meat industry is as much in need of purification as is that of ham and bacon curing. The Davieses use carefully selected animals – such as the Tamworth pigs from Mrs Dalton's farm in Cheshire (see page 163), and only use the traditional ingredients such as salt, saltpetre, brown sugar, honey and woodsmoke to cure and preserve. As a result, the bacon and hams are superlative, and naturally very much in demand, with customers driving over the hills from miles around. They sell by post too. Their 'special offer' is worth noting: 'Buy a half-pig from us and we will cure any part specially for you.' Telephone first if you are coming from a distance, to be given exact directions. Longnor is on the B5053, between the main Buxton to Ashbourne and Leek to Ashbourne roads.

Nelson's pork pies, bacon and sausages

J H Nelson & Sons,
Buxton Road, Bakewell, Derbyshire
Tel. Bakewell (062 981) 2044
JOHN NELSON

Nelson's was established in 1842, and has been family-run ever since. It is delightfully old-fashioned, and so are the *pies* – hand raised, 'of supreme and superb standards', with no additives, and plenty of mace and other spices. The *bacon* is very good and very fat, so that bread fried in the 'dip' is particularly delicious. The shop is the only retail outlet, and shop hours are 8.45a.m.–5.30p.m., Monday, Tuesday, Wednesday and Friday, 8.45a.m.–1p.m., Thursday and Saturday. Buxton Road is the A6 from Bakewell to Buxton.

Thornton's chocolates

J W Thornton Ltd,
Derwent Street, Belper, Derbyshire
DE5 1WP
Tel. Belper (077 382) 4181
THE THORNTON FAMILY

Thornton's is a family firm, with a special atmosphere of friendliness, and with pride in a business which began as a small sweet shop in Sheffield in 1911, and now produces the finest chocolates this side of the Channel. The family are Stanley Thornton, inventor of *Special Toffee* (so full of butter that it can only be transported in slabs and broken into pieces with a toffee hammer once it is safely in the shop), and President of the Company, his son Michael (Deputy Chairman), and his nephews Peter (Chairman) and John (Managing Director). But

Telephone No.
2044

THE CELEBRATED PORK PIE ESTABLISHMENT

Established
1842

J. H. NELSON & SONS
Pork Butchers
WHOLESALE HAM & BACON FACTORS
Buxton Road ... BAKEWELL
Home.cured Hams and Bacon :: Fresh Sausage Daily

perhaps the most important member of the team is Walter Willen, the Swiss confectioner who came to England for six months to learn English in the 1950s and luckily for us all stayed to create the chocolates for which Thornton's are famous – their *Continental Selection*. His latest *tour de force* is his *Chocolates of Distinction* range, hand-made chocolates with sophisticated and mouth-watering centres, some of which, like the *Pear Brandy Truffle* and the *Walnut Kirsch Marzipan*, are flavoured with Walter's native Swiss liqueurs. This range is only available in some of the 159 Thornton shops round the country. More widely available is their newest range, *Regency Plain* – very dark chocolate with natural centres, including two from Joseph Thornton's original range, to celebrate their seventy-fifth anniversary in 1986, *Rose* and *Violet Creams*. I particularly liked the *Bitter Sweet Truffle*, a sort of double concentrated chocolate for chocoholics. Because of the very short shelf life of their chocolates (that of the Chocolates of Distinction is only seven days), Thornton's like to own and run their retail outlets, in order to ensure that the stock is strictly controlled. Recently they have opened more shops in the South of England – Basingstoke, Bournemouth, Bromley, Canterbury, Exeter, Guildford and Ipswich. They do a mail order service for some of their lines, and make *diabetic chocolate* too, as well as delicious *ice cream*.

Matthew Walker fruit cakes and Christmas puddings

Matthew Walker (Derby) Ltd, Heanor Gate Road, Heanor, Derbyshire DE7 7RJ Tel. Ripley (0773) 760121
BARRY PAGE, MANAGING DIRECTOR

Although this firm is now part of a large group, it still operates autonomously, as a family firm. The present managing director, Barry Page, is only the third person to hold this position in the eighty-seven years that Walker's have been famous for their *fruit cakes, plum puddings* and *mince pies*, and is deeply involved and committed to continuing that tradition. The recipes are as old as the firm, no additives are used, and the ingredients are of the best quality and specially selected. The company is very highly regarded as a supplier of quality products, and makes many of them under famous labels both in this country and abroad. Retail outlets are too numerous to list, but they include House of Fraser stores, Selfridges and top quality grocers.

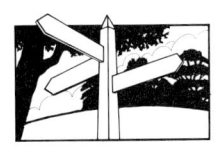

NOTTINGHAMSHIRE

Christy's stoneground flours

Grange Farm Mill, Hockerton, Nr Southwell, Nottinghamshire NG25 0PJ
Tel. Southwell (0636) 812193/812982
SIMON CHRISTY

Although the Christy family has been farming for over 300 years, milling is a new venture for them. They felt that the most sensible use for their copious supply of wheat was to grind it themselves, using a fine pair of French burr-stones. They produce traditional stoneground 100% wholemeal flours in various blends – *organic*, a *strong bread flour* and a lighter textured *pastry flour*. They deliver to Leicester, Sheffield, Nottingham and Derby, or 'by arrangement to anywhere'. Flour is also available from the farm, Monday, Tuesday, Wednesday and Friday 10a.m.–5p.m., Saturday 9a.m.–1p.m., which is just off the A617 from Newark to Mansfield, half a mile past Hockerton towards Mansfield.

The Colston Bassett & District Dairy Stilton

Harby Road, Colston Bassett, Nottingham NG12 3FN
Tel. Kinoulton (094 97) 322
E T WAGSTAFF

This dairy and Webster's (see page 127) are the only independent *Stilton* producers, and Colston Bassett is the only one using *unpasteurised milk*, which makes a very distinctive cheese with a very rich flavour and a brown powdery crust. This company, too, was formed by a farmer's co-operative and remains so. It was started in 1912, with Tom Loy, Mr Wagstaff's predecessor, first producing Stiltons in 1920 – he continued as manager/cheesemaker until his retirement in 1960. Mr Wagstaff points out that, although the number of farms supplying the dairy has declined from sixteen to five over the years, Colston Bassett now produce three times the quantity of cheese they were producing in 1960. But those remaining five farmers still supplying milk to the dairy are the descendants of five of the original families who formed the co-operative. Both Mr Wagstaff's maternal and paternal grandfathers were founder members. The list of retailers is very large, and includes the best cheese shops. Locally, stockists include: M. Moulds, The Post Office, Colston Bassett, Nottinghamshire; J & R Watson, Long Acre, Bingham, Nottinghamshire; The Cheese Cottage, Loughborough. The dairy is open to those wishing to buy cheese, but the management are not able to give tours of the factory. Hours are 7.30a.m.–12.30p.m., 1.30–4.15p.m. Monday to Friday, 7.30a.m.–12p.m. Saturday. Colston Bassett is on the Nottinghamshire–Leicestershire border, 2 miles from the A46 (Fosse Way).

'Mrs Elizabeth King' pork pies and sausages

The Lodge, Cropwell Butler, Nottinghamshire NG12 AG3
Tel. Radcliffe-on-Trent (060 73) 2233
KENNETH PARR

Mr Parr has Emerson's inspirational words framed on the counter of his shop: 'If you write a better book, preach a better sermon or make a better mouse-trap, though you build your house in the middle of a wood, the World will beat a path to your door.' Mr Parr makes better pork pies than most, having learnt the techniques from Melton Mowbray pie-makers when he was seventeen, fifty-six years ago, and finds it exciting that more and more of the World are

> *Gracious Goodness Since 1853*
> **KING'S ENGLISH SAUSAGE MINI-BOMB**
> All the meat is Pure Pork and it contains NO PRESERVATIVE. The crust is SUPERCRUST which is also sold separately. Thaw and bake for half an hour at 200°C, 400°F or gas Mark 6. Add a further 7 minutes if you put it in the oven frozen.
> Made and sold in
> **Cropwell Butler Nottingham**
> *Mrs. Elizabeth King's English Supercrust and Bomb are trade marks*

taking the trouble, and the petrol, to come to this small village for the products. Mr Parr has a long history of baking and butchering – his grandfather taught him that 'a baker can always be a butcher, if he wishes, but a butcher can seldom be a baker', and so insisted that he qualify first as a baker. Now, in his mid-seventies he has officially retired, but is in fact still producing superb pies and sausages with the help of his grandson, winning the First Prize in the great Melton Mowbray Pork Pie Exhibition, and the Roper Challenge Cup. He has adopted a technique which simplifies problems of freshness, and of distribution – all his products, *pork pies*, *Sausage Bombs* and *rolls*, *Eccles cakes* and '*Supercrust*' *pastry*, are uncooked but oven-ready, with clear instructions on every pack. The meat is pure pork, with no preservatives, and the pastry recipe a secret, but based on his lifetime's experience of pie-making. The only retail outlet is his own small shop, open 9.30a.m.–12p.m. every morning except Sunday and Monday. Cropwell Butler is off the A46 between Leicester and Newark, about 9 miles east of Nottingham. The Lodge is down a conifer-lined drive in Hardigate Road, 'next to Barratt & Swann, the well-known furniture makers'.

Somerset Creameries' Stilton

Somerset Creameries Ltd,
Nottingham Road, Cropwell Bishop,
Nottinghamshire NG12 3BQ
Tel. Nottingham (0602) 892986/892350
D S D SKAILES, I M D SKAILES, H R HACKLAND

This is a family company founded by Frank Strickland-Skailes in the 1920s. Since his death, the company has been run by the above team, and extensive modernisation is being carried out. So although the *Stiltons* (*pasteurised* and *unpasteurised*, *white* and *blue*) are made in the traditional manner, the factory is the newest in the industry. The territorial cheeses – Leicester, Double Gloucester, Derby, vegetarian Cheddar – are made both in 40-pound blocks and in traditional rounds. Sales are either wholesale or by mail order, visitors by arrangement.

Cropwell Bishop is the next door village to Cropwell Butler (see previous entry).

LINCOLNSHIRE

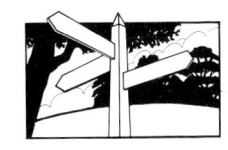

Belvoir elderflower cordial and raspberry cordial

*Belvoir Fruit Farms Ltd,
Belvoir, Grantham, Lincolnshire
NG32 1PB
Tel. Grantham (0476) 870286*
LORD JOHN MANNERS

This delicate and scented cordial started life as a kitchen product, made for home consumption at the rate of only twenty bottles a year. When the fruit farming side of this mainly sheep and arable farm of 2200 acres was started four years ago, it was decided to manufacture the cordial in a small way – 2000 bottles to begin with. This has now trebled, and is growing so fast that 15,000 bottles are anticipated soon. The cordial contains a little citric acid and is pasteurised, otherwise the contents are exactly the same as any home-made recipe. It makes a wonderful sorbet, either in the proportions of one-third cordial to two-thirds water, or half and half. Topped up with iced champagne or sparkling wine it makes a magical summer drink, and is also recommended as a winter warmer when mixed with spirits and hot water. *Raspberry cordial* is a more recent development and is made from the farm's own fruit with the addition of lemon juice, sugar and a little preservative. Retail outlets include: Alan Porter, Farnley, Otley, West Yorkshire; Justin de Blank, 42 Elizabeth Street, London SW1; Thoughts of Food, 60 Wellby Street, Grantham, Lincolnshire; Hobson's Choice, Queen Street, Bottesford, Nottinghamshire. Sales are also from the fruit farm – open all day, but the office is only manned in the morning; there is a telephone answering service. The farm is ½ mile below Belvoir Castle carpark on the Redmile road, about 7 miles east of Grantham.

Curtis's Lincolnshire Chine

*A W Curtis & Sons Ltd,
164 High Street, Lincoln LN5 7AF
Tel. Lincoln (0522) 30802*
THE CURTIS FAMILY

Lincolnshire stuffed chine is a purely local delicacy, or so I was told, until I found recipes for it in Northamptonshire too, and a reference to 'sage-stuff'd chine' in that Northamptonshire poet John Clare's 'The Shepherd's Calendar'. It is a dish for celebrations, for christenings, and in John Clare's case, Christmas (hence the sage). It is a cut of brine-cured pork, in between the shoulder blades, which forms an oblong block which is then deeply slashed, and each slash packed with a mixture of chopped fresh herbs. In the old recipes, the mixture was very varied and included currant leaves as well as the more usual parsley, thyme and sage. It is simmered until tender, then eaten cold. Mr Dickens, of Curtis & Sons, says that it should be eaten with that time-honoured English standby – a little vinegar, and brown bread. I preferred it with a mildly mustardy vinaigrette. Curtis & Sons make another local speciality – Lincolnshire Plum Bread. Their recipe (secret) is yeast-based, with sultanas, currants, raisins and spices. 'Simply buttered it is delicious, eaten with a slice of mature Cheddar cheese, it is superb,' says Mr Dickens. Lincolnshire is also the home of good sausages and pork pies, two more Curtis specialities. All their products are for sale in their eighteen retail shops and their seven mobile shops, in Harrods, and Bonne Bouche Pâtisseries throughout West London. A mail order service operates from the following address: A W Curtis, Mail Order Dept, Long Leys Road, Lincoln LN1 1EA, Tel. (0522) 27212. The shops are all open from 8.30a.m.–5.30p.m., Monday to Saturday, with outlying shops closing at lunchtime on Wednesdays.

present for anyone with a June birthday. For further details, ring, or write to the above address.

Michael Paske farm asparagus

Michael Paske Farms Ltd,
The Estate Office, Honington,
Grantham, Lincolnshire
Tel. Honington (0400) 50449
MICHAEL AND CHRISTINE PASKE

The Paskes supply their top quality *English asparagus* by post – a marvellous service for those who live far away from sources of this best-of-all vegetables. It is cut, packed and despatched the same day, and comes in *three different pack sizes* – Jumbo (fat spears 20mm thick), Long Green Extra (16–20mm thick), and Long Green Selected (10–16mm thick – my own preference, as the flavour of asparagus always seems better the thinner the spear). A parcel of asparagus would be a wonderful

EASTERN ENGLAND

Essex
Suffolk
Cambridgeshire
Norfolk

As though to counteract the suffocating agribusiness which blankets the wide flat landscapes of the region, there are plenty of producers in this area working hard to provide fortunate easterners with a wonderful range of good food and drink. Local game is made into opulent pies by the Camplings of Essex Larders*. Turkey has always been an East Anglian product, Derek Kelly of Kelly Turkeys* is introducing the Bronze variety to restore faith in this overworked bird. Further north, in Norfolk, Valerie Green* is re-introducing the Norfolk Black Turkey for the same reason – both aim to make the Christmas turkey a treat once again.

North Norfolk, with its annual influx of appreciative visitors, has a number of producers placed strategically along the coast. In Burnham Market, Susan Elston* runs a very good food shop, stocking interesting things from all over the country, including a range of farmhouse cheeses. She also makes her own jams and chutneys from local produce. At Wells-next-the-Sea, Marian Cartwright* presides over the making of more excellent chutney and jam – the scent of simmering chutney hung in the air all round when we visited in August. Her partner, Charles Butler, supervises the blending of herbs, spices, teas and coffees. Stop at Morston to buy oysters, whitebait or mussels, depending on the season, from Major Athill*, who also runs a sailing school, then park the car somewhere at Blakeney and spend time wandering among the creeks on the marshes, blue with sea-lavender, picking samphire. The season for this delicious sea 'asparagus' is the late summer, and although you can buy it from local fishmongers, it is much more fun to pick it for yourself. Trim off the muddy stalks and roots, then cook it and serve it as you would asparagus, with plenty of melted butter. At Cley-next-the-Sea you can buy particularly good taramasalata and sweet pickled herrings, and a range of smoked fish, from the Cley Smokehouse*, where Michael Rhodes is always glad to discuss his products with you. You can buy freshly boiled and dressed crab almost anywhere along this coast road in the summer months –

people sell them from their cottages and caravans, from garages and ice cream vans. With some rolls from a nearby baker and a bottle of Robin Don's Norfolk Apple Wine* you can have an impromptu picnic – we chose the edge of an over-sized cornfield, with the spire of one of Norfolk's many beautiful churches silhouetted against a lowering thunderous sky.

Suffolk, too, is packed with good food, and is home to two of the best apple juice producers in the country – John Chevallier Guild of Aspall Hall*, who makes cyder as well, and the Peake family at Boxford, who make Copella* – a wonderful blend of Cox's and Bramleys. These apple juices go very well with the famous Suffolk hams, and at least one ham producer, Jerrey's of Peasenhall*, uses local cider and apple juice for pickling hams.

Two smokehouses – Leggett's of Beccles* and The Raglan Smokehouse* in Lowestoft – produce the traditional smoked fish of the area – bloaters, red herrings and kippers, legacies of the once-huge Lowestoft herring industry.

You need considerable time to explore the food finds of this huge area, and to enjoy the pubs too, where the food may not always be good, but the beer is usually excellent. And take the Diary of the Rev. James Woodforde with you as reading matter; his descriptions of huge meals eaten either in his rectory at Weston Longeville, north-west of Norwich, or with friends in the area, cover a cross section of all that is still the good food of East Anglia.

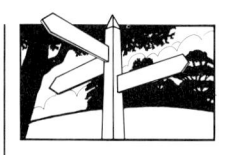

ESSEX

Adam's Rib Farm goats' dairy produce

The Paddock, Ulting, nr Maldon, Essex
Tel. Chelmsford (0245) 380328
MRS J LYNN EVE

The Eves produce *milk* from their herd of goats, and *meat* too – kid meat is like rather gamey lamb, and as well as good flavour has the added advantage of being very low in fat. They also distribute goats' dairy products from other producers in the area – yoghurt, cheese and ice cream. Local Essex retail shops supplied include: Nature's Table, Unit 8, The Walk, Billericay; Perfect Health, Victoria Road, Romford; Supreme Health Food Co., 235 Cranbrook Road, Ilford; Burton's (grocers), Broomfield Road, Chelmsford; John Chesham, 164 Heath Park Road, Gidea Park, Romford, and 120 Aldborough Road South, Seven Kings, Ilford. Callers by appointment only, please.

Cole's Traditional Christmas Puddings

A J Cole & Sons,
19 & 52–54 High Street,
Saffron Walden, Essex
Tel. Saffron Walden (0799) 22126
C J COLE

So good are the Coles' puddings and mincemeat, and so ingenious is their packaging, that last year three different companies tried to steal their ideas, making it necessary for Cole's to take out a copyright on both the labelling and packaging. But some important details are not in the least secret – such as the fact that the only liquid in the *Christmas pudding* is strong Suffolk Ale, brewed by Greene King & Sons of Bury St Edmunds. This is the only preservative used, as all Cole's products are free from artificial additives – the *health food puddings* are free from gluten, too, and all animal derivatives. The *mincemeat* is particularly unusual and good, made with an apricot base blended with rum and sherry, and there is a *vegetarian version* made with vegetable suet. All these sprang from the bakery business founded in 1939 by A J Cole and his wife. The bakery still specialises in producing home-made bread and confectionery for the two Cole's shops in Saffron Walden's High Street, where you can also buy the full range of products. The shops are open from 9a.m.–5p.m. every working day. Otherwise, look for Cole's elegant black and gold packaging in Harrods and other London food halls, and in good grocers all round the country (300 retail outlets).

Crape's specialist apples

Crape's Fruit Farm, Rectory Road, Aldham, Colchester, Essex CO6 3RR
Tel. Colchester (0206) 210406

JOHN R TANN

John Tann's fruit farm is a fascinating 'library' of *unusual fruit* and in particular *apples*, of old varieties in danger of extinction, and new varieties not usually available in shops. His lists make absorbing reading; the wide range of apples – about 160, of which some are represented by one tree only and others are newly planted – includes such dessert varieties as White Joaneting, Ribston Pippin, d'Arcy Spice, Irish Peach, Cornish Gilliflower, Norfolk Royal, Cornish Aromatic, Court Pendu Plat (one of the oldest varieties, dating back to the Roman occupation), Upton Pyne and Winter Lemon. Cooking varieties include Rev W Wilks and Roundway Magnum Bonum. The preservation of older varieties is often assisted by interested customers and others who (by arrangement, stresses Mr Tann) contribute graftwood of 'good old sorts in danger of being lost and are not yet in our collection'. This is an enthusiasts' fruit farm, supplying *medlars* and *quinces* too, quite apart from *pears*, *cherries*, *plums*, *gages*, *damsons*, and *soft fruits including white currants*. *Do telephone first*, especially if you are coming any distance, to check on availability, and also to pre-order if you require large quantities (boxes of apples approximately 10, 20 and 30lbs). The fruit farm is open Monday–Saturday, 8a.m.–5p.m., from June to April, always closed on Sundays. To find it, from the A12 and A120, turn off at Marks Tey, 5 miles west of Colchester; at the roundabout take the Aldham and Marks Tey Station road for 1¼ miles to Rectory Road, which is off on the left beside an orchard. From A604, west of Colchester, turn off almost opposite Aldham Post Office, up by Aldham Garden Centre. Go up to the village, straight ahead at the church crossroads, past the housing estate and ¼ mile on to Rectory Road, going off to the right. The farm is on the left, 300 yards up Rectory Road.

J C Dixon – meat from extensively-reared animals free from growth promoters

North Hall Farm, Quendon, Saffron Walden, Essex CB11 3XP
Tel. Rickling (079 988) 429

John Dixon started his hormone-free meat production in 1979 as a part-time adjunct to his 'self-sufficiency' life-style, and now applies the same principles to this commercial full-time occupation, now in its eighth year. He rears Gloucester Old Spot pigs for pork and bacon, Soay lambs and Angus steers; their meat is available to order only, sold as halves or quarters for the freezer. Free-range eggs are available from the farm at any time. Quendon is 2 miles south of Newport on the B1383 – take the Henham/Elsenham road, ¾ mile to the telephone kiosk on the left. The farm drive is opposite.

Essex Larders pies and quiches

Pyes Farm, Hounslow Green, Dunmow, Essex CM6 3PR
Tel. Great Dunmow (0371) 830272
JOHN AND ZINNIA CAMPLING, JANE MALINS

In 1979, Mr Campling was wondering when and how to retire from twenty years of fruit farming when he was inspired to contact Mrs Thomas, of Devon Larders (see page 27), after reading an article about her in a farming paper. The Camplings obtained planning permission to turn the tractor shed of their erstwhile fruit farm into a kitchen and bakery, and with Mrs Thomas's advice and encouragement, baking equipment, and a 32-pound bag of flour, they launched themselves as Essex Larders. Their 'retirement' has been so successful that, with the help of their daughter Jane, two full-time and eight part-time workers, they won the Pub Food Award at the Cookery and Food Catering Exhibition at Newmarket in 1984. Their pies, while based on Mrs Thomas's recipes, are modified to suit East Anglian taste. The range includes *seven cold jellied pies, eleven hot pies, twelve varieties of quiche, nine dessert pies* – all made from the best quality local ingredients, with no additives or preservatives. *Steak and kidney* and *game* pies now carry the range right through the season. Sales are wholesale only, to shops in the area, including: Ffitch & Son, Ware, Hertfordshire; Bon Appetit, Hertford; Cossticks, Tacket Street, Ipswich; Peter Dominic, Bridge Street, Cambridge. Personal callers are welcome by appointment, between 9.30a.m.–4p.m. on weekdays.

Fullers' Jersey farm produce

Brickwall Farm, Sible Hedingham, Halstead, Essex CO9 3RH
Tel. Hedingham (0787) 60329
MR AND MRS R FULLER

The Fullers were driven into processing the milk from their 80-strong herd of Jersey cows in the summer of 1976, when the terrible drought almost brought about the end of their farm. By chance, they produced a very good yoghurt, using a Burco boiler, stainless steel bucket and the skimmed milk left from their cream production. More than ten years later, with more expertise and better equipment, they produce a range of *low-fat* and *gold top soft cheese* and *yoghurt, a natural set yoghurt, cultured buttermilk, Jersey* and *soured cream* and *cottage cheese*, even *cheesecakes*, which they deliver to over two dozen shops in the area, as well as to local hotels. Their farm shop also sells the produce. Visitors are always welcome to watch the milking, or the calves being fed, and groups are shown round the farm and dairy during April and May – please ring for details. Sible Hedingham is about 8 miles north of Halstead on the A604 Halstead to Haverhill road.

Kelly Turkeys

Springate Farm, Bicknacre Road, Danbury, Chelmsford, Essex CM3 4EP
Tel. Danbury (0245 41) 3581
DEREK AND MOLLIE KELLY, PAUL KELLY

Perhaps Derek Kelly's experience working for one of the largest turkey

Maldon salt

*The Maldon Crystal Salt Co. Ltd,
The Downs, Maldon, Essex CM9 7HR
Tel. Maldon (0621) 53315*

CLIVE OSBORNE

I used to buy Maldon salt twenty years ago, when as more of a medicine than a condiment it was still packed in beautiful brown cardboard boxes covered with Victorian lettering extolling its virtues. The virtues remain the same despite the rather less attractive but more contemporary packaging. The manufacture of Maldon salt still relies on the favourable conditions which have existed in Essex for centuries, the dry windy climate of the coast which causes rapid evaporation of the sea-water trapped on the salt marshes. This produces high salt levels in the rivers which drain the marshes, and it is from these rivers that water is transferred to huge holding tanks, usually after periods of dry weather when the salt content is at its highest. The processes for procuring those beautiful inverted crystals that are the unique feature of Maldon salt have changed very little; natural gas is now used instead of the coal brought by sea from the North of England to heat the water in the evaporating pans, but the same degree of skill is needed to keep the temperature constant for the fifteen–sixteen hours it takes for the crystals to form. The process is entirely natural, the salt is totally pure and free from any of the additives usually found

producers in Europe prompted him to start up his own business, in 1971, producing the best instead of the cheapest. His *turkeys* are 'Traditional Farm Fresh' i.e. they are fed an extra four to six weeks and killed when they are mature and have developed more flavour, then hung for at least seven days before being prepared by hand without any added water or chemicals. He is also introducing the *bronze turkey*, which has an even better flavour, a little gamier is perhaps the best description. Kelly Turkeys is very much a family firm; Derek's wife Mollie writes the recipe leaflets, and there is a small dedicated staff. Sales are wholesale to top quality outlets, and retail direct from the farm. They also supply turkeys as company Christmas presents. Contact the Kellys to find out your nearest stockists. The farm is 1¼ miles south of Danbury, which is 5 miles east of Chelmsford on the A414.

in table salt. The Maldon Crystal Salt Co. is the only company still manufacturing sea salt, and it is flourishing – 25% is exported, largely to Sweden. In this country it is widely distributed through health food and delicatessen wholesalers as well as some supermarket chains. The company regret that they aren't able to accommodate visitors, but it is worth walking the fields surrounding the town of Maldon, looking for the 'red hills' of Essex, the remains of the Saxon salt industry, when the water was trapped in clay pans and partially evaporated before being put into earthenware pots. The 'hills' are the spoil tips of burnt earth and broken pots.

Peartree pork products

High Birch Farm, Weeley Heath, Nr Clacton-on-Sea, Essex CO16 9BU
Tel. Clacton-on-Sea (0255) 830921
PAUL ERNST

Mr Ernst's father and grandfather processed and marketed their home-produced poultry until the growth of food processing began about thirty years ago. The threat to farming livelihoods from cheap imported foods was steadily erosive, but in order to turn the tide, the Ernsts realised that the answer lay in quality, not quantity. They stuck to their traditional methods of producing *hams, sausages, bacon* and other *pork products* from their home-reared pigs, and have proved that there is a constant demand for such products. 'I feel there is a relatively small, though quite adequate and very secure market amongst a sector of the public who are becoming more aware of the food that they eat. This interest now, of course, extends to a concern with the way the animals are reared.' Mr Ernst's words sum up his confidence in the future of his products, which include boxed *freezer packs of game, poultry, beef* and *lamb* as well. Sales are within a 50-mile radius to wholesale customers, and there is a significant trade from the farm shop, as well as a limited but growing mail order trade. The farm shop is open all year, Monday to Friday, 9.30a.m.–1p.m., 2–5p.m., Saturday, 9a.m.– 12.30p.m. From the A133 ¾ mile south of Weeley, take a right turn to Aingers Green. After ¾ mile turn left to St Osyth, High Birch Farm is on the left after ½ mile.

SUFFOLK

Aspall cyder and apple juice

Aspall Hall, Debenham, Stowmarket, Suffolk IP14 6PD
Tel. Debenham (0728) 860510
J M & J I CHEVALLIER GUILD

John Chevallier Guild resigned his commission in the Navy in 1970 to restore his fine family house, and fortunes, by reviving the 250-year-old family cider business. He has succeeded too, by catering for a market concerned with quality – Aspall Organic Apple Juice came top out of forty-five major brands in a national newspaper tasting recently. This is juice from freshly pressed English apples, and not merely a concentrate. Apples are supplied from the Aspall Hall orchards and others in the neighbourhood, and are all unsprayed (the firm holds the Soil Association Symbol). The range of products includes *cyder* (medium, sweet, dry and extra-dry, all still), *Organic and English fresh pressed apple juices*, and *speciality vinegars* (organic cyder, red and white wine, and pickling malt). Additional juices include *freshly pressed pear juice, apple and blackcurrant* and other blends. The cyder is not as widely distributed as the other products, but most are found in good health food shops and delicatessens throughout the UK (with export to Europe and Japan). The shop at Aspall Hall is open on weekdays, 9a.m.–12.30p.m., 1.30–3.30p.m. 1½ miles north of Debenham on the B1077.

The Butley-Orford Oysterage

Market Hill, Orford, Woodbridge, Suffolk IP12 2LH
Tel. Orford (0394) 450277
WILLIAM PINNEY

The founder of this remarkable place, Richard Pinney (William's father), describes it succinctly on the final page of his book *Smoked Salmon and Oysters – a Feast of Suffolk Memories* – as having 'four corner stones – oyster growing, salmon smoking, catering and extensive fishing'. This in no way does justice to the influence Richard Pinney has had on the smoked salmon of Britain – Jane Forestier-Walker of Minola Smoked Foods (see page 57) worked under him, as did the founder of what is now the largest producer of smoked salmon in Scotland, which still bears his name – Pinneys (see page 220). The oysters are the Pacific *gigas*, the salmon Atlantic, the catering 'our sampling kitchen, our little Orford restaurant', where the produce of the oyster beds, the smokehouse and the sea is served and eaten by appreciative customers. For opening times for the restaurant and shop (which sells delicatessen goods as well) ring (0394) 450277, and to contact the smokehouse, oysterage and fishery departments ring (0394) 450322. Orford is at the junction of the B1084 with the River Alde, about 5 miles south of Aldeburgh.

Cavendish Manor 'Ambroseia'

Cavendish Manor Vineyards, Nether Hall, Cavendish, Sudbury, Suffolk CO10 8DX
Tel. Glemsford (0787) 280221
B T AMBROSE

Ambroseia (note the pun) is a blend of *grape and apple juice*, non-alcoholic, but a wonderful base for alcoholic drinks, as well as being delicious in its own right. Mr Ambrose also makes an *English white wine* called *Cavendish Manor*, and both products are made from home-grown fruit. Although the venture is fairly recent (1972), Mr Ambrose points out that the Romans grew grapes here – he is the first to do so since the Roman occupation, however. Visitors are always welcome, and the vineyard has its own off-licence which is open daily. For further details on retail outlets and trade enquiries, please telephone. The shop hours are 11a.m.–4p.m. throughout the year; both vineyard and shop are on the A1092, 100 yards north of Cavendish church.

Copella fruit juices

*Copella Fruit Juices Ltd,
Hill Farm, Boxford, Suffolk CO6 5NY
Tel. Boxford (0787) 210348/210496*
MRS DEVORA PEAKE AND FAMILY

Copella apple juice (named after the Cox's Orange Pippins which are its chief ingredient) is one of the best on the market – a delicious essence of apples. It is cloudy because it is unfiltered, thus retaining all the goodness, and it is wonderfully flavoured not simply because of the variety of apple, but because of a super-fast method of production. Hand-selected fruit is washed, pressed, flash-pasteurised and then immediately bottled (or boxed – it also comes in cartons) in a non-stop operation which means that from apple to bottle takes only two hours. Devora Peake herself was born in Russia and came to England from Palestine in 1938; she has the drive necessary to run this family empire and make something out of every corner of the farm's poor soil which covers 800 acres. Organic farming, which Devora and her second husband Bill tried well ahead of the current wave of thinking, and which nearly ruined them, is now paying dividends; *Peake's Organic Products* – apple juice, apples and stoneground wholewheat flour, are all produced from an area of the farmland which has been set aside for organic husbandry. And an infertile area has been made into two money-spinning 18-hole golf courses which form Stoke-by-Nayland Golf Club – landscaped round four reservoirs which provide irrigation for the fruit and arable areas. Morello cherries and blackcurrants are also grown for the fruit juice blends. Devora's son Jonathan is technology manager, while daughters Susanna and Tamara are company secretary, and sales and marketing director respectively. Susanna's husband Roger Rendall is general manager both of the farm and of fruit processing, and Tamara's husband Stephen Unwin is head of production and development of Copella Fruit Juices. It all reads like a soap-opera saga. Their 'Beaujolais Nouveau' is their *Discovery Blend*, only made in September from the first apples of the season. Copella products are very widely distributed – you can find them at better motorway service stations, as well as in National Trust properties and healthfood shops. There is a shop at Hill Farm, too, open from 9a.m.–5p.m. on weekdays. Take the B1068 turning off the A134 Colchester–Bury St Edmunds road, then turn left to Boxford to find the farm shop on your right.

Emmett's Suffolk hams

*Emmett's Store, Peasenhall,
Saxmundham, Suffolk IP17 2HJ
Tel. Peasenhall (072 879) 250*
F G AND N R JERREY

The Jerreys specialise in one Suffolk speciality – hams – combined with another – cider. Their *cider-pickled hams* are as good as they sound, being cured in a mixture of local cider and apple juice. They also do sweet pickled and oak-smoked hams, sweet pickled back bacon, and fresh and smoked sausages. Halves, as well as whole hams are available at Christmas, and both these and the bacon are available by mail order – an area which is expanding fast, with the demand for 'real' food. 'The future looks bright,' says Mr Jerrey cheerfully – he is continuing an old family business. The shop is open from Monday–Friday, 8.30a.m.–1p.m., 2–5.30 p.m. Saturday, 8.30a.m.–1p.m., 1.30–5.0p.m. To find Peasenhall, turn off the A12 at Yoxford on to the A1120 to Peasenhall – the shop is on the crossroads in Peasenhall.

Leggett's bloaters and kippers

A J Leggett & Sons,
35/37 Blyburgate Street, Beccles, Suffolk NR34 9TF
Tel. Beccles (0502) 712192
R I AND D A LEGGETT

Roy and Douglas Leggett are the third generation of Leggetts to satisfy the public's demand for fresh and smoked fish and shellfish, and to win prizes for it: for five years running they've won the Broadland Partnership Award. In their own smokehouse they use only oak wood and sawdust, buying the herring daily from Lowestoft Fish Market (Douglas's job) to ensure a regular supply of the freshest and best for transforming into bloaters and kippers. They also supply fresh fish, their own boiled shellfish (lobsters, crabs, shrimps, cockles, whelks,

according to season), and seasonal local poultry and game. Sales are mainly to local shoppers (Roy Leggett serves in the shop), with shop hours 7.30a.m.–5.30p.m. every day except Wednesday (early closing) and Saturday, when they close half-an-hour earlier. Beccles is 9 miles inland from Lowestoft on the A146.

Ostler ewes' dairy products

The Laurels Stables, Horringer, Bury St Edmunds, Suffolk IP29 5SN
Tel. Horringer (028 488) 281 evenings, or before 9a.m.
MRS ANN JAMES

Mrs James keeps hunters for hire to experienced riders in the winter, and for her summer income, she decided to keep dairy sheep on a small acreage of pasture. She produces a range of *fresh soft cheeses* (plain, chive or wrapped in fig-leaves), *plain yoghurt* and *milk* from the ewes along with *paddock* (i.e. *real* free-range) *eggs*, and *spiced apple chutney* made before the hunting season starts. The name 'Ostler' (horse-handler) was an obvious one for the products, for which there is a good market in the locality. Despite all the demands on her time (Mrs James is managing director of a firm of flooring contractors, and a committee member of the British Friesland Sheep Society), visitors are welcome – either to serve themselves on a 'trust' basis if everyone is busy, or by appointment, to see round the farm, and to learn hand-milking. The milking is done with a mobile parlour, taken out to the flock, and then brought back to the purpose-made dairy for processing. Some quiet ewes are for sale as 'house cows'. Horringer is on the A143 Bury St Edmunds to Haverhill road, 2 miles from Bury, and the farm is just past the Beehive pub on the right hand side.

A R Paske – seakale plants

The South Lodge, Gazeley Road, Kentford, Newmarket, Suffolk CB8 7QA
Tel. Newmarket (0638) 750613
A R PASKE

The absence of seakale in the shops is something which Mr Paske is planning to remedy. At the moment, he encourages you to grow this delicious vegetable for yourself. Like asparagus, it was moved from its natural seashore habitat into English gardens in the eighteenth century, but for some reason has not regained the popularity it had when Carême was serving it to the Prince Regent, and seakale pots, forcing the shoots to succulent pallor, could be found in every large kitchen garden. It is indeed easy to grow, even in our black, acid Cumbrian soil, and is a wonderful treat to have in April and May before the English asparagus season starts; and it is very decorative when it grows beyond the edible stage. Mr Paske also sells globe artichoke plants (variety 'Green Globe'), and sends out informative leaflets with both plants. Roy Paske describes his enterprise as 'more of a hobby', so all sales are by post – write for details.

The Raglan Smokehouse

Raglan Street, Lowestoft, Suffolk
Tel. Lowestoft (0502) 81929
D MULLENDER AND G BUCKENHAM

Gordon Buckenham was brought up in the fish smoking business and has forty years of experience; David Mullender comes from a long line of fishermen and was a trawler skipper himself for fifteen years before coming ashore to join the retail fish trade where he has been for the last thirty-five years. Eight years ago they formed a partnership to save an eighteenth-century smokehouse from demolition when the owner became too old to run the business, and they now have a year-round production of *cold-smoked kippers, red herring, smoked haddock, cod, whiting, prawns* and *salmon*. The fish is sold wholesale to fish-markets, and through the smokehouse shop (which also sells wet fish) sales are direct from the smoke-room. The methods are traditional to this area – no additives or colouring, of course, and pre-1940 standards are maintained. Gordon and David feel that the healthy future of their business can only depend on the general future of the fishing industry in England. To make that industry grow instead of decline, we must all increase our fish consumption. The smokehouse shop is open 8a.m.–5p.m. Monday to Friday, 8a.m.–noon on Saturdays.

Stiff's Suffolk bacon and chaps

R *Stiff & Sons,*
Kersey, Ipswich, Suffolk IP7 6DY
Tel. Hadleigh (0473) 822147
J STIFF

The recipe the Stiffs use for their Suffolk cures is well over 100 years old, and until the middle of 1984 they cured hams by that recipe, as well as bacon, before illness called a halt to that side of the business. The bacon is very good, and fortunately, available by post for anyone who would rather forgo the bacon offered in supermarkets. Buy some now, while you can, as Mr Stiff is worried about the continuity of the business after his retirement in a few years' time, as neither of his children are involved in the work. The shop is open in summer from 9.30a.m.–5p.m., six days a week, in winter from 9.30a.m.–1p.m. on weekdays and all day on Saturdays. Early closing is on Thursdays. The shop is in the middle of Kersey village, to the west of the A1141 about 2 miles north-west of Hadleigh. Mr Stiff will also cure bacon for private customers.

CAMBRIDGESHIRE

The English Provender Co. preserves and condiments

Aldreth Farm, Aldreth, Ely,
Cambridgeshire CB6 3PG
Tel. Ely (0353) 740069
ANNE AND EDWARD PARKER

I had formed a very favourable impression of English Provender products when I tried them, but it was somewhat dispelled by the marketing 'blurb' that I was sent through the post, which said that English Provender had been started 'to exploit the rapidly growing market for speciality foods both in the grocery and gift areas'. What damage the ad men do with one mis-chosen word – in this case, 'exploit'. However, there are some very good things in the product range, which covers a wide range of jams, marmalades, fruit and herb jellies, mustards, chutneys, relishes, ketchups, herb vinegars and mayonnaise. There is a good *Strawberry Vinegar,* unsweetened, for instance, and a *Spiced Wine* vinegar which adds zest to casseroles. There is a very good *Apple with Coriander Chutney,* and while I shall be glad when the craze for adding liqueurs to jam is over, I found the *Dark Plum Jam with Brandy and Walnuts* made a wonderful filling for a dark chocolate cake. The fruit used is local, and the preserves are made in small batches; the packaging is very decorative, and they do own-brand labels for other companies. Their products make very acceptable gifts. Visitors are welcome by appointment between 9a.m.–5p.m. on weekdays. Aldreth is 2 miles south of Haddenham, which is on the A1123, which crosses the A10 about 7 miles south of Ely.

Fitzbillies' Chelsea buns

Fitzbillies, 52 Trumpington Street, Cambridge CB2 1RG
Tel. Cambridge (0223) 352500
MR AND MRS CLIVE PLEDGER

Fitzbillies' *Chelsea buns* have played an important part in many people's memories of Cambridge since the bakers and confectioners opened at the time of the First World War. Jane Grigson can remember queuing for them in the grey days after the Second World War, and even now thinks them the best she's ever eaten. The recipe is a secret – not even written down, say Clive and Julia Pledger, the third generation of 'Mr & Mrs Fitzbillie', and so it should remain.

Fitzbillies, under the Pledgers' ownership, now send their own *chocolates,* made on the premises to recipes of their own devising from butter, fresh cream and liqueurs, *by post,* as well as their *fruit and Genoa cakes,* beautifully packed in Fitzbillies' cake tins. The Pledgers, rightly, do not try to compete with Sainsbury's and Marks and Spencer; they supply consistent quality at prices which everyone seems happy to pay, and steer clear of any artificial additives, limiting their use of food colours to birthday cakes: 'Our goods are as wholesome as cakes and pastries can be.' One of their specialities that I found very interesting, although I wasn't able to try it for myself, is the Fitzbillies *Sponge,* made each Christmas for as long as anyone can remember – a completely plain cake traditionally eaten with cheese. There are two shops now – one at the above address, the other in a new shopping precinct, 50 Regent Street (between the University Arms Hotel and the Catholic Church). Both are open between 8.30a.m.–5p.m., Monday to Saturday.

Over Mill stoneground wholemeal flour

The Mill, Over, Cambridgeshire CB4 5PP
Tel. Willingham (0954) 30742
G G WILSON

It had been Mr Wilson's ambition to own a windmill ever since he was at school, and in 1960 he was at last able to fulfil that ambition by buying Over Mill, unused since 1929. Refitting the mill meant making two new sails and re-flooring the tower, among many other things; now the mill is once again grinding corn, using two sets of under-drift stones. The flour is packed in 10, 14 and 70lb bags, and is either *wholemeal* or *plain*; wind dictates availability, of course. Sales are from local health or wholefood shops, or from the mill door – usually between 9a.m. and 4p.m., but it is best to telephone first as the mill is sometimes unmanned. To reach Over, leave the A604 6 miles north-west of Cambridge by the B1050 to Longstanton and Willingham. Just before Willingham turn left for Over.

NORFOLK

Major Athill – oyster farmer

*Scaldbeck Barn, Morston, Holt,
Norfolk NR25 7BJ
Tel. Cley (0263) 740306*
ANDREW ATHILL

Major Athill combines oyster farming (his are Pacific oysters, resistant to the oyster disease, bonamia), with a sailing school and boat hire business, and is as picturesque a character as you would hope to find on the north Norfolk coast, his sea-dog appearance belying his army rank. Since oysters do not appreciate me, I was unable to appreciate those sold by Major Athill, and we called on him out of the *mussel* season which lasts from September to March. But his *whitebait*, caught by seine netting in the estuary, were the best I have ever tasted and came complete with little wisps of seaweed which when deep-fried tasted as good as the fish. Blakeney Harbour had an old-established oyster business until the 1920s, when the beds became sanded over. Andrew Athill, advised by the Ministry of Agriculture, Fisheries and Food, began on-growing his Pacific oysters in 1974, using the rafting method (hanging the oysters in mesh containers below rafts which float on pontoons) in the tidal creeks of Blakeney Harbour, a haven from pollution. The oysters are available year round, and the whitebait (fresh or frozen) from June to October. Sales are to personal callers, who are welcome at any time. Look for a small sign on the roadside as you drive along the coast road (A419) between Wells-next-the-Sea and Blakeney, at Morston.

Black Sheep Ltd, black Welsh lamb

*Black Sheep Farm Store, Ingworth,
Norwich, Norfolk NR11 6PJ
Tel. Aylsham (0263) 733142/732006*
MRS R CLARE HOARE

Mrs Clare Hoare's flock of Black Welsh sheep are now famous as much for their wool and woollen goods, and their record ('Baa, Baa Black Sheep', of course) as for the *lean, sweet-flavoured and fine-textured meat* which they also produce. The Ingworth and Blickling flock began less than twenty years ago from an original purchase of only six black sheep and is now one of the largest of the 200 registered flocks of Black Welsh mountain sheep throughout Britain and around the world. The meat is a seasonal product, available between August and December, and order forms are mailed annually to those who are interested. Orders are booked for *collection* (please notify) from the farm store. This might seem a great deal of trouble, but the meat is well worth it, and there is an enormous range of Black Welsh wool garments, fabrics, even wool fat soap to buy at the same time. The sheep themselves can be seen grazing round the charming church at Ingworth, opposite the farm store, which is open daily (except Mondays, unless a Bank Holiday) all the year round from 9a.m.–5.30p.m. Ingworth is about 1 mile to the west of the A140 from Norwich to Cromer, halfway between the two.

Cartwright & Butler Ltd, preserves, herbs and spices

The Spice Mill, Wells-next-the-Sea, Norfolk NR23 1DB
Tel. Fakenham (0328) 710144
MARIAN CARTWRIGHT

Another jam-making business, but this time it seems cosier and nearer its kitchen origins than some. Marian Cartwright, 'housewife, mother of three, concert pianist, ceramic designer and lover of food', as she is described, began making chutneys in 1980. Her partner, Charles Butler, bought an ailing herb and spice packing business in 1979 and transformed it into a success. Marian and Charles, whose families had long been close friends, pooled their resources at The Spice Mill, Wells-next-the-Sea, and now have a very viable enterprise producing Marian's original *chutneys, herb and spice blends, mincemeats, fruit butters, marmalades, preserves*, as well as *biscuits, both sweet and savoury*, and *teas and coffees*. All are made and blended on the premises – as you can see, and certainly smell, if you visit the Spice Mill. The 'factory' shop sells 'bin ends' and trial lines; the whole range is well distributed throughout the country in good grocers as well as gift shops. Packaging is pretty but modest. The Spice Mill is open Monday to Friday, 9a.m.–5p.m. It is situated on the A149 at Wells-next-the-Sea.

Cley Smokehouse

High Street, Cley-next-the-Sea, Holt, Norfolk NR25 7RF
Tel. Cley (0263) 740282
MICHAEL RHODES

The tiny shop sells the produce from the kilns outside – *kippers, bloaters, smoked cod's roe* and *salmon* – and the by-products – *taramasalata, bloater paste* and *salmon pâté*, as well as *crab pâté* and *sweet pickled herrings*. No colouring is used. Local herring are used for bloatering, the curing of ungutted herring, giving a delicious gamey flavour, when the autumn shoals arrive. The sweet pickled herring are prepared to a Scandinavian rather than a traditional English recipe – using cider vinegar and spices. They are either sold in large jars, or ladled from tubs on the counter. The pâtés and pastes are prepared daily depending on available ingredients – crab during the summer months only, bloater paste when there is time 'as it is a lot of trouble'. The taramasalata is a year round product and we liked this one's flavour, and its lovely *pale* colour – no artificial pink in sight. All retailing is done from the shop, with distribution to about a dozen local fish shops, delicatessens and restaurants. The Rhodeses value their customers' comments and interest and find 'the interchange of ideas essential for the continuation of quality'. The shop is open every day including Sunday, 9a.m.–6p.m. from spring to autumn, and in winter 10a.m.–4p.m. It is in the main street in Cley, next to a pottery called Made in Cley, and almost opposite the butcher's. As it is right on the busy, winding coast road, parking is a problem. Persevere, however, as the kippers are delicious and Cley is a charming village.

Custance goats' produce

Hainford Place, Hainford,
Norwich, Norfolk NR10 3BX
Tel. Norwich (0603) 898456
ELIZABETH DOWNING

Ted and Elizabeth Downing began keeping a cow to provide dairy products for their family of four children, then the excess milk encouraged them to take in orphan lambs and pigs. After that, it was calves, then a single suckler herd to provide beef, and now these have made way for goats – for *milk* and *soft cheese* production, and, more latterly, for Angora and cashmere fibre production too. Not surprisingly, Elizabeth Downing has been able to write a series of books for Pelham Publishing – *Keeping Goats*, *Keeping Pigs*, *Keeping Sheep* and *Keeping Rabbits*, with *Keeping Cows* in the pipeline. Apart from the *fresh* and *frozen milk*, and *soft cheese*, *beef*, *lamb*, *pork* and *goat meat* are also available. All animals are fed on additive-free foods, and kept free range. Retail outlets include Womens' Institute markets in local towns (Aylsham and Norwich); Mousetrap, Norwich; and personal callers – although there is usually someone there, it is best to telephone first to check on availability of produce. Hainford is 6 miles north of Norwich, between the A140 and B1150.

Elmham House Norfolk apple wine

*Elmham Wines Ltd,
Elmham House, North Elmham,
Dereham, Norfolk NR20 5JY
Tel. Elmham (036 281) 571*

ROBIN DON

Robin Don is a Master of Wine, and a wine merchant, and has been in the wine trade for twenty-eight years. He planted the first vines at Elmham twenty years ago, on a trial and error basis, throwing out the Müller Thurgau since it clearly wasn't happy in Norfolk. He now grows Madeleine Angevine, Bacchus and Schönburger for his Elmham Park wine. But it was his Norfolk Apple Wine which caught our eye in the Norwich wine merchants, and which we enjoyed enormously. Its label used to proclaim that it was 'The Pale, Still Vintage Cider for the Wine Drinker' – now it is simply called Apple Wine, a name which much more accurately describes its character. It is made from 70% Cox's and 30% Bramley apples, using fine white wine technology. The apples are mostly from Robin Don's own orchards, but if he needs any extra, he buys apple juice from the Peakes in Suffolk (see page 146), as the Cox's/Bramley balance in their apple juice is just right. Hicks & Don are sole agents and sell to the trade, both at wholesale and trade terms. Visitors are welcome by appointment – telephone the number given above (ansaphone), or Elmham 616 (evenings), or Elmham 363 (mornings). North Elmham is 5 miles north of East Dereham on the B1110 – the drive gates are almost opposite the church.

Fir Tree Farm milk-fed pork

*Fir Tree Farm, Darrow Green, Denton,
Harleston, Norfolk IP20 0AY
Tel. Homersfield (098 686) 324*

IVAN AND MANDY SMITH

The surplus milk and milk by-products from the Smiths' herd of British Saanen and Golden Guernsey goats goes to feed the farm-bred and raised pigs. This produces exceptionally tender meat, full of flavour, but quite free from antibiotics and growth promoters. Slaughtering is done at an approved abattoir, and the meat is then sold by the side, cut and bagged, from the farm. The *goats' milk* is also for sale and there is a *lightly-pressed waxed cheese* too, mildly flavoured with an Edam-like texture. Mrs Smith's mother, who lives with them, offers bed and breakfast to visitors during the summer. All the products are for sale from the farm, but please note that the meat is to order only, and batches are ready every six to eight weeks. Hours are Monday to Thursday, evenings from 5–7p.m., Fridays and Saturdays all day, closed on Sundays. To find Darrow Green, turn off the A143 about 7 miles south-west of Bungay, to Alburgh at the Bell pub in Wortwell. In Alburgh bear right, in front of the Tradesman's

Arms pub, then left, by the church. Just after Paynes Hill Farm, turn left, then left again. Fir Tree Farm is distinguished by an 80-foot fir tree.

Hockwold Manor black turkeys

Manor Farm, Hockwold-cum-Wilton, Thetford, Norfolk IP26 4ND
Tel. Feltwell (0842) 827037
MRS VALERIE GREEN

The Norfolk black turkey is reputedly the direct descendant of the first turkey brought to this country in the sixteenth century, and said to have been landed at an East Anglian port – hence the name. Mrs Green breeds them for the Christmas market; breeding, hatching, and rearing during the year, killing and dispatching in early December. These are turkeys for the connoisseur – they take longer to mature, which of course helps the flavour, and Mrs Green uses the farm fresh techniques of proper hanging for a week or more, too. She finds she has a good market for these turkeys, despite the fact that they might cost 25% more than their supermarket rivals. 'So many of our people stick with them when once they realise what they are eating. It isn't unusual for people to order for next Christmas before they have finished the carcase for this Christmas,' she told me. A real Christmas treat, in other words. A flock of these splendid birds looks like a gaggle of flamenco dancers, red wattles, beautiful black feathers, and a far more elegant shape than the breast-heavy supermarket victims at the cheap end of the market. Mrs Green prefers people to ring before coming so that special arrangements can be made. And ring or write for details of the mail order service, but don't leave it too late, as the turkeys are not reared in large numbers. Hockwold is on the B1112 about 7 miles north of Mildenhall.

Humble Pie preserves

Humble Pie Foods,
Market Place, Burnham Market,
King's Lynn, Norfolk
Tel. Fakenham (0328) 738581
SUSAN ELSTON

This shop impressed me when I first visited it three years ago, and continues to do so. Susan Elston combs the country in search of good food, and what she doesn't buy from others she makes herself. Her own range of *jams and chutneys* is wide, but only small quantities are made of each – using fresh local garden and farm produce in the summer and dried fruits in winter. She evolves interesting combinations of flavours – *apple, pear and quince jam*, for instance, or *greengage, orange and walnut*. The *lemon*, and *orange chutneys* are sharp and delicious with rich meats such as goose, pork or hare. The labels are simple and beautifully hand-written – Sue Elston says 'you have to have nice handwriting to work here!' Open from Tuesday to Saturday, 9a.m.–1p.m., 2–5p.m., with half days on Wednesdays. Burnham Market is on the B1355 to Fakenham, and the shop is in the centre of the village.

NORFOLK NOBS
(LOCALLY KNOWN AS HOLLOW BISCUITS)

Traditional Norfolk Fare!

THEY'RE BOUND TO PLEASE WITH BUTTER AND CHEESE

Ashworth's of Norwich
THE BAKERY
LIVINGSTONE STREET
NORWICH NR2 4HE
TEL: 20391

NET WEIGHT 184 g 6½ ozs
INGREDIENTS: FLOUR, WATER, VEGETABLE FAT, YEAST, SUGAR, SALT

Norfolk Nobs

Ashworth & Stannard Ltd,
The Bakery, Livingstone Street,
Norwich NR2 4HE
Tel. Norwich (0603) 620391

MR ASHWORTH

The *Norfolk Nob* is very similar to the Dorset Knob (see page 50), a hard, small, rusk-like roll, known locally as 'hollow biscuits' and very good with cheese. Ashworth & Stannard's come in both white and brown, more as a concession to current eating habits, I think, rather than for any traditional reason. They also make *Easter Fair Buttons* – not available when I was there in August, of course, but another Norfolk speciality. The Bakery was established in 1907 by the grandfather of the four brothers who run the business now. They have four shops in Norwich – 97 Dereham Road; 173 Plumstead Road; 9 St Augustine Street, and 39 West Earlham Centre. All are open 8.30a.m.–4.30p.m. Monday to Saturday.

Norfolk Porkers

Mill House, Bressingham, Diss,
Norfolk IP22 2BE
Tel. Bressingham (037 988) 266

K J WEATHERBURN

Mr Weatherburn's aim is 'simply to make the best sausage in Britain' – whether he has succeeded or not is so much a matter of personal preference that I hesitate to say. However, *Norfolk Porkers* are made from the best cuts of pork (those more usually sold as joints) and natural skins, have a high meat and a low fat content, and no preservatives, additives, colouring or chemicals are used. There are four varieties, *sage*, *tomato*, *spicy* and *mild*; special recipe batches can be made to order. Sales are wholesale to hotels, and via Essentially English, 10b West

Street, Oundle, Northamptonshire; Spearings' Delicatessen, Dedham, Essex; F D Dunnet & Son, Little Clacton, Essex.

Norfolk Punch

Welle Manor Hall, Upwell, Norfolk
PE14 9AB
Tel. Wisbech (0945) 773333

ERIC ST JOHN-FOTI

Called a '*Medieval Monastic Herbal Drink*', Norfolk Punch is the modern version of an ancient Benedictine recipe and is said to contain at least thirty different herbs and spices. It tastes a little like the Dandelion & Burdock which you can still buy in Northern chip shops. A wineglassful of 'Nature's answer to Tension, Tiredness and Depression' drunk hot in the evening certainly made me feel relaxed, but Mr St John-Foti wisely makes no claims on medicinal grounds for his non-alcoholic drink, which he first began making for charity. It is now widely distributed, with retail outlets such as Harrods, Holland & Barrett, and Nature's Way. Confectionery is made too, called *Norfolk Delight*. All the products are available at Welle Manor itself, which dates from the thirteenth century and is a rare example of a medieval fortified manor house. Groups can tour the manor at any time by prior appointment, otherwise it is open on the *first Sunday of every month at 3p.m.* Upwell is on the B1412, about 6 miles south of Wisbech.

Prospero Fine Ices

Wiveton Barn, nr Holt, Norfolk
Tel. Cley-next-the-Sea (0263) 740673

DEREK AND CAROLYN NEWMAN

The Newmans started their sorbet venture in 1984, and now distribute their delicious products all over the country. They chose Norfolk as their location because of its abundant fruit farms, and taught themselves the art and technique of sorbet production, taking some recipes from nineteenth-century cookery books, and testing each carefully. They use a wide range of fruit – some exotic, such as mangoes, some local such as blackberries, for their *Blackberry and Apple with Blackberry Liqueur*. They also make *savoury sorbets* from avocados, tomatoes, and cucumber. Despite the very sophisticated machine to freeze the sorbets, each mix is hand-made and checked for flavour and quality – colourings, additives and artificial emulsifiers are never used. Their products are distributed nationally through Hales Snails Ltd to outlets such as Harrods, and the London Superstore in Notting Hill Gate, London W2, and they distribute to local shops. They do not sell from the above address, 'But if anyone has a real interest in sorbets or would like us to supply them they are most welcome to make an appointment.'

SUFFOLK FARMHOUSE RASPBERRY JAM
NO PRESERVATIVES NO COLOURING
INGREDIENTS: RASPBERRIES, SUGAR
NET WEIGHT 1lb 454g
MILL LANE FARM, WEYBREAD, DISS

Suffolk Farm Produce

Mill Lane Farm, Weybread, Diss, Norfolk
Tel. Fressingfield (037 986) 288

C N POTTER

The Potters dug a reservoir to supply water for their soft fruit, and now use it to rear *table trout* and *crayfish*. They sell these, together with raspberries, gooseberries, and strawberries in season (either ready-picked, or pick-your-own), fresh and frozen poultry, free-range eggs, and really excellent jam made from their own fruit. They only supply a limited number of retailers in the immediate locality (including Beanos Wholefood Shop, Harleston), as most of their selling is done through their own farm shop – open every day from 10a.m. to dusk during June to October. From November to May they are open from 12–5p.m. Weybread is on the B1116, just south of the A143 Beccles road.

THE NORTH-WEST

Cheshire
―
Greater Manchester
―
Lancashire

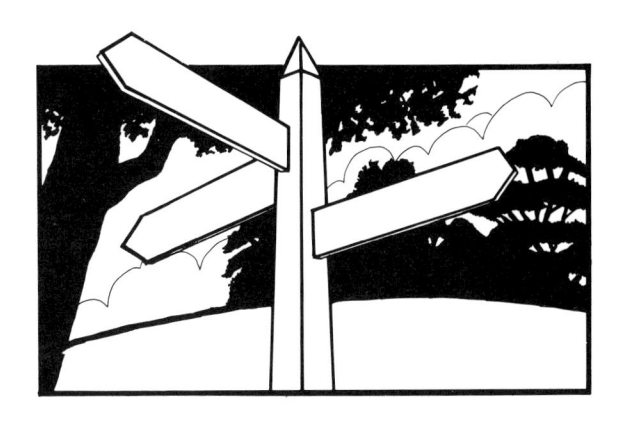

Cheshire has lost a good many of its culinary traditions, but has gained one or two new ones as well. The best Cheshire cheese is being made just over the border in Shropshire, but up in the hills near Macclesfield, Mary Gregory* is making an excellent goats' cheese – called Blackwood. In Lancashire, one or two farms continue doggedly to make real farmhouse Lancashire cheese, an increasingly rare delicacy since 'new' or 'single acid' Lancashire flooded the market, travesties of this great and mellifluous cheese.

Manchester itself, like London, is a good centre for ethnic food – Indian, Armenian and Chinese, and to the south, where it meets the softer Cheshire countryside, taste is sophisticated. This is commuter country, where a taste for smoked salmon and often rather pretentious restaurants means that not enough call is made on local food producers – with the exception of the Stanneylands Hotel, near Wilmslow, which sets an altogether higher standard. And south of Manchester there are two superb confectioners – Jean Durig in Hale*, and Martin Wienholt* in Alderley Edge. Jean Durig came to this country from Switzerland and has been drawing customers to his small shop for at least twenty-five years, to treat themselves to his wonderful cakes and chocolates. Martin Wienholt is by now thoroughly English, but still bakes to the best traditions of his German great-grandfather, and returns regularly to Germany to collect new ideas.

Sadly, the last remnant of Cheshire's once-thriving salt industry, the independent Lion Salt Works at Northwich, has just closed. There are faint hopes that it may continue to produce a little of its excellent block salt on a 'museum' basis, demonstrating old techniques to visitors. The presence of salt-works all over the county is indicated by town names ending in 'wich' – the seventeenth-century local term for a salt-pit. Some of the salt traditions remain, however – for example in Nantwich, Welch's cure their bacon with Cheshire salt, although for a better supply of dry-salted hams and bacon, as for Cheshire cheese, it is to Shropshire you must go, where the rural traditions are more lively.

However, at Quarry Bank Mill, Styal, twelve miles south of Manchester, the market gardening traditions of Cheshire are being kept alive. This is an old cotton mill, surrounded by its worker housing and Apprentice House. It is here, in the garden of the Apprentice House, that old local varieties of vegetables are being grown with the help and guidance of the Henry Doubleday Research Association. The Altrincham carrot, Timperley Early rhubarb, Staffordshire Lad broad beans and Lancashire Lad peas are all being saved from extinction – these are varieties which were certainly grown in the area, probably by the mill workers themselves, who were encouraged to produce their own vegetables. Some of the crops are incorporated into the menu of the mill tea-room, particularly the salad vegetables in the summer, and if there is any surplus, it is sold to visitors to this museum of the cotton industry. This is a National Trust property, but is managed and run by a separate independent charitable trust; although it is open throughout the year, the growing season is clearly the best time to see the vegetable allotment.

Once north of Manchester, approaching the Pennines, the food becomes more northern in character – in Stalybridge there is a tripe shop which sells udder and cowheel too, and next to it a cooked meat shop – huge joints of cold roast ham and pork in enormous blackened roasting tins, and piles of muffins, big and round with a 'thumb-print' in the middle. In Salford, Bellamys* still make potato cakes, muffins and crumpets – they are the last of the hot-plate bakers. Lancaster offers Morecambe Bay shrimps smoked by Lune Smoked Foods*, and Chorley is proud of Thornley's* prize-winning black puddings. Barnoldswich* still has a bakehouse where the oatcakes are 'thrown' on to the hotplate. Farms in the Trough of Bowland continue to make real Lancashire cheese, and that wonderfully salty whey butter which is the best of all to spread thickly on crumpets and muffins.

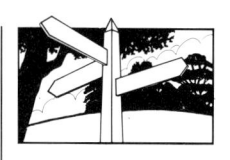

Cheshire and Greater Manchester

Cheshire Larders

*17 Snowden Road, Eccles,
Manchester M30 9AS
Tel. 061-789 0646*
JONATHAN DAVEY

For the history behind Cheshire Larders, see the entry on Country Larders (page 27). Jonathan Davey took over Cheshire Larders from Tony Morton in November 1985, and is producing pies to the same impeccable standard, using most of Mrs Thomas's original recipes. These are the pies I use myself when time is short. Jonathan has worked in catering for some years, and says he developed his feeling for good food whilst working at Chisholme House, near Hawick, 'a residential centre in which taste and beauty are of paramount importance'. Sales are wholesale, mainly to hotels and pubs, with a retail outlet at Country Delicacies, Tarporley, Cheshire.

Cheshire Wholefoods sugarless muesli

*Cheshire Wholefoods Ltd, Unit B6,
Stadium Industrial Estate, Chester
Tel. Chester (0244) 375205*
J G GORNALL

I first came across this muesli when I was desperately seeking a sugarless brand amongst the over-sweet supermarket brands, and now buy it in preference to many others. It contains no salt or preservatives either. Cheshire Wholefoods also do a *high-fibre muesli, plain bran,* and a *fruit and fibre cereal.* Look for their products in Asda, the Co-op, Tesco, Waitrose, Sainsbury's and William Morrison.

Cromwell's chocolates

*15 King Street, Knutsford,
Cheshire WA16 6DW
Tel. Knutsford (0565) 54832*
MRS J LAYFIELD

The chocolates here are in fact made at Alan Crowe's branch of Cromwell's in Upton-upon-Severn (see page 106). The story of Cromwell's is one of happy accidents. Mrs Layfield was marketing manager for Cordon Bleu Freezer Centres when she met Alan Crowe (an erstwhile accountant) and fell in love with his chocolates. She quickly appreciated their marketing potential, and Cromwell's in Knutsford was born. Alan Glover, a friend of Mrs Layfield, met Alan Crowe by chance, and from this meeting Cromwell's in Bath evolved (see page 41). All three are dedicated to quality and to the purity of their chocolates, and will not sacrifice standards for price. This does not mean Cromwell's chocolates are prohibitively expensive – they are more of an affordable luxury. The quality *is* very high; they are made from the finest Belgian Callibaut chocolate, and the range includes some unique centres, such as *Passion Fruit*, and *Kiwi Fruit*. Truffles are a speciality, with a very unusual *Mint and Pernod* flavour; marzipans are light and delicate, and the pretty flower-shaped *Caraques* are *solid chocolate pieces in dark, milk and white chocolate*. There are seasonal specialities, of course, Father Christmases, Easter rabbits and eggs, chocolate hearts, and for very special occasions the chocolates can be packed in one of the really beautiful satin boxes from Paris which the shop stocks. The shop is in the main shopping street in Knutsford (which is Mrs Gaskell's 'Cranford'), and has a distinctive canopy. It is open from 9a.m.–5.30p.m. from Monday to Saturday.

Dalton's 'Farmhouse Country Delicacies'

The Homestead Farm, Pott Shrigley, Macclesfield, Cheshire
Tel. Macclesfield (0625) 72331
THE DALTON FAMILY

A visit to the Daltons' farm – ten acres of Peak District hill and valley – is a delight. Red-gold Tamworth pigs, Angora goats, some Herdwick sheep (the Daltons originate from Cumberland) – all are as welcoming as the Daltons themselves. Go there for *sausages*, *ham* and *bacon* from the Tamworths (made by Maynard Davies, see page 130), for *goats' milk*, charmingly decorated *soft cheeses*, and *kid meat* from the goats, and for delicious *lamb* from the Herdwicks and Black Welsh sheep. The bacon and ham are much sought after, and

you will need to place an order. The sausages are very good – regional specialities include *Cumberland Ring*, and *Manchester Sausages* to a recipe taken from a Victorian book on the subject. The emphasis is on good food from happy animals. The milk and cheese are sold through various local shops, and supplied to local hotels. The Stanneylands Hotel, Wilmslow, one of the best places to eat in Cheshire, takes their ham, sausages and cheese. Visitors are very welcome. 'We are always open if someone wishes to call,' says Joyce Dalton. Pott Shrigley is just off the A5002 from Macclesfield to Whaley Bridge. Just past Pott Shrigley church, take the right hand turning to Whaley Bridge – you will see the signs for The Homestead Farm on your left as you go up the steep hill.

De-Lite potato cakes, muffins and crumpets

W W Bellamy Ltd, Greenwood Street, Salford, Greater Manchester M6 6PF
Tel. 061-737 5133
ROGER AND GEORGE BELLAMY

This is an old-established family hot-plate baker (i.e. they don't use ovens), started by Wallace Bellamy (father of Roger and George) in the 1930s; Wallace's father was also a hot-plate baker. I was introduced to De-Lite crumpets in the bitterly cold February of 1986, as I was compiling this book, and found them to be the best I had ever eaten – apart from their flavour, which is wonderfully yeasty, they are exceptionally light. I asked Mrs Bellamy about this, suspecting some chemical. No, she said firmly, just flour, water, yeast and salt, but the secret is to let the batter stand overnight. Their muffins are wonderful too, and come in both brown and white – they are good toasted, dripping with butter, of course, but I like them very much cold, used instead of a soft roll for summer picnics. Look for their products – potato cakes and Scotch pancakes too, in small bakers' shops in the North-west and the Midlands.

Durig Swiss Pâtisserie and Chocolaterie

2 & 4 Broomfield Lane, Hale, nr Altrincham, Cheshire WA15 9AQ
Tel. 061-928 1143
JEAN AND EVE DURIG

A fellow chocoholic introduced me to Durig's, and greed led me to try their cakes as soon as I saw them. Particularly recommended is the *Dunham Forest Gâteau* (named after a local stately home), a wonderful hazelnut sponge with praline. Local people have fond memories of Durig's *honeycake houses*, a Christmas speciality for almost twenty years. But apart from the chocolates (Jean Durig's province), and the excellent pâtisserie, Eve Durig herself makes a very good range of condiments – a lovely *Apricot and Lemon Chutney* which is perfect with cold ham and turkey, *Piccalilli* to a Victorian recipe, *pickled walnuts*, *jams* and *preserves of seasonal fruits*, at least six marmalades, four curry powders, five vinaigrettes, raspberry vinegar (another Victorian recipe), coarse grain mustards, and *biriani*, *pilau*, *Spanish rice and mushroom risotto* ready mixed to cook at home.

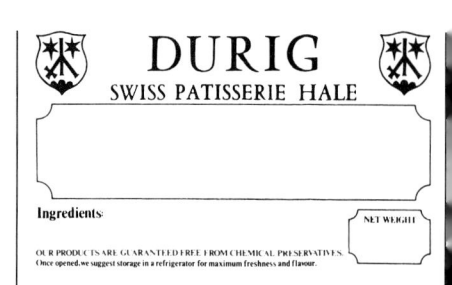

DURIG
SWISS PATISSERIE HALE

Ingredients: NET WEIGHT

OUR PRODUCTS ARE GUARANTEED FREE FROM CHEMICAL PRESERVATIVES
Once opened, we suggest storage in a refrigerator for maximum freshness and flavour.

Stuffings are also available, made from their own French bread – *walnut and celery* is particularly good. There are also frozen products from the bakery – pizzas, pies and so on. This is a wonderful shop, and one whose future looks secure, as the Durigs' son, Dani, is now in charge of the bakery, and develops new products with his father. The double shop in Broomfield Lane is the only retail outlet, and is open Tuesday to Saturday, 9a.m.–5p.m.; *closed* for staff holidays for the *week after Easter* and the *first three weeks of August*. The shop is near Hale Station, the last two shops in a row of five at the end of Broomfield Lane where it joins Victoria Road. Hale itself is just south of Altrincham.

Elstone's home-made foods

38 Princess Street, Knutsford, Cheshire WA16 6BN
Tel. Knutsford (0565) 3125
MRS SHEILA ELSTONE

Elstone's is an established greengrocers in Knutsford, and Mrs Elstone is now promoting a range of home-made foods helped by her sister-in-law, Mrs Sheilah Wilkinson. The range includes *cottage* and *fisherman's pies*, *lasagne*, *moussaka*, *fish cakes*, *prawn rolls*, *various salads* and *prepared vegetables*. *Jams*, *pickles* and *chutneys* are made from seasonal fruits and vegetables. This is good simple home-cooking – just the sort of thing to buy for a family supper, without having to worry about E numbers on the packet. The shop in Princess Street is the only retail outlet, but Mrs Elstone's *Lemon Cheese* is sold through David Mellor, King Street, Manchester. The shop is open from 8a.m.–5.30p.m. every weekday.

Moorlands goats' cheese

Blackwood Hill, Rushton Spencer, nr Macclesfield, Cheshire SK11 0RU
Tel. Rushton Spencer (026 06) 336
MARY GREGORY

Mary Gregory admits that her first attempt at cheesemaking resulted in 'some rather boring cheeses'. Fortunately, her husband's company sent the family to France for a year, where they both gleaned valuable experience from visiting large and small cheesemaking concerns. Trying out French recipes on an English market they discovered that there had to be a happy medium. They found it, christened it *Moorlands goats' cheese*, and entered it for a Speciality Soft Cheese class, where it won First Prize, beating competitors from all over Europe. This cheese comes *plain*, or with *horseradish, capers, green* or *black peppercorns, herbs* (in summer) and *garlic*. The Gregorys' newest cheese is *Blackwood*, a more mature cheese with a bluish rind, a connoisseur's cheese, as Mary Gregory terms it. The milk is all pasteurised, and comes from various herds in the district with high standards of hygiene. Cheese is sold via wholesalers: The House of Callow Ltd, Wholesale Market, Freemens Common, Ayleston Road, Leicester, Tel. (0533) 541637 (Midlands and South), and Foster Food and Wine Agencies, 2 Trafford Road, Alderley Edge, Cheshire, Tel. (0625) 585561 (North). Or telephone Mary Gregory for your nearest stockist. Visitors are welcome 'at any reasonable time – including weekends – but to save a wasted journey, it may be better to telephone beforehand'. To find Blackwood Hill, take the A523 towards Macclesfield from Leek; after 4 miles turn left towards Congleton. Blackwood Hill is 1½ miles along that lane, on the left.

Smythe's Purveyors of Taste – smoked foods

Units 7 & 8, Oakfield Road Industrial Estate, Oakfield Road, Altrincham, Cheshire WA15 8EW
Tel. 061-928 8822
MICHAEL HYMAN, JYTTE RAFF

Michael Hyman's grandfather survived the wreck of the *Titanic* to found his Goodfare smoked salmon business at Strangeways in Manchester. Michael Hyman recently sold Goodfare and has now started a new food smoking company in Altrincham, with the help of Jytte Raff, who used to run the popular Danish Food Centre in Manchester. Her responsibility is to use Michael's smoked products for high-class take-away meals, for board room lunches 'and prestige gatherings' – all delivered to the door in a replica vintage van. Smythe's list of smoked products is long, and includes *Pastrami*, *Lamb smoked with rosemary and mint*, *Scotch and Pacific Salmon*, *Smythe's Mistake* (hot smoked poached salmon, now a popular item), and delicious *smoked sliced halibut*, a Scandinavian speciality. Various wholesalers are supplied, or sales can be direct to the public from the factory – telephone for details of the Outside Catering Service. Factory hours are 10a.m.–5p.m., Monday to Friday. It is next to the Sports Centre, and to find Oakfield Street, from the A560 heading west, turn left into Stockport Road after passing playing fields on the left. Oakfield Street is the third left.

Titterton's pork products

J *Titterton & Sons Ltd,*
Ann Street, Reddish, Stockport
Tel. 061-480 6887 or 061-480 2889
THE TITTERTON FAMILY

James Titterton began by selling pork from a handcart in 1875 in Reddish – now his firm has a number of retail shops in the South Manchester area, and is still in the hands of James's grand and great-grandsons. They pride themselves on their *traditionally produced hams* (their *cooked ham* is wonderful), *sausages* which are made properly from pork steaks and shoulder, with no emulsifiers or water, and only the minimum of preservatives. The *pork pies* are good, too, and use belly pork and bacon, with a crust made with vegetable fat. There is *home-cured bacon* too. Shop early at weekends, or you will have to join a long queue. All their shops – in Edgeley, Stockport, Cheadle, two in Reddish, Hazel Grove, Macclesfield, Chorlton, Didsbury, Levenshulme and Wythenshawe market – are open from 8.30a.m.–5.30p.m., with some closed on Wednesdays.

Welch's home-cured bacon

A T *Welch, 45 Hospital Street,*
Nantwich, Cheshire
Tel. Nantwich (0270) 625491
W H AND M B AUSTIN

Welch's is an old-fashioned grocer, where you can have your bacon sliced to the thickness you prefer (they cure their own here, lovely and fat and full of flavour). This is a service becoming increasingly rare, as commercially cured bacon, soft with added water, will not slice easily. It is always a good test of quality, if you can have bacon sliced thinly on No. 5 on the bacon slicing machine. The sausages are good, and you can even watch them being made. There is a good selection of farmhouse (*real* farmhouse) cheeses, and of coffee and tea. The Austins (who bought the shop from the

Welch family in 1966) have long collected old grocery ephemera, and a few years ago assembled these at the far end of the main shop, as a reconstruction of an old grocer's shop. It is a good idea, very popular with children and the elderly who can remember the items being used. Shop hours are 9a.m.–5.30p.m. on Tuesdays, Thursdays and Fridays, 9a.m.–1p.m. on Wednesdays and 9a.m.–5p.m. on Saturdays. Hospital Street is in the centre of Nantwich, and Welch's is near the Methodist church.

G. Wienholt, Continental Pastrycook

25 London Road, Alderley Edge, Cheshire SK9 7JT
Tel. Alderley Edge (0625) 583275
KATHLEEN, MARTIN AND ROSEMARY WIENHOLT

Alderley Edge is a pleasant place to shop, with an exceptional book shop, a good cheese shop, and Wienholt's. Martin Wienholt's great-grandfather came to England in the 1860s, and older members of the family speak of him as the person who introduced real vanilla slices to England. Every male descendant since has been a confectioner – the present business in Alderley was started just after the war by Martin's father. The quality is superlative – everything from the *pâtisserie* to the *pies and quiches* is produced from a not over-large kitchen behind the shop, spotlessly clean and highly organised, with old machines still in use, where they clearly do a job better than their modern counterparts. Although the family is by now thoroughly English, they keep the memory of their Germanic origins bright in their *Continental pâtisserie*, and return to Germany regularly to pick up new ideas. Some of these have to be Anglicised according to the availability of ingredients. 'We have always concentrated on confectionery as opposed to bread,' Martin Wienholt told me. 'We feel this area is sadly neglected in Britain, and that this road, although lonely, is more profitable for a small family business like ours than competing with the big boys.' Certainly the fact that the shop is always busy demonstrates the public's appreciation of the Wienholts' lonely road. Beautiful packaging is a speciality of their seasonal products, and for Christmas and Easter Martin Wienholt makes chocolates – truffles, Easter eggs, etcetera. But, *note the opening times*: the shop is only open on *Thursdays, Fridays and Saturdays*, 9a.m.–5.30p.m. Preparation and baking take place on the other days of the week, and as a large range of products is prepared on the premises, days must be set aside to concentrate on this. Their customers are used to this, and travel long distances on the 'open' days. Alderley Edge is 5 miles south of Wilmslow on the A34 (London Road).

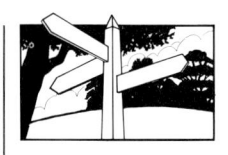

LANCASHIRE

Butler's farmhouse Lancashire cheese

Lower Barker Farm, Inglewhite, Preston, Lancashire PR3 2LH
Tel. Brock (0995) 40334
THOMAS BUTLER

Lower Barker Farm is tucked away in the Trough of Bowland, on the western slopes of the Forest of Bowland. Here the Butlers make lovely crumbly mellow *Lancashire cheese*, in the traditional way, by hand, using the 'two-day curd' method. This produces an incomparably better cheese than the mass-produced 'single-acid' New Lancashire cheese most often found in the less reputable shops and supermarkets. If you think you don't like Lancashire cheese, then taste some of the Butlers', and see if you don't change your mind. The milk used is from the Butlers' own herd of Friesians, unpasteurised; they also make *Sage Lancashire*, which used to be a Christmas speciality, and *whey butter*, deliciously salt and the perfect accompaniment to the cheese itself. Personal callers are welcome, and can buy the cheese and butter from the farm; the cheese is distributed via Mendip Foods, Park Avenue, Whitchurch, Cheshire; Mollington Farm Cheese Co. Ltd, Grange Farm, Mollington, Chester. To reach Inglewhite, leave the M6 at junction 32. Follow the A6 to Broughton, then follow the Beacon Fell/Inglewhite signs. Lower Barker Farm is situated 1½ miles through Inglewhite village.

Fayre Game quail

Lodge Lane Nurseries, Lodge Lane, Lytham, Lancashire FY8 5RP
Tel. Lytham (0253) 738640
M G B KAY

Quail have become increasingly popular, and therefore increasingly available, thanks to specialists like Fayre Game. These small birds have taken the place that pigeons held in days when most meat supplies were seasonal, that of year-round availability combined with perfect portion control. Quails' eggs have filled an epicurean gap, too, left by plovers' and gulls' eggs, providing an almost perfect, versatile, first course. I must admit I like the look of them best of all – they are the most beautiful of eggs with their brown, blue and grey blotches. Fayre Game supply every *permutation of quail – fresh, frozen, smoked* and *boned*, and their *eggs*. They also supply a variety of *seasonal game* – grouse, snipe, partridge, mallard, teal, wigeon, pheasant and woodcock – as well as *game with year-round availability* – venison, hare, rabbit, pigeon; *guinea fowl* are also available. Fayre Game, founded only eight years ago, now supply 50% of the UK market. Sales are via wholesale markets and retail outlets (telephone for your nearest supplier). The Nurseries lie just off the A584 from Preston to Lytham – just beyond Warton turn right into Lodge Lane, the Nurseries are on the left.

S & G Fowler, specialist dairy produce

*Ferrocrete Farm, Carnforth, Lancashire
LA6 1AU
Tel. Hornby (0468) 21965*
SIM AND GEOFF FOWLER

The Fowlers have made a considerable name for themselves in the nine years since they started selling their goat produce; they are founder members of the English Goat Breeders' Association, and have the biggest herd of English goats in the country. They also run a small flock of milking sheep and a cow, to offer a complete range of dairy products. Their products include *live yoghurt* (using Lactobacillus bulgaricus and Streptococcus thermophilus), live *low fat yoghurt*, a *soya yoghurt*, *cheese*, *lemon curd* and *rum butter* (both using half the normal sugar content, and raw cane sugar), *free range eggs* and *organically grown vegetables* and *herbs*. Sim Fowler is herself a qualified physiotherapist and both are knowledgeable about wholefoods and alternative medicine, so are able to advise their customers on 'many and various diets to help with certain ailments', as well as to offer additive-free food to the healthy. Their products are distributed throughout the North of England via Transpennine Wholefoods (Tel. (0524) 381038 during office hours, Thursday to Sunday; there is an ansaphone service at other times). White Cross Natural Foods (Tel. (0524) 388323) distribute throughout north Lancashire. Personal callers are very welcome at the farm – open all year round, seven days a week, 1.30–9p.m., and at other times by arrangement, 'or take pot luck'.

EWES MILK

500 ml
Keep frozen, thaw slowly and use within 3 days

Towers and Sons
Manor Farm,
Borwick, Lancashire
Tel : Carnforth
(0524) 732960

Ferrocrete Farm is on the B6254 (Carnforth to Kirkby Lonsdale) at the Arkholme crossroads, next to the Post Office.

The Golden Fudge Co.

*Peel House, Peel Road, West Pimbo, Skelmersdale, Lancashire
Tel. Skelmersdale (0695) 32086*
HAROLD BROWN

Mr Brown's fudge was recommended to me by Mrs Layfield of Cromwell's Chocolates in Knutsford (see page 162); it is the only one that she feels is good enough to share space with her chocolates. The recipe used is a family one 'that goes back to my grandmother at least, and I am sixty years of age'. In fact, the business was started by Mr Brown's son, who has been a fudge enthusiast from a very early age and used to make the recipe for himself, before later manufacturing fudge commercially with a Buckinghamshire company. Harold Brown took early retirement from his work as a civil servant to form a fudge-making partnership with his son in 1983. The Golden Fudge Co. also makes *fruit bars* (called *Fiona's Favourite*, after their co-inventor) in two flavours, *Date & Apricot*, and *Tropical*. Neither these, nor the *fudge*, which comes in six flavours, including *ginger*, contains any additives, and all are hand-made. Despite the small size of the company, its products are sold as far afield as Jerusalem, Iowa, and Holland, as well as through London outlets: Naturally British, 13 New Row, Covent Garden, London WC2, and Selfridges. Local outlets include The Toffee Shop, Royal Arcade, Wigan. Much is sold for own-label packaging. Mr Brown, although once or twice tempted to expand the business, likes to do all the purchasing, manufacturing, marketing and accounting himself, finding these occupations more satisfying than simply making money. 'The quality of the fudge could suffer through large-scale production, and it is very important that I make healthy products,' he told me. But it leaves him no time to entertain personal callers any more, so please telephone for further details of supply, and stockists.

Lune Smoked Foods Ltd

Duke Street, St George's Quay, Lancaster, Lancashire
Tel. Lancaster (0524) 69563

PETER FLUDE

Local produce – *Lune salmon, local chickens* and *poussins, Morecambe Bay shrimps* – are smoked over oak chips in the traditional manner, although using modern kilns. They also produce *smoked salmon, lobster*, and *crab mousses*, and delicious *smoked silverside of beef*. Freshly caught *Morecambe Bay brown shrimps* (the best-flavoured of all) are boiled in sea-water before being picked (shelled) and *vacuum packed*, and have a much better flavour than those often bought from local fishermen, which have sometimes been frozen. Lune Smoked Foods also sell these *potted*, or *garlic potted*, or *buttered and spiced*. *Manx queenies* are also available – these are the small scallops (half the size of those generally available), which we used to buy so often in Whitehaven (further up the Cumbrian coast) twenty years ago. They were too cheap, alas, and are now sold to markets much further afield, at premium prices. The excellent restaurants of the Lake District buy from Lune Foods, and their products are also distributed to: Vin Sullivan,

11 High Street, Abergavenny, Gwent; J & J Graham, Market Street, Penrith, Cumbria; Gill's Fish Shop, Sea Road, Pevensey Bay, East Sussex; Winn's Fish, 18 The Arcade, Retail Market, Queensgate, Huddersfield, West Yorkshire. A mail order service is available, and you can buy from the factory (a very handsome stone-built 300-year-old warehouse), open 8.30a.m.–5p.m., Monday to Friday.

Martin & Grafton marmalades and preserves

Barn Lane, Golborne, Warrington, Lancashire WA3 3NT
Tel. Wigan (0942) 711615

W R MOLYNEAUX AND R S VINE

Preserve-making has been carried out on the premises here for nearly a hundred years, and although in the 1960s and early 70s it seemed that traditional preserves were no longer a viable proposition, public awareness of quality has rescued firms like Martin & Grafton. That, and of course the ability of the company to adapt. The new Common Market ruling on the fruit content in jams and preserves (one of the few sensible food rulings) has resulted in 'Extra' jams. All Martin & Grafton's varieties are made to this 'extra' standard, in seven flavours, with three marmalades (including *Lemon &*

Lime Marmalade with Gin), as well as *mincemeat, lemon cheese,* and *English honey*. There are three varieties of *chutney* – the *apple chutney with cider* we found was very good with Cumberland sausage. There is a wide distribution of these products throughout the north, via food halls, gift shops, garden centres, craft shops, hampers and 'stately home' shops. Please telephone for your nearest stockist.

Stanley's oatcakes

Well House Bakery, Back North Avenue, Barnoldswick, Colne, Lancashire
Tel. Barnoldswick (0282) 813180/812023

NICHOLAS RUMBOLL

A friend, born and bred on the southern outskirts of Manchester, was bemoaning the loss of real Lancashire oatcakes, oval (not round like the Staffordshire variety), grey and dusty with oatmeal, that she remembered from her childhood. So I took her to Stanley's. The smell of slightly burnt oatmeal greets you from some way away – follow it, and you come to the tiny Well House Bakery. In the bakery, a comfortable place full of sacks of flour and oatmeal, with crumpet rings hanging on the walls and crates of that morning's production of oatcakes, crumpets and muffins standing on the stone flags,

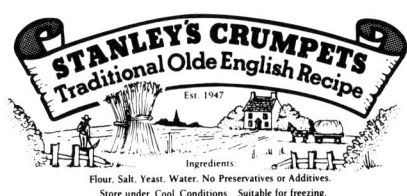

Mrs Wordsworth is practising her craft. This is the last remaining bakery where the oatcakes are 'thrown' on to a bakestone, giving that distinctive oval shape. Previously, this throwing was done with a practised flick of the wrist, using a floured cloth. Mrs Wordsworth uses a sort of canvas roller on wheels; this, dusted with a mixture of oatmeal and flour, has ladlesful of the batter poured carefully on to it in neat circles, and is then rolled forward over the heated bakestone. As each circle of batter reaches the edge, it is projected on to the bakestone to form an oval pancake. Then comes the flick of the wrist, as each is turned in order to cook the other side. The loose, browned oatmeal is dusted off and the oatcakes are hung on racks to cool before being folded into half-dozens for delivery. Stanley's *crumpets, muffins, potato and milk cakes*, and *Scotch pancakes* reach a wider public, but the oatcakes continue to be made for the traditional Lancashire markets: Pauline Davis's Tripe Stall, Colne Market; Alan Johnson, Burnley Market; and to local pubs for the Saturday night snacks of 'stew 'n' 'ard'. 'Stew' being a sort of beef brawn, and 'hard', oatcakes dried until they are crisp, rather than hard. The bakery itself is only open in the mornings, Monday–Friday, 9a.m.–12p.m., and is worth a visit. The oatcakes freeze well, so it is worth buying them in quantity.

Thornley's black puddings

Ridgewood Farm, Flag Lane, Heath Charnock, Chorley, Lancashire PR6 9ED
Tel. Chorley (025 72) 71251

BILL, JACK AND ARTHUR THORNLEY

Thornley's list their products as 'the pig and everything appertaining to the pig', but their real triumph is *Thornley's Prize-winning Black Pudding*, made to a recipe of Grandad Thornley who started the firm at the end of the last century. It has indeed won many prizes; Jack Thornley has been competing in the International Black Pudding Festival, Confrérie de Chevalier du Goute Boudin (or Knights of Black Pudding Tasters) for almost twenty years. The *pork pies* and *sausages* are prize winners too, and this prize-winning tradition is clearly going to continue, as Jack Thornley underlined in his letter to me:

'Thornley's will continue to be run as a family business; the fourth generation now work for the company. Also, Jack Thornley will continue to

enter international competitions.'
There are four Thornley shops: 24
Chapel Street, Chorley; 51 Newport
Street, Bolton; 38 Hough Lane,
Leyland; and 6 Orchard Street,
Preston. All are open from
8a.m.–6p.m., six days a week.
Thornley's products are widely
distributed to other shops in the
North-west.

Westmorland smoked salmon

*Westmorland Smoked Foods,
Cragg House, High Casterton, Kirkby
Lonsdale, via Carnforth, Lancashire
Tel. Kirkby Lonsdale (0468) 71551/41906
(ansaphone)*

J M THOMPSON

The only salmon smoked here is fresh
Scottish farmed salmon – no frozen or
imported fish are used at all. Oak
sawdust is used in a cold smoking
process over a very long period.
Westmorland Smoked Foods also
specialise in *smoking cheese –
Lancashire, Cheddar* and *goats' cheese*.
Products are sold either as

Westmorland Smoked Foods, or
under the Debrett trademark, and
sales are mainly wholesale to top Lake
District hotels and restaurants – Miller
Howe, at Windermere, for example.
Some is sent by mail order. Personal
callers are welcome, from
8.30a.m.–5p.m., or telephone for an
appointment. High Casterton is on the
A683, about 2 miles north of the A65
(junction 36, M6) to Kirkby Lonsdale
and Settle. The new smokehouse,
opened by Barbara Cartland in 1985,
is at Ingleton, 15 miles from Junction
36, on the A65, about 1½ miles on
the B6255.

WESTMORLAND
SMOKED FOODS

Cragg House, High Casterton
Kirkby Lonsdale, Via Carnforth, Lancs.
Telephone 0468 71551 or 41906

THE NORTH-EAST

Yorkshire and Humberside

A trip to Halifax market is enough to reassure anyone that everything they had ever heard about Yorkshire appetites is true. I have never seen such beef – whole sides lie like bolts of cloth, thickly wrapped in yellow fat. There are few neat cubes of trimmed topside here! This is the roast beef of old England and it is very good to see it. The cheese stalls are piled high with Wensleydale, both blue and white, and the cake stalls with parkin, tea-cakes and curd tarts. This is food that beats the cold, the stuff of central eating – much needed to counteract the wind that can blow straight from Siberia in the winter, and where summers are rarely too hot to enjoy a good Yorkshire tea.

But there is more elegant food to be found – Alan Porter stocks much of it in his admirable shop in Boroughbridge. He distributes, as well as sells, much of the good farmhouse cheese made in this area – Iain and Chris Hill's Ribblesdale* goats' cheese, Inez Vermaas's unpasteurised Botton* cheese, a full-flavoured hard cheese, especially good when flavoured with celery seeds, and the Atkinsons' Thixendale* goats' cheese. Crayfish, as well as huge golden trout, are being reared near Skipton, at Kilnsey Park*, and near Harrogate, Ivan Holmes* is rearing hormone-free meat. Father Edmund Hatton* is growing a fine range of apples in the Ampleforth Abbey orchards, and Tim Wilson's Yorkshire Dales* ice cream, free from additives, has taken the North of England by storm, and is now found even in rural areas which were once only served by the large companies and their non milk-fat confections.

But I still feel that for most Yorkshire people, the real stuff of life is not in goats' cheese and crayfish, but in black puddings and Longley Farm's* extra thick cream (wonderful with a piece of apple pie and Wensleydale). Barnsley chops* – a double thickness chop cut from the best end to weigh well over a pound – make any other lamb chop seem a waste of time, and are best accompanied by a glass of Theakston's Old Peculier, brewed still, and for a long time to come, I hope, at Theakston's small brewery in Masham.

The story of Wensleydale cheese is sad, however, as is so often the case with regional cheeses – it is now only made on a large scale by the Kirkby Malzeard dairy near Ripon, and is sent to Derbyshire to be blued by Nuttall's of Hartington. Mark Robertson, in Northumberland, is trying a revivalist farmhouse version. Swaledale is once again being made, by the Bottomleys in Daleside, but they cannot make enough to meet demand, and so I have not given them their own entry in this book, although I would like to have been able to.

York hams have also suffered, as the term 'York' now simply means a particularly mild cure, and can be applied to the most degraded of reconstituted ham-flavoured blocks. But Scotts of York sell the real thing, as do Johnsons of Whitby* and the firm that used to be called The Vale of Mowbray Bacon Factory, and is now part of the Harris* group. They also have obtained the rights to make Bradenham ham. And the pork pie is alive and well too – the best, undoubtedly, are to be bought in Skipton, at Stanforth's*. There is something particularly good about the crust, which we found hard to pinpoint, as well as the succulent pure pork filling. The custard tarts are a triumph, too – light and delicate real custard (not a wodge of custard powder) with a powdering of nutmeg. But for real Yorkshire food, particularly at tea time, go to any of Betty's* tea-rooms – in Ilkley and Harrogate, York and Northallerton, all in the Good Food Guide – and eat your way through tea-cakes and parkin, with Fat Rascals thrown in for good measure – good Yorkshire food.

Ampleforth College Orchard

*Ampleforth College, Ampleforth, Yorkshire
Tel. Ampleforth (043 93) 206*

The orchard at Ampleforth College was started in order to provide apples for the school and staff for as much of the year as possible. There is no artificially cooled store so many varieties were planted with natural keeping qualities, to give a succession of dessert apples of good quality from August to Easter. Currently a programme of grubbing up the original planting, acre by acre, and replanting with newer varieties is in progress. Some of the original varieties have been discarded and have been replaced by newer and more suitable ones. Any surplus of apples over and above the needs of the school is sold off in part by farm gate sales. Irish Peach, Vista Bella, Ribston Pippin, Brownlees Russet and Flanders Cox are among the varieties already available or are included in the planting plan. An excellent book of apple recipes is available, collected by members of the community, and with a foreword by Dr Joan Morgan, scientist and apple enthusiast. Priced £2.25 plus 34p postage and packing, it is obtainable by post from: Ampleforth Abbey Publications, Mrs E C Lumsden, Deepdale, Skewsby, Yorkshire YO6 4SG.

Betty's Café Tea Rooms

*1 Parliament Square, Harrogate HG1 2QU. Tel. (0423) 64659
6–8 St Helen's Square, York YO1 2QP. Tel (0904) 59142
32–34 The Grove, Ilkley LS29 9EE. Tel. (0943) 608029
188 High Street, Northallerton DL7 8LF. Tel. (0609) 5154*

During the five years our daughter was at school in York, Betty's acted as an invaluable *pied à terre*, a place for coffee, lunch (lovely Yorkshire rarebit with Theakston's ale and ham), for tea (Earl Grey, and Bronte cake), and a place to buy treats to take back to school, or to take back home across the

Betty's

CAFÉ TEA ROOMS
NORTH YORKSHIRE
Est 1919

Pennines. The first Betty's Café was the Harrogate one, opened by Frederick Belmont, who came to England from Switzerland in 1919; the York tea-rooms followed in 1935, decorated as a replica of one of the great 1930s ocean liners. Apart from the cream cakes and pastries, Betty's are proud of their regional food – their *Yorkshire cheese lunch* offers *blue and white Wensleydale cheese*, they make use of Theakston's powerful Old Peculier Ale, brewed in Masham, in *Christmas Puddings and Cakes*, and list *Yorkshire Curd Tart*, *Fat Rascals*, a thick biscuit clotted with currants, *Parkin* and *teacakes*. They also make their own *Petit Fours*, and *chocolates* and *truffles*, and their confectioners are sent back to the homeland of their founder, to the Richemont College in Lucerne, to train. They now offer *wholefood products*, too, and an enormous range of *tea* and *coffee*. Retail sales are through their own cafés, and their shops: Taylors in Stonegate, 46 Stonegate, York; Kings Master Bakers, Old Market Place, Ripon; and Taylors of Harrogate, Pagoda House, Prospect Road, Harrogate. They also offer a mail order service.

Botton Creamery & Bakery

*The Camphill Village Trust Ltd,
Danby, Whitby, North Yorkshire
YO21 2NJ
Tel. Castleton (0287) 60885 [Bakery];
60871 [Creamery]*
PATRICK FRENCH

The Camphill Village Trust is a charity, founded in 1954 by Dr Karl König to provide a constructive way of life for the mentally handicapped within a community. There are many such Camphill communities round the world now, but this one in Danby Dale was the first of its kind. Part of the financial support is earned by the sale of products and farm surplus – farming is one of the leading occupations for Camphill Village residents. Members work on the land, then feed their fellow members on the produce and sell any surplus to the local district. The Botton cheeses have won customers from far outside their own locality. *Botton* is a hard full cream unpasteurised cows' milk cheese made to a traditional Dales recipe, using vegetable rennet; it comes plain or flavoured with such things as celery seeds. *Danbydale* is a soft cheese, also flavoured or plain, with a thin wax coating. Inez Vermaas is cheesemaker here, and her expertise has produced a cheese sold in the best shops in the country: Neal's Yard Dairy, Covent Garden, London WC2; Wells Stores, Streatley, Berkshire; as well as local outlets which include: Shepherd's Purse, Church Street, Whitby; Jumbo, 8 Park Street, Pickering; Gouldings Health Food Shop, 454 Marton Road, Middlesbrough, Cleveland; Country Fayre, 83 Station Road, Redcar, Cleveland. The village's own shop is open Monday to Friday, 9a.m.–12p.m., 2–4p.m., and also sells the creamery's *live yoghurt*, and *fresh curd*. The *bakery* makes *wholemeal breads* from *stoneground organically grown English wheat*, and a *herb and cheese bread*, using Botton cheese. They sell all they can make at the moment, via their own shop and fifteen retail outlets in the area – some of these are the same as the cheese stockists, and in addition: Scarth's Shop, High Street, Castleton, North Yorkshire; King's, Helmsley, North

YORKSHIRE AND HUMBERSIDE

Yorkshire; Electra's Delicatessen, 30 Westgate, Guisborough, Cleveland. The bakery is open Monday to Friday, 9a.m.–12p.m., 2–5p.m. and on Saturdays, 9a.m.–12p.m. Danby is just south of the A171 Guisborough to Whitby road. NB: Funds are currently being sought to build a new, larger creamery and food centre. Contact Patrick French if you would like to help.

Farmhouse Preserves

Stumps Lane, Darley, Harrogate, North Yorkshire HG3 2RR
Tel. Harrogate (0423) 780996

JOHN AND PAM DAWSON

The Dawsons bought the business as a going concern just over three years ago, as escape for John after twenty years as a travel agent; as he explained, 'to make money for ourselves instead of making money for other people.' The Dawsons found it was an uphill battle, and for the first eighteen months 'we had little to show for our efforts, but we always knew that if we gave the best possible service and kept a high quality in all that we did we would succeed'. This is proving to be true, and the Dawsons' 'venture into the unknown' is now so successful that they are offering to franchise their recipes and formula to other parts of the country. Their range of preserves includes *lemon curd* (their top seller in Yorkshire), seven marmalades (including a lovely *lemon* variety with *stem ginger*), nine jams, five exotic preserves (i.e. with the ubiquitous liqueurs), and items such as *stem ginger in syrup, honey,* and *mincemeat*. There are no artificial additives or preservatives used. Their list of outlets in the area is very long, so please telephone for shops nearest you. Visitors are welcome, 'whenever we are there manufacturing'. They are situated 5 miles outside Harrogate, 2 miles from the main A59 Harrogate to Skipton road.

Goats' Dairy Produce

In Yorkshire, as in Cumbria, there are a number of dairies producing goats' dairy produce; I will list, briefly, the following, which I know are making good quality cheese and yoghurt.

Beamer Dairy Goats

Chapel Farm, Thixendale, Malton, North Yorkshire YO17 9TG
Tel. Driffield (0377) 88340

KEVIN AND SUSAN ATKINSON

Mr Atkinson 'gave up a normal way of life' as he puts it, to keep goats. He now makes three fine cheeses: *Thixendale*, a hard, cloth-bound matured (two to six months) cheese; *Wold Roll*, a 'Swiss roll' soft lactic continental cheese, rolled in herbs, garlic and black pepper; and *Beamerdale*, soft, lactic, matured, red waxed (also chive flavoured, in yellow wax). Sales are wholesale and retail, with some mail order. Retail outlets include: Neal's Yard Dairy, Covent

Garden, London WC2; Peter Gott, Sillfield Farm, Kendal, Cumbria, and others in the York/Malton area. Visitors by appointment only at the moment. Thixendale is north of the A166 York to Driffield road.

Cerin House Products

Cerin House, Back Lane, Dishforth, North Yorkshire YO7 3LH
Tel. Thirsk (0845) 578002
MR AND MRS R W MATTHEWS

The Matthews sell *milk* and *yoghurt* (plain and fruit flavours), *cheeses*, *cream* and *ice cream* (during the summer months when extra milk is available), and also *free-range poultry* (chickens and geese), *eggs*, and *home-grown vegetables*. Stockist: The Natural Food Store, 23 North Lane, Headingley, Leeds. Visitors are welcome after 6.30p.m. on weekdays, and any time on Saturday and Sunday. Dishforth is off the A168, near the roundabout with the A1. Back Lane is marked, 'but asking for the couple who keep goats usually leads to us.'

Levens Farm Products

Levens Farm, Lund Lane, Killinghall, Harrogate, North Yorkshire HG3 2BG
Tel. Harrogate (0423) 500268
GUY AND PAT ROSS

Levens is one of the largest goat farms in the UK. *Yorkshire goat cheese* is produced in four flavours and in miniatures as well as larger sizes for cutting. *Wharfedale Blue* cheese is also made. Distribution is by mail order and through wholesalers – please telephone for further details. Levens Farm also sells Yvonjean ointment (made from goats' milk), recommended for the treatment of eczema, psoriasis and varicose ulcers. It is also available by post. Visitors are welcome either individually or in parties. Please telephone for an appointment. Killinghall is on the A61 just north of Harrogate.

Ribblesdale Dairy Goat Cheese

Ashes Farm, Horton-in-Ribblesdale, Settle, North Yorkshire BD24 0JB
Tel. Horton (072 96) 231
IAIN AND CHRIS HILL

The Hills make a very good *pressed cheese*, waxed, in three variations – *original*, *vegetarian* (microbial coagulant), and *smoked*. Blue and mature variations are sometimes available. Distribution is mainly via cheese factors, and is countrywide to the best cheese shops. Visitors are no longer encouraged to drop in, as the cheese production suffers. This is the cheese I use for preserving in olive oil with herbs and garlic, in the French manner.

Robrock Dairy Goats

Folly Lane Farm, Thurlstone,
Sheffield S30 6QF
Tel. Barnsley (0226) 765515
MRS ROSEMARY BROCKLEHURST

Fresh and *frozen milk, live natural* and *fruit yoghurt, feta,* and *cream cheeses, Robrock Red, Blue, Mature* and *Stripey Cheese* are all available here. The red colouring is annatto, otherwise no additives or thickeners are used. The yoghurt is largely unsweetened. The products are well distributed in the area – and to Harrods too. Visitors are welcome at any time, but for personal attention it is best to call between 4.45 and 9.30p.m. on weekdays, or any time at weekends. Visitors coming from a long distance should ring first to check on availability. Thurlstone is off the A628 Manchester to Barnsley road, 14 miles north-west of Sheffield. In the village bear left at Towngate Stores. At the top of the steep hill Ingbirchworth Road becomes Folly Lane – look for a large bungalow on the left.

Hirst's Black Puddings and Barnsley Chops

Swinhill House, 36 Queen's Road,
Barnsley, South Yorkshire
Tel. Barnsley (0226) 284851
ALBERT DICKINSON HIRST

The name Hirst has been synonymous with black puddings in Barnsley since 1887. The famous Barnsley chop originated here in 1933 when Albert Hirst senior was asked to produce a cut of meat to celebrate the opening of Barnsley Town Hall by the then Prince of Wales. The Barnsley Chop weighs 1lb 6ozs and is taken from the best end of a loin of lamb – not surprisingly, there are only two of these chops per lamb. The once-great Hirst empire went into liquidation as a result of the miners' overtime ban and strike (fewer black puddings and pork pies served in the NCB canteens), but Albert Dickinson Hirst, the third generation, is rebuilding it all. He is selling the Hirst prize-winning black pudding, and the Barnsley chop, from Stands 14/17 in the Barnsley Meat Market – and he has brought out a low-fat and a garlic black pudding. It may take some time, but Hirst's name will surely, once again, grace Barnsley with the products to which it had become accustomed.

Jon's Toffee

Jon's Toffee Ltd,
Victoria Road, Sowerby Bridge,
West Yorkshire HX6 3AQ
Tel. Halifax (0422) 831515
DAVID WHITEHOUSE

The originator of Jon's Toffee was John Watson who started the business in 1938. He specialised in traditional toffees and fudge, selling to local shops and Northern shows and fairs. David Whitehouse (who has many years' experience in manufacturing quality sweets) bought John Watson's business in 1977, and has expanded its sales nationally and abroad. He maintains the quality – the old recipes are still used, the sweets are mainly hand-moulded, and boiled in open copper pans – and carries on the tradition of selling fudge and toffee in places of public recreation, namely in up-market tourist outlets such as stately homes, National Trust shops, and museums. Much is sold under own-label packaging, and the latest venture in this field is to produce individually ('From one up,' says David Whitehouse) gifts of toffees and fudge in personally printed cartons. Callers are welcome, between 8.30a.m.–4.30p.m. on weekdays. Sowerby Bridge is on the A58 on the southern outskirts of Halifax – the factory is off Victoria Road (behind the Open Market).

Kilnsey Park & Trout Farm

Kilnsey, Skipton, North Yorkshire
Tel. Skipton (0756) 752150
JOE POPE (MANAGER)

Mr Pope feels that the quality of the clear spring water here, rising in the limestone hills, gives *Kilnsey trout* a 'flavour of unusual quality'. The owners of Kilnsey Estate, Peter and Anthony Roberts, have been rearing trout for ten years (including the large *'golden' trout*, up to 15lbs in size), and the development of a modern farm shop has accelerated this process. Other estate products are for sale – *smoked trout* (smoked on the premises), *crayfish*, *pheasants*, *grouse*, *wild duck* and *rabbit*. The shop also stocks freshly produced local items such as pâtés, jams, honey and natural ice cream. The shop is open every day of the year (except Christmas Day) from 9.30a.m.–5p.m. It lies between Kettlewell and Grassington on the B6160, 11 miles north of Skipton.

Longley Farm dairy products

Longley Farm, Holmfirth,
Nr Huddersfield HD7 1RS
Tel. Holmfirth (0484) 684151
JOSEPH AND EDGAR DICKINSON

Joseph and Edgar inherited the small, 20-acre Pennine farm from their great-uncle, together with ten cows, a horse, and debts greater than the whole farm's worth. From these small beginnings they created a progressive dairy unit with some of the best milk yields in Yorkshire, and in 1954, when rationing controls ended, they started to separate cream. Northerners are familiar with *Longley Farm extra-thick double cream*, 'Yorkshire expatriates crave for it,' and neither this nor the *whipping cream* is homogenised. Their *yoghurt*, both *plain* and *fruit flavoured*, won first prize at the great Nantwich Show last year, and they make *kosher yoghurt* too. ('All production from milking to packing the end product is under rabbi control, and each pot is individually marked with the rabbi's seal, so is suitable for orthodox Jews.') They were the first people to make *cottage cheese* in the UK after the War, and they continue to make 'the real thing', using vegetable rennet. Some is even exported to Paris and Monte Carlo. They are one of the few dairies which continues to produce *Yorkshire curd*, for curd tarts. When I asked the Dickinsons how they saw the future, they said, wisely, 'People change all the time, as does what they want to eat. Milk is a wonderful raw material to be used to satisfy these changing needs. At the moment, the emphasis is on the non-fat part of the milk, yesterday it was the fat part, tomorrow

– well, who knows.' Longley Farm products are very widely distributed in the North, via wholesalers, and cash and carry outlets. There is some direct delivery in the immediate locality – telephone for your nearest retail outlets.

PORK BUTCHERS

Yorkshire is truly a pig county. 'We specialise in the pig and its products' is the boast of more than one pork butcher, and this applies to them all. As with the goats' products, here is a brief summary of a few of the many good pork butchers in this ample county. I found while compiling this book that a pork pie crawl (and that is what it became, late in the day, after stopping at shop after shop), is almost as much fun as a pub crawl, and certainly as fattening.

T Appleton & Sons

Yore Pork Products Ltd,
6 Market Place, Ripon, North Yorkshire
Tel. Ripon (0765) 3198

DAVID SUDDARDS

This is an old established family firm. 'From a pig carcase we produce a large variety of products, both fresh – *sausages, joints,* et cetera – and manufactured – *pork pies, small pasties, cooked meats,* et cetera. All to handed down recipes, locked secretly in the head, not in a book.' The shop is open 8.30a.m.–5.30p.m. every weekday.

Harris, Leeming Bar – York and Bradenham hams

20 Leases Road, Leeming Bar,
Yorkshire DL7 9AW
Tel. Bedale (0677) 22661

STEPHEN SMITH (DEVELOPMENT MANAGER – SPECIAL HAMS)

Part of the Harris bacon group, this firm has been producing *Marsh York ham* for several years, and obtained the rights for Bradenhams only recently, relaunching this 'aristocrat of hams' in 1984. The York ham is a traditional dry cure; the Bradenham is made to a copyright recipe unchanged since the eighteenth century and a closely guarded secret – the curing is very lengthy and expensive. Both are available raw and cooked, whole or half. The York is also sold boneless. Please telephone for stockists.

Hopetown House – sausages and black pudding

Hopetown House, Burneston, Bedale, North Yorkshire DL8 2JN
Tel. Thirsk (0845) 576252
S C AND J H GIBSON

The Gibsons are relative newcomers to pork and pork products. Their *Hopetown House sausage* is a family recipe – coarse cut and spicy in thick or thin links. The *black pudding* is a traditional recipe. Both are the first of a range of delicatessen products to be produced from their own pigs. Sales are currently via local deliveries and from the farm gate.
Monday–Thursday, 8a.m.–6.30p.m.; Friday, 8a.m.–6p.m., Saturday, 8a.m.–5p.m. Hopetown House is adjacent to the northbound carriageway of the A1, approximately 4 miles south of Leeming Bar, 1 mile south of the Burneston turn-off.

Johnson's of Whitby – York hams, hand-raised pork pies

89 Church Street, Whitby, North Yorkshire YO22 4BH
Tel. Whitby (0947) 603117
RICHARD A BARKER

The supply of Johnson's traditionally cured *York hams* frequently cannot meet demand, but you may be luckier with their *Standing Pork Pies*, seasonally produced for Christmas. They also make the patriotically named *Empire Roll* (locally known as sliced polony, and known until the First World War as German sausage, when the name was diplomatically changed), *saveloys*, et cetera, smoked in their own smokehouse. No preservatives are used, so deliveries and sales are limited to a 30-mile radius. The shop is open daily except Wednesdays (half-day closing). Church Street is in the old part of Whitby, on the east side of the harbour.

Stanforth's Celebrated Pork Pie Establishment

9 Millbridge, Skipton, North Yorkshire BD23 1NJ
Tel. Skipton (0756) 3477
DAVID AND ELAINE JUBB, AND DAVID HOLMES

The name is larger than the shop, which is tiny, with a constant but fast-moving queue. Quite simply the best *pork pies* we tasted *anywhere* (for a fuller description see p. 176), and the *custard tarts* were wonderful too. Well worth a detour, but Skipton is delightful anyway. The shop is open every day except Tuesday, which is half-day closing. It is at the top of the town; turn left by the parish church, and the shop is on your left.

G P Stonehouse & Son – sausages

1a Stamford Street East, Leeman Road, York YO2 4YD
Tel. York (0904) 55061
MR GEORGE R STONEHOUSE

Mr Stonehouse is a sausage innovator – promoting such unusual blends as *lamb and mint*, *tomato and onion* (voted the Most Beautiful Sausage in Britain, coming first in the *Daily Mirror* Great British Banger contest in 1985), and *curried sausages*. Hours are 8a.m.–5.30p.m. daily, with 1p.m. closing on Wednesday and Saturday, and the shop is situated about 250 metres past the National Railway Museum.

Thornton's Champion Sausage

G E Thornton & Sons,
39 Main Street, Crosshills, Keighley,
West Yorkshire BD20 8TA
Tel. Crosshills (0535) 33108
SAM AND PETER WHITAKER

'Super sausage and excellent home cooked meats, particularly ham and pork,' said the enthusiastic friend who recommended Thornton's. Established over 100 years ago and still in the hands of the same family, this is the sort of pork butcher's which withstands all competition from supermarkets – bacon is cut to order, and there is a very good range of cheeses, with many true farmhouse cheeses from the small dairies. Other retail outlets for the Champion sausages – The Roasting Pot, Swadford Street, Skipton, North Yorkshire; Rushtons Delicatessen, Keighley Road, Colne, Lancashire. Thornton's is open 8.30a.m.–5p.m., Monday to Friday, but closed for lunch every day between 12.15–1.45p.m. Early closing is on Saturday. Crosshills is about 6 miles north-east of Keighley, at the junction of the A6068 with the A629.

Weegmann's pork pies and hams

6 Market Place, Otley, West Yorkshire
Tel. Otley (0943) 462327
C W AND E SMITHSON

Pork pies are a speciality here, as are the home-fed and cured *hams* and the home-made *sausages*, and all are additive-free. The shop was started by Weegmann (a German immigrant) in 1867, and its present owners, the Smithsons, took it over in 1969. Otley is on the A660, about 5 miles north of Guiseley.

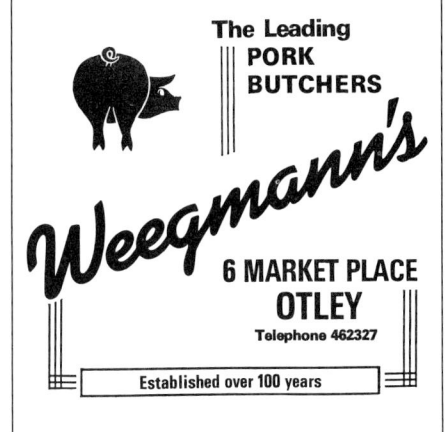

The Leading PORK BUTCHERS

Weegmann's

6 MARKET PLACE OTLEY
Telephone 462327

Established over 100 years

Raywell Organic stoneground flour

York Grounds Farm, Raywell, Cottingham, East Yorkshire
Tel. Hull (0482) 657342
M AND R J THOMPSON

York Grounds Farm has been run organically since 1949; the flour mill was installed a few years ago to enlarge the family enterprise and to supply a growing demand from interested consumers. Traditional horizontal stones are used to mill the farm-grown wheat; the flours are organically-grown 100% wholewheat flour, and conservation grade 100% wholewheat flour. Organic potatoes and cabbage are available from October to March. Sales are via wholesalers Hider Food Imports Ltd, Wiltshire Road, Hull, Humberside, who distribute in the north of England, and to personal callers by arrangement.

RAYWELL
STONEGROUND
ORGANICALLY GROWN
WHOLEWHEAT FLOUR

GROWN & MILLED BY
M. & R.J. THOMPSON
YORK GROUNDS FARM
RAYWELL COTTINGHAM
E. YORKS

Strawberry Farm pick-your-own organic fruit and vegetables, honey, and charcoal

Birstwith, Harrogate, North Yorkshire
HG3 3AW
Harrogate (0423) 771360
IVAN HOLMES

Set in Nidderdale, one of the most beautiful of the Yorkshire Dales, Strawberry Farm is an idyllic place to spend a day picking soft fruit. As it is well away from large towns and busy roads, it is the reputation for tranquillity, its range of fruit and the amenities it offers (tea-shop, children's play area, tractor transport in the fields) which attracts customers from all over the Pennines. The crops are all grown on 'as near an organic basis as possible, consequently our customers, our earthworms and our bees are all equally happy,' says Ivan Holmes. Added to this, the larger farm to which Strawberry Farm is attached produces hormone-free meat from traditional breeds of sheep and cattle, and markets this, and the potatoes and other Strawberry Farm produce, through Metcalfe Parker, King's Road, Harrogate. And finally, charcoal is prudently made from woodland thinnings during the winter months for sale in the strawberry season to fuel summer barbecues. Open during the season (approximate dates) 1 July–14 August, 9a.m.–8p.m.; 15 August–30 September, 9a.m.–6p.m. Birstwith is midway between Harrogate and Pateley Bridge.

Yates' parkin and curd tart

Yates & Son (York) Ltd,
75 Low Petergate, York YO1 2HY
Tel. York (0904) 22018
MR AND MRS M W MACKOWN

This bakery was established in 1833, and the old bakery behind the shop has been preserved, and is used as the tea-room. The products are traditionally regional – *parkin* to an 1836 recipe, *Yorkshire curd tarts* and pies, oven bottom bread made by overnight fermentation of sour doughs. The retail outlets are: Hollands, 96/98 Carlton Street, Castleford; Hollands of Castleford, 16 Northgate, Wakefield; Mackowns, 130 Dib Lane, Leeds; Yates, 19 New Street, York. Shop and tea-room are open Monday to Saturday, 9a.m.–5.30p.m.; Sunday, 9a.m.–6p.m.

Yorkshire Dales Old Fashioned Ice cream

Aireside Mills, Cononley, Keighley,
West Yorkshire BC20 8LW
Tel. Crosshills (0535) 36363
TIM WILSON

The speed with which Tim Wilson's ice cream has covered the North of England since he began the enterprise in July 1984 is testament to its quality, and his energy. This 'old fashioned' high quality dairy ice cream comes in seven flavours, including *passion fruit* and *hazelnut*, and does not contain any artificial colouring, flavouring or preservatives, and is all made in small batches. Latest lines are an additive-free *milk ice lolly* and a range of *natural fruit sorbets*. There are now over 250 outlets in Yorkshire, Lancashire, Derbyshire, Lincolnshire and Cheshire. Ring for your nearest retail outlet. Personal callers to the dairy are welcome, and supplies are by Yorkshire Dales' own van delivery service. Open Monday to Saturday, 9a.m.–5p.m. Cononley is 2 miles from Skipton off the A629.

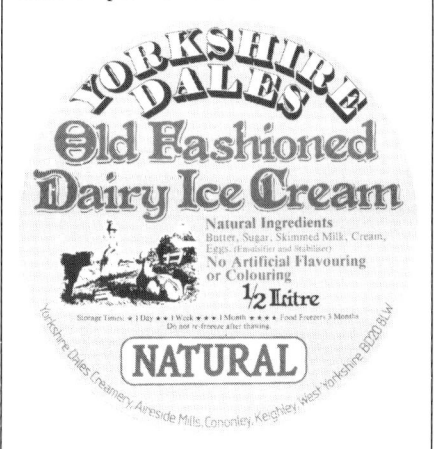

NORTHERN ENGLAND

Cumbria
(including Isle of Man)
—
Northumberland
(including Tyne & Wear and Durham)

This is the part of the country in which I have spent most of my cooking life, and one that has changed quite a lot in the last twenty years. When I first came to Cockermouth it was, as it still is, a small and relatively prosperous farming town, untouched by the unemployment which had hit the coastal towns like Whitehaven and Maryport during the 1930s and after, and as yet unscathed by Lake District tourism, which stopped at Keswick. There were at least four good grocers – one sliced bacon from good fat sides with a long knife, sold fresh yeast, and sugar in blue paper; there was a marvellous pork butcher, selling boiled ham on the bone, and all the chemists sold alcohol – some in the form of some very fine single malts. Now, the town has become diluted in one way, but strengthened in another, by 'incomers' – middle management from the industry (what there is of it) on the coast, professional people, and people who have retired to this quiet, pleasant and pretty town. They want different food, which is rarely supplied by the indifferent supermarkets. One of the good grocers remains, but is now classed as a delicatessen, and health foods have taken the place of the fat bacon and sugar in blue bags. This is a major development, as delicatessens can supply the sort of simple foods which appeal to the sophisticated – additive-free yoghurts and fruit juices, granary flour and pine kernels, tahini and chick peas – although not necessarily to the Cumbrian farmer.

Some traditions remain – good Cumberland sausage, for instance. I haven't listed any one maker in particular, as every town in Cumbria has a butcher who makes sausage to his own recipe, and one man's choice may well not be another's. Most are good in their way – many Cumbrians swear by the sausage made by the Cumbrian Co-op – we like that made by Bar Woodall* of Waberthwaite, and by Relph's of Cockermouth, and again that served with chips at the Horseshoe in Lorton. The best thing to do is to buy a little every time you see the long glistening ropes hanging up or lying coiled in a butcher's window, and decide for yourself. Provided it is made of coarse cut, pure pork, contains little or no cereal, and is wrapped in natural skins, it will be real Cumberland sausage – it is best to avoid the packaged varieties in the cold cabinets of supermarkets, however.

The traditional food of Cumbria contains many of the exotic ingredients brought to the region because Whitehaven, the second largest port on the north-west coast after Liverpool during the late eighteenth and early nineteenth centuries, traded with the West Indies. Whitehaven's remaining fine Georgian houses and its elegant grid system town-plan testify to once-held status. Rum butter, which now forms part of Cumbrian mythology because it has so many customs bound up with it, combines all the major imports in one dish – sugar, nutmeg and rum. Grasmere Gingerbread is another example, and Sweet Lamb Pie, which contains a mixture very much like that of the original mincemeat – lamb and its fat, dried fruit, sugar, and, of course, spices. Hawkshead Cakes are like large Eccles cakes, cushions of pastry, stuffed with dried fruit, sugar, and spices, and Clipping Time Pudding is a rice pudding enriched with bone marrow, dried fruit, cinnamon and nutmeg. These regional dishes are more often produced for tourists than eaten at home, although most households make or buy rum butter for Christmas. Bar Woodall* cures the traditional Cumberland hams down near Ravenglass, and nearby, Harry Fellows* is reviving smoked Herdwick mutton hams – called macon – which were made on the many fell farms. Near Wigton, Carolyn Fairbairn* makes Cumberland farmhouse cheese, and at Melmerby, Lis and Andrew Whitley are carrying the Cumbrian baking tradition shoulder-high into the new fibre age by using local stoneground wholemeal flour to bake a superlative range of cakes and breads in wood-fired ovens.

The restaurants of the Lake District are some of the best in the country: John Tovey's Miller Howe, Francis Coulson and Brian Sack's Sharrow Bay, the late Bronwen Nixon's Rothay Manor (ably continued by her family). All draw on the abundance of local delicacies provided by the many good food producers in the area, and in turn they support each other: the Whitleys use flour from the Jones's mill at Little Salkeld*, Harry Fellows smokes Bar Woodall's hams and Carolyn Fairbairn's cheeses, and so on. It would seem a good idea, perhaps, to form a marketing organisation like Devon Fare, to promote their goods further afield.

Northumberland is a fishing county, as Cumbria was an importing one, and the Berwick Salmon Fisheries*, one of the oldest in Great Britain, still sends locally netted wild salmon to London, just as it did in the eighteenth century when boiled and salted salmon was shipped to London in the 'Berwick Smacks'. Kippers continue to be cured in the late summer at Craster* as they have been for over a hundred years.

Up in Coquetdale, Mark Robertson is reviving farmhouse Wensleydale, as well as making two locally named ewes' milk cheeses which carry on the custom that only died out at the turn of the century. Gastronomy centres on Eggleston Hall*, where Mrs Gray runs a cookery school at which famous chefs give demonstrations and run courses. The shop run by the same team is called Partners, and stocks local Cotherstone cheese, Marsh's Bradenham hams, as well as dishes from the Eggleston Hall kitchens.

CUMBRIA

Alston Cheese

Back Garth, The Butts, Alston,
Cumbria CA9 3JU
Tel. Alston (0498) 81931
KATE WEBB

Kate Webb's practical approach is one that will keep her cheeses in existence longer than many who have embarked on cheesemaking over the past few years. She 'wondered about making cheese' while watching an Alston neighbour feed her surplus goats' milk to her dogs. She already had a scientific background and had been a bacteriologist for a number of years – an invaluable skill for cheesemaking. To this she added knowledge gained during a commercial cheesemaking course at the West of Scotland College of Agriculture. 'I then came home and made a great deal of very bad cheese before I discovered a method and a recipe that worked. I still make a lot of mistakes which are enjoyed by local pigs.' Nonetheless, she now supplies her cheese to some very discerning retail outlets. The cheeses are made daily by hand, using vegetarian rennet, in 40-gallon batches, and matured for six weeks before selling. The recipe is basically a Caerphilly one, much modified to suit the various milks she uses. *Tynedale* is a buttery cheese made from unpasteurised Ayrshire milk; *Smoked Tynedale* is lightly oak-smoked by Harry Fellows of Ashdown Smokers (see following entry), *High Pennine* is a summer-only goats' cheese using pasteurised milk; a *mixed cheese* is made from a combination of cows' and goats' milk: 'A most difficult cheese to produce, but at its best well worth the trouble.' This is only available from May–December. Kate markets her products 'any way I can' – she has a mail order service operating at Christmas, and sells wholesale and to personal callers. Retail outlets include: Alan Porter, Farnley, West Yorkshire; Peter Gott, Sillfield Farm, Nr Kendal (and Kendal and Barrow markets), Cumbria; Food for Thought, Land of Green Ginger, Tynemouth, Tyne and Wear; Grahams, Market Square, Penrith, Cumbria; Neal's Yard Dairy, Harrods and Paxton & Whitfield, all in London. Not all these shops carry the full range, of course. She now has a small shop next to the dairy to sell her own and other cheeses from small cheesemakers in Cumbria, Northumbria and the Borders. Open during normal shop hours in the summer season, in winter 'knock and see if I'm there'. Alston is on the Northumberland/Cumbria border, 36 miles from Penrith on the A686.

Ashdown Smokers

Skellerah Farm, Corney, Millom,
Cumberland LA19 5TW
Tel. Bootle (065 78) 324 (24-hour answering service)
E H (HARRY) FELLOWS

Ashdown Smokers produce some of the most imaginative smoked products I have come across. Pride of place must be given to their *Macon*, or smoked local native Herdwick mutton – a traditional product eaten 'summer dry and winter wet' in Cumbrian farmhouses: thinly sliced, and sometimes fried, in summer; and boiled with root vegetables in winter. Mutton it is, not insipid lamb, and it takes these high-fell sheep two years to gain the weight and flavour necessary. Following a 130-year-old recipe, the legs are then put into an aromatic dry cure for up to three weeks before being washed, air-dried and slowly smoked over local oak and juniper. They really have a wonderful flavour – aromatic, slightly gamey, just a little sweet. Harry Fellows and his wife, Kathleen, were 'hobby' smokers until they decided that the hobby had got out of hand, and in order to contain it they turned their fourteen years' experience into a full-time business, backed up by their additional experience in the wine trade. So successful has it been that they have moved to larger premises where they can also bring on their own stock, so that the quality of the material is assured – few smokers I have come across are this dedicated. The product range includes *sirloin* and *fillet of beef, pork, venison, ox tongue,* superlative *bacon and hams* (for further details of these see Bar Woodall, page 200), *sausage* and *venison sausage, wild rabbit* and *mallard, pheasant, pigeon,* locally caught *wild trout, sea-trout, salmon* and *eel.* They also smoke *cheese* from local cheesemakers. Local customers can be supplied with fresh game and fish of the same high quality. Customers' own produce will also be smoked for them and a wide range of cures is offered – there is no use of chemicals, artificial substances or colouring. Sales are through wholesalers to retailers and hotels, and by mail order – vacuum packing makes this possible. Retail outlets include: Vin Sullivan, Abergavenny, Gwent; Mostly Smoked, 47 Elizabeth Street, London SW1; T O Williams, 17 High Street, Wem, Shropshire; Alston Wines, Front Street, Alston, Cumbria; E H Booth & Co, Victoria Street, Windermere, Cumbria. Their produce can also be seen at some of the county shows and fairs. Personal callers are welcome, 9a.m.–5p.m. all year round, but as most things are freshly smoked, telephone first to check on availability. Corney is to be found on the English Lakes Ordnance Survey Map SW sheet 115917.

ASHDOWN

TRADITIONAL OAK SMOKERS OF FINE FOODS

Cumberland Mustard

Tyne Willows, Alston, Cumbria
Tel. Alston (0498) 81135
MARILYN AVENS

This is the mustard recommended by Harry Fellows of Ashdown Smokers for serving with several of his smoked products, and described by its makers as a *coarse-grain mustard 'relish'*. The black and white mustard seed is ground at the Watermill, Little Salkeld (see page 199), mixed with honey, cider vinegar, water, salt and nutmeg. Three further flavours are added – *garlic, horseradish* or *green peppercorns*. The product, which began as a Christmas present for the family, can now be seen in all the local delicatessens. Other retail outlets in Cumbria include: Wordsworth House National Trust Shop, Cockermouth; The Village Bakery Foodshop, Melmerby; Eden Valley Wholefood stalls at Penrith and Carlisle markets; market stalls run by Peter Gott of Sillfield Farm, Endmoor, Kendal (Tel. 04487 328).

English Ice Creams

Gipsy Well, The Banks, Staveley, Nr Kendal, Cumbria LA8 9NE
Tel. Staveley (0539) 821562
COLIN COOPER ENGLISH

Shortly after his second book, *The National Trust Book of Sorbets, Flummeries and Fools*, was published by David & Charles in May 1985, Colin Cooper English started English Ice Creams. He felt there was a need in the Lake District for really good ice cream, and his first season proved him right. Although still in its infancy, the business now supplies several hotels and restaurants regularly, and a distributor has shown an interest in marketing the sorbets throughout the Lake District. Colin's experience is enormous – he is a Swiss-trained restaurateur, and his own restaurant gained entries in the Good Food Guide and Michelin, and an Egon Ronay star. He has now joined forces with three freelance catering experts to form Lakeland Banquets, as the ice cream trade is largely seasonal. There is a range of ten flavours, including *pear, greengage*, and, in season, *damson*, which makes use of the local Lythe Valley fruit, a speciality of this part of the Lake District. These ice creams and sorbets are freshly made to order, so 24–48 hours' notice should be given. Also available are *parfaits*, and *iced mousses*, with *bombes, cassatas* and *iced vacherins* again made to order, according to customer specifications. No artificial substances are used. No personal callers, please, 'as there's no time to be sociable'.

Goats' Dairy Produce

Cumbria has become, over the past few years, a county of goat-keepers, all producing milk, yoghurt and sometimes cheese. I list a few for the interest of those allergy sufferers who may like to know where to buy supplies. Cumbria is now so large, since it includes Westmorland and North Lancashire, and its population so scattered, that I have tried to locate a producer in most areas.

Ghyllside Herd

Ghyll Farm, Westnewton, Aspatria, Cumbria
Tel. Aspatria (0965) 21081
CAROLE YATES

Traditional hand-made cottage-type *soft cheese*, and a *hard cheese*; *fresh and frozen milk, yoghurt*; *kid meat* in season are available here. Local stockists: The Granary, Market Place, Cockermouth; W I Market, Aspatria; Michael's Delicatessen, Keswick. Personal callers are welcome at most reasonable times, with a phone call first if possible. The farm is in the middle of Westnewton, midway between Aspatria and Allonby (on the coast).

Noblestone Herd

Sark Hall, Longtown, Carlisle, Cumbria CA6 5NJ
Tel. Longtown (0228) 791428
MRS C NOBLE

Frozen milk, milk in bulk to cheesemakers, and *colostrum* (the first milk produced after the birth of a kid, and in demand for lambs and calves) from this herd of Saanen goats are for sale. Local stockists: Holland & Barrett, The Lanes, Carlisle; Harkness Store, Longtown. Most sales are direct from the door, but please telephone first to check on availability. Longtown is north of Carlisle on the A7, and Sark Hall is 3 miles beyond Longtown.

Wardle's goats' dairy produce

Tottlebank Farm, Blawith, Ulverston, Cumbria
Tel. Lowick Bridge (022 985) 287
ELIZABETH WARDLE

Wardle's sells *fresh, frozen* and *skimmed* milk, *butter* (with and without colouring), *cream, soft cheese, hard cheese* (May to December), *low* and *full fat yoghurt, ice cream, sorbets* and *mousses, cheese cakes*, and *whey biscuits*. All products are made to order, and deliveries can be arranged; please telephone. Blawith is on the A5084, on the west side of Coniston Water.

See also: Alston Cheese, page 192, Thornby Moor Dairy, page 198.

Kendal Mint Cake

Robert Wiper, Kendal Mint Cake Works, Entry Lane, Kendal, Cumbria
Tel. Kendal (0539) 20427
HARRY WIPER

Although there are four competing manufacturers of this curious confectionery in Kendal, Wiper's claim that Joseph Wiper (the great-great-uncle of the present proprietor) originated the now renowned Kendal Mint Cake in 1869, in his premises in Stricklandgate. It was Robert Wiper, Harry's father, who realised the value of supplying expeditions with this high-energy sweet – the British Imperial Trans-Antarctic Expedition, 1914–17, the first major Everest attempts, and the Canadian Everest Expedition of 1982, among many others, have all been fuelled by Wiper's Kendal Mint Cake. The ingredients remain the same – sugar, glucose syrup and oil of peppermint, and it is still hand-made and hand-wrapped. It is sold mainly in the Lake District and Kendal itself, although mountaineering and outward bound schools all over the country are supplied with it. It can be bought directly from the works, too, but there are no facilities for visitors to watch the manufacturing process.

Manx kippers

It has always been illegal to dye kippers on the Isle of Man, although since 1983, under the Manx Kipper Rules for that year, 'approved colouring matter' has been allowed. Nevertheless, the sweet Manx kipper is still a pale fawn brown, rather than the mahogany brown of the dyed varieties. The kippers, small (as herring caught off the north-west coast of England are very small) are at their best during the late summer. There are three traditional curers on the Isle of Man whose kippers are worth asking for:

John Curtis Ltd, 10 Woodbourne Road, Douglas
Tel. Douglas (0624) 73875
Mr John A Curtis

Geo. Devereau & Sons Ltd, 38 Strand Street, Douglas
Tel. Douglas (0624) 73257/6360
Mr P A Canipa

T Moore & Sons Ltd, Mill Road, Peel
Tel. Peel (0624 84) 2214
Jim Coulson

All are distributed via wholesalers to fishmongers and markets throughout the North-West. Moore's are supplied to Harrods, too.

Muncaster Mill stoneground organic flour

Muncaster Mill, Ravenglass, Seascale, Cumbria CA18 1ST
Tel. Ravenglass (065 77) 232
PETER ELLIS (MANAGER)

Muncaster Mill has been renovated to form an additional tourist attraction next to the Ravenglass and Eskdale narrow gauge railway. It was the manorial mill for Muncaster Manor,

Stoneground Natural Bran

MUNCASTER MILL

Milled from Organically Grown Wheat
500 g   1.1 lb
METRIC PACK

and the present building, dated about 1700, stands on a site used since 1455, and the 1845 millstones are now grinding *organically grown English wheat* to produce *flour of various grades*. Because of the lack of demand for the flour in the immediate locality, the mill is likely to continue rather more as a tourist attraction than as an important producer of flour. Nevertheless, Peter Ellis hopes to reintroduce *traditional stoneground oatmeal*, and possibly some *barley products* to the range. Sales are mainly to personal callers, with a limited number of local Cumbrian retail outlets. These include: T F Barnes, Gosforth; K M Bennett, 8 Sautergate, Ulverston; Better Livin', The Parade, Seascale; Brocklebanks, 79a Market Street, Dalton-in-Furness; The Good Food Store, 153 Queen Street, Whitehaven; Tysons, Princes' Street, Broughton-in-Furness. The mill is open daily in the tourist season, except on Saturdays: April, May and September, 11a.m.–5p.m.; June, July and August, 10a.m.–6p.m. Flour is available out of season, but please ring first. The mill is by the side of the main A595 coast road 1 mile north of Ravenglass, by the Ravenglass and Eskdale railway.

Roundthorn Farmhouse Foods

Roundthorn Farmhouse, Beacon Edge, Penrith, Cumbria
Tel. Penrith (0768) 62299
MR AND MRS J MATHEWS

Mr Mathews's stall is a welcome sight amongst those selling lurid shoes and vacuum cleaner innards at the open markets round the fringes of the Lake District. His wife Jane bakes the *cakes*, *bread* and *scones*, and makes the *jams*; there is usually poultry – *chickens*, *ducks*, and sometimes a boiling fowl or two – and *free-range eggs*, as well as *game in season*. Added to these products, Mr Mathews specialises in very good cheese, an invaluable service. Mr Mathews's PhD in chemistry sharpened his awareness of the growing dangers of chemicals in food and he chose his present way of life after a disillusioning spell in the Civil Service. He has recently added a cheese distribution service to top Lake District restaurants to his market stall activities. He can be found on the following markets, *all year round*: Cockermouth, Mondays; Penrith Covered Market, Tuesdays; Brampton, Wednesdays; Whitehaven, Thursdays; Keswick, Saturdays. The products can also be bought from the farmhouse, 9a.m.–10p.m. (except Sundays). At Penrith take the A686 to Lanwathby and Alston, take the third left turn, then the first right up a narrow lane. The farmhouse is through a farmyard on the right, behind an hotel.

Sarah's Lakeland Fudge

Lanefoot Cottage, Pardshaw Hall, Cockermouth, Cumbria
Tel. Cockermouth (0900) 823708
NORMAN SMITH

Mr Smith, at seventy, has a new career, that of fudgemaker to the fudge-hungry tourists of the Lake District. Using his grandmother Sarah's recipe, he now makes 300 6oz-bags a day, on the system of having six pans boiling, and six pans cooling, all in his not over-large kitchen. And he can barely keep up with demand. Wet cold summers like that of 1985 are best for his business: 'In hot weather everyone buys ice cream, but in cold weather they all buy my fudge.' As a true Cumbrian, born and bred, his motto is 'Wordsworth left his poetry, I want to leave my fudge'. He supplies all the National Trust shops in the Lake District, together with thirty-eight other retail outlets, including in Cumbria: the Ravenglass Railway; Santon Bridge Crafts; Appleby Castle; and The Coffee Bean Cafe, Grasmere. Personal callers are welcome at all times 'except when producing or delivering'. Pardshaw Hall is a small hamlet, to the east of the A5086 Cockermouth to Cleator Moor road, about 3 miles out of Cockermouth.

Slack's Cumberland ham and sausage

Newlands Farm, Raisbeck, Orton, Penrith, Cumbria CA10 3SG
Tel. Orton (058 74) 667
MICHAEL SLACK

The Slacks use their own home-bred pigs to produce *hams* and *bacon* as near the traditional texture and flavour as possible, with a slow curing in salt followed by drying in the fresh air. The sausage is made to a 150-year-old Cumbrian recipe, and contains a very small amount of preservative. Everything is made on the farm. The curing side of their 18-year-old business only began about twelve years ago, and it took some eight years to perfect their present cure. There are some mail order sales, but most of the wholesale and retail selling is done from their farm shop in Tebay: Slack's Farm Shop, Tebay, Penrith, Tel. Orton (058 74) 446. Open January–March, Tuesday, Thursday and Friday, 8.30a.m.–5p.m.; Saturday, 8.30a.m.–1p.m. April–December, Monday to Saturday, 8.30a.m.–5p.m. Newlands farm is in the centre of the village of Tebay, ¼ mile from Junction 38 on the M6, on the A685 Kendal to Kirkby Stephen and Appleby road.

Thornby Moor Dairy cheese

Thornby Moor Dairy, Aikton, Wigton, Cumbria CA7 0JZ
Tel. Wigton (0965) 43160
CAROLYN FAIRBAIRN

Carolyn Fairbairn produces both goats' and cows' milk cheeses, using unpasteurised milk in both cases. There are six cheeses in the range, five matured and one lactic cheese made from either milk. All the matured cheeses are made with animal rennet as Carolyn feels this works better for any cheese that is to be ripened for two to three months, as hers are. *Cumberland Farmhouse* is a Friesian milk cheese with a smooth texture and full flavour. Clothbound, it comes in 20lb, 10lb and also in 2.5 and 1lb 'gift size' cheeses. *Cumberland Herb Cheese* is the farmhouse cheese individually flavoured with fresh herbs, Garlic, Sage, Fennel and Dill. Waxed, in sizes as before, and there is a *Smoked Farmhouse* as well, smoked in their own smokehouse. The *Lactic Cheese* is either plain or flavoured with herbs. *Allerdale Cheese* is a semi-hard goats' cheese, moist and sweet-flavoured. Waxed, it is made in

5lb, 2.5lb and 1lb sizes. The cheeses are widely distributed both locally and nationally, and by mail order. Stockists include: E H Booth & Co., in Kendal and Windermere; La Charcuterie, 25 High Street, Yarm, Cleveland; Comrie Cheese Shop, Comrie by Crieff, Perthshire; Wells Stores, Streatley, Berkshire. Personal callers are welcome from 8.30a.m.–2p.m. on weekdays and at other times by appointment. Aikton is north of the A596 Maryport to Thursby road, about 5 miles north-east of Wigton.

in the bakery and restaurant. The Whitleys also make ice cream and sorbets, and send their Christmas puddings and cakes by mail order. Retail outlets in Cumbria include: Granary Wholefoods, Market Place, Cockermouth; Stokoe's Stores, Armathwaite; Sundance Wholefoods, Keswick; George's Wholefoods, Brampton; Holland & Barrett, The Lanes, Carlisle; The Shop in the Shelter, Caldbeck. The Village Bakery has a shop in Penrith, too (Angel Lane, just off Market Square, by the clock tower), which stocks a wide range of cheeses and delicatessen

The Village Bakery

The Village Bakery, Melmerby, Penrith, Cumbria CA10 1HE
Tel. Langwathby (076 881) 515
LIS AND ANDREW WHITLEY

Wholemeal croissants seemed a contradiction in terms until I tasted those from this bakery – how could anything made with a brown flour be as light and rich as a croissant should be? I still don't understand how, but these are. The Whitleys' range of *breads*, *rolls*, *cakes* and *pies* are made with organic English wheat flour stoneground at the Watermill, Little Salkeld (see following entry), and baked in a brick, wood-fired oven built to a 'Scotch' design. The yeast and pastry products are baked first when the oven is hottest, then cakes and biscuits use the oven's declining heat, with pizzas and stotties (flat loaves) baked on the brick 'sole'. A place well worth visiting for lunch, tea, or, best of all, breakfast. Behind the bakery is a small-holding which produces vegetables, fruit, milk and meat for use

goods; open 9a.m.–5p.m. every weekday except Wednesday. The bakery is open from 8.30a.m.–5p.m. on Tuesday, Thursday, Friday, Saturday, Sunday and Bank Holiday Mondays, closed on ordinary Mondays and all day on Wednesdays. Melmerby is on the A686 Penrith to Alston road, 9 miles from Penrith.

The Watermill stoneground organic English flour

The Watermill, Little Salkeld, Penrith, Cumbria CA10 1NN
Tel. Langwathby (076 881) 523
NICOLAS AND ANA JONES

This is one of my favourite mills, tucked down below the level of the nearby road, alongside Sunnygill Beck, the tributary of the River Eden which provides power for the water wheel. Nick and Ana wanted, from the start twelve years ago, to use the mill for its original purpose, 'The grinding of high quality, organically grown cereals using the clean self-renewing power of water. But we wished to combine this with a place of entertainment and education.' This has not been easy, but they have achieved it. The mill is a fascinating place to see and learn how grain becomes flour, and how the flour is used; half-day courses in milling and baking are held. Local farmers have been persuaded to grow more and more wheat to Nick's specifications, and it is part of the pleasure of the place to see the wheat growing in the fields around the mill itself. The tea-room serves scones, biscuits, cakes, pies and breads baked from the freshly ground flour. The range of cereal products is wide and includes, apart from the 100% and 85% *wholewheat flours, a 100% rye,* and *85% barley flour. Granarius* is their own combination of barley malt flour and wheat flour together with cracked wheat and wholewheat grains – it makes lovely nutty bread. They also sell a range of oatmeal products – The Watermill was once famous for its high quality oatmeal in the days when oats were the main cereal crop in the North of England, and local legend insists that a regular consignment was sent to Fortnum & Mason. Sadly, oats now have to be milled elsewhere, but three grades of oatmeal are available, as well as oatmeal-based muesli, giant oatflakes, whole oat groats, et cetera. Their products are widely distributed throughout Cumbria and Northumberland, but it is best to telephone for your nearest stockist.

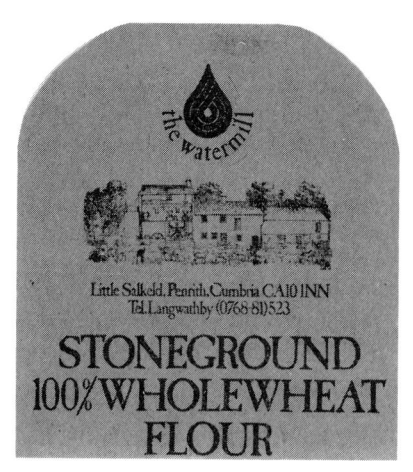

Little Salkeld, Penrith, Cumbria CA10 1NN
Tel. Langwathby (0768 81)523

STONEGROUND 100% WHOLEWHEAT FLOUR

The Watermill is open on Monday, Wednesday, Thursday and Sunday, and Bank Holiday Saturdays, between Easter and the end of September, from 2.30–5.30p.m., for visits to the mill itself. To collect orders, call between 9.30a.m.–12.30p.m., Mondays to Fridays except Christmas and Bank Holidays. Little Salkeld is 1 mile from Langwathby off the A686 Penrith to Alston road.

Woodall's Cumberland hams

Lane End, Waberthwaite, Nr Millom, Cumbria LA19 5YJ
Tel. Ravenglass (065 77) 237
BAR WOODALL

Lane End Post Office is very unremarkable from the outside, and inside sells the usual tinned pears and peas, cough sweets, frozen foods, and rather nice old sepia postcards of the area. But look at the pork products and you will see the difference – hanging over the counter are some mahogany-coloured hams, stamped with Bar Woodall's mark, famous now well outside their native Cumbria. The sausage, in neat coils, is more speckled than is usual, and the bacon is clearly not composed of a large proportion of water, and will slice as thinly as you like – a true test of quality. For Bar Woodall is a pig farmer, and a fisherman, but a ham curer *par excellence*. His contented pigs live 'behind the shop', fed on unadulterated feed – barley, now, rather than oats, but strictly no antibiotics, 'something I set a great deal of store by'. He feels the nature of the feeding contributes to the flavour of his hams, together with the curing, of course. The hams are a month in a salt and sugar cure, then dried and hung for a further two months to mature, all very traditional, as is the recipe he uses for his sausages, very secret and dating from 1828. He will tell you the ingredients, but not the proportions: 100% pure pork, salt, pepper, cayenne, mace and sage – making a spicier sausage than most, but one of my particular favourites.

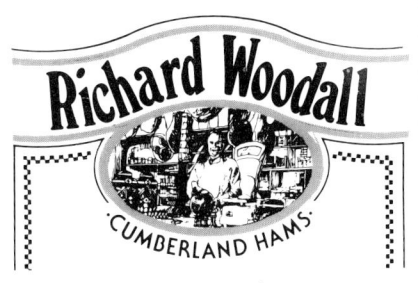

But he flouts tradition when it comes to his new venture, that of producing a Cumberland ham that is eaten raw, like Parma or Bayonne ham. These he vacuum packs so that they remain at their peak, and sends them by post, either on or off the bone, sliced or whole. So good are they that Chris Bonington took one of these hams with him up Everest – Bar Woodall will show you the photographs to prove it. He also does a Cumbria Royal Ham, cured in old ale, molasses, vinegar, salt and sugar, and there is a smoked version of this, too. The smoking of the hams and bacon, and some of the sausage, is done by his colleague and neighbour, Harry Fellows, of Ashdown Smokers (see page 192). There is a certain amount of mail order, and the list of stockists is very long, so it is best to telephone for details of a stockist near you. The Post Office and shop are open from Monday to Friday, 8.30a.m.–12.15p.m., 1.15–5.30p.m., closed on Saturday afternoons and Bank Holiday Mondays. Waberthwaite is just off the A595, 20 miles south of Whitehaven, 4 miles south of Ravenglass, 11 miles north of Millom.

NORTHUMBERLAND

Berwick Salmon Fisheries 'Scotwild' smoked salmon

Berwick Salmon Fisheries plc,
1 Main Street, Spittal,
Berwick-upon-Tweed
TD15 1QY
Tel. Berwick (0289) 307474

K M ANDERSON (MANAGING DIRECTOR)

This company, one of the oldest in Great Britain, began life in the eighteenth century when a group of local men took shares in a small fleet of sailing ships; these 'Berwick Smacks' carried large quantities of boiled and salted salmon to London. After the railway network reached Berwick in the mid-nineteenth century, the shipping trade declined. However, the directors of the company concentrated on improving the salmon fisheries they had acquired earlier to supply the cargoes for their ships, and it is this aspect of the company that continues to form the principal business. Throughout the legal netting season (from 15 February to 14 September on the Tweed), *salmon* are netted, then despatched by road or rail to markets all over the country. Some selected fish are used for 'Scotwild' *smoked salmon*. Sales are via wholesalers, mail order, and personal callers (prior notification, please), 9a.m.–5p.m. on weekdays and 9a.m.–12p.m. on Saturdays. Spittal is just to the south of Berwick.

Eshott Milk

Eshott Home Farm, Felton, Morpeth, Northumberland NE65 9EP
Tel. Felton (067 087) 432
T N H SANDERSON

Long before the Milk Marketing Board was in existence, Eshott was selling 'certified milk' – the highest grade of milk in the 1920s and 30s, and a premium product, sent specially by train to Harrods and Selfridges. Mabel Lucie Atwell designed the trademark used by Eshott Milk in the 1930s, when the 'Eshott Babies' symbol was recognised throughout the North-east as representing farm fresh quality. The War brought a halt to this expansion, and after the War large dairy companies were buying out the private dairies. But Eshott has remained independent, its managers realising

ESHOTT FARM
HOME FARM, FELTON, MORPETH, NORTHUMBERLAND. NE65 9EP

that their customers would prefer a more personal service, and a more varied range of milk and other products than the big dairy networks are prepared to offer. Accordingly, the Sandersons, father and son, did a trial run, taking twenty-seven pints of farm fresh, untreated milk round the local township. This proved so popular that they now distribute over 140 gallons of milk a day, from *full fat Jersey gold-top* to *blue-top fully skimmed milk*, as well as *green-top unpasteurised Ayrshire*. They carry *Jersey cream*, too, and distribute *Longley yoghurt* (see page 182), and *cottage cheese*, *Wensleydale butter* and their own *home-grown potatoes*. Their successful battle against the giants has just won them a National Farmers' Union Gold Marketing Award. For distribution details in the North-east, please telephone. Farm visits by parties are welcome; please ring for a date and time. Felton is just east of the A1, on the B6345 to Amble on the Northumberland coast.

Morrelhirst Dairy Goats

Morrelhirst, Netherwitton, Morpeth, Northumberland
Tel. Rothbury (0669) 20230
JILL HARRISON

Mrs Harrison wanted her own enterprise which would fit in with her husband's hill farm, and fulfil her deeply held beliefs in organic and extensive farming. She has a small herd of Anglo-Nubian and British Toggenberg goats which graze on the Simonside Hills south of Rothbury – from the milk she makes *soft herb cheese*, *plain yoghurt*, and sells *fresh* and *frozen milk*. The herbs are organically grown (Mrs Harrison holds the Soil Association Symbol for organic produce), the goats homeopathically treated, and vegetarian rennet is used for the cheesemaking. Stockists include: Food for Thought, Land of Green Ginger, Tynemouth, Tyne & Wear; Heighly Gate Nurseries, Morpeth. Mrs Harrison also visits local agricultural shows. Personal callers by appointment, please. Morrelhirst is on the B6342 Hexham road, between Rothbury and Scots Gap.

Northumbrian Duck

W G Lough & Son Ltd,
1, 2, & 5 Holly Avenue West, Jesmond,
Newcastle-upon-Tyne NE2 2BH
Tel. Newcastle (0632) 811351

HUGH LOUGH

A friend introduced me to Mr Lough's '*Northumberland Duck*', bringing one back for me after a visit to her family in Jesmond. So I was delighted when Jane Grigson featured this 'bit of fun' in her *Observer Guide to British Cookery*. For in fact it isn't duck, but lamb – shoulder, to be exact – boned out to look much more duck-like than the real thing. Lough's have been producing this mythical beast since the 1920s, using the knuckle bone to form the duck's head and neck, and removing the blade bone altogether. This has the added advantage of making a shoulder much easier to carve, and produces a near-perfect joint for a dinner party, as well as a conversation piece, should you need one. Lough's have been trading in the wealthy suburb of Jesmond for over thirty years; Hugh Lough is the third generation, and is justly proud of their reputation. Apart from the 'ducks', they do *crowns of lamb, guard of honour,* and *noisettes,* all using best English lamb from local farms, *superlative beef,* hung for at least twelve days before selling, *osso bucco* and *calves' liver,* their own *sausages, home-cured bacon,* and *game.* The shop is open from 8a.m. every weekday morning (except Wednesday when it opens half-an-hour later), closing at 5p.m. on Monday, 5.30p.m. on Tuesday and Thursday, 6p.m. on Friday, and 1p.m. on Wednesday and Saturday. Holly Avenue runs across the B1309 Osborne Road in the centre of Jesmond.

Redesdale farmhouse cheeses

Soppitt Farm, Elsdon,
Newcastle-upon-Tyne NE19 1AF
Tel. Otterburn (0830) 20276

MARK ROBERTSON

Mr Robertson's two ewes' milk cheeses are *Redesdale* – a semi-hard cheese – and *Coquetdale,* a soft cheese. They are called after the two rivers which drain the area, the Rede and the Coquet. Mark Robertson is reviving the old Northumberland tradition of ewes' milk cheeses; he thinks that in isolated hill farms the practice only died out at the turn of the century. But he is also reviving a much more famous cheese – *farmhouse Wensleydale* – which has died out, with the exception of that produced by the Kirby Malzeard dairy near Ripon, North Yorkshire. Mr Robertson supplies: The Corbridge Larder, Corbridge, Northumberland; Straker & Leatham, Hexham, Northumberland; Almonds & Raisins, Queens Square, Newcastle-upon-Tyne; Harrods and Neal's Yard Dairy, Covent Garden, London WC2. The farm shop is open daily from 10a.m.–6p.m. all year round, and sheep milking can be seen at 4p.m. daily from May to September. The farm shop also sells other dairy products, made from both ewes' and cows' milk – *yoghurt, cheesecakes, whey biscuits,* etc. There is a tea-room, too, which serves ploughman's lunches and afternoon teas. Soppitt Farm is on the B6341 2 miles east of Otterburn.

Robson's Craster kippers

L Robson & Son Ltd,
11 Haven Hill, Craster, Alnwick, Northumberland
Tel. Embleton (066 576) 223
K L ROBSON AND A ROBSON

Craster kippers are as famous as Manx or Loch Fyne, and are just as innocent of artificial colouring, with a lovely light, mild cure – a salmon cure adapted for herring by a Mr John Woodger in the mid-nineteenth century. Robson's have been curing for more than a hundred years now – since 1856 – using nothing but oak smoke. The sad thing is that the kippers are only produced from June to September – like all the best foods they are still very seasonal. The smoked salmon that Robson's also cure is available all the year round. Visit the smokehouse, down by the harbour, from Monday to Friday, 9a.m.–12p.m., 1–5p.m.; Saturday, 9a.m.–12p.m., 1.30–5p.m.; Sundays, 1.30–5p.m.

Shaws 'Northumbrian' biscuits

Shaws Biscuits Ltd,
Dukesway, Team Valley,
Tyne & Wear NE11 0QP
Tel. Tyneside (091) 482 2611
RICHARD ADAMS (CHAIRMAN),
G P KEEN (SALES DIRECTOR)

In 1987, Shaws will be celebrating their fiftieth birthday as a private independent company, one of the very few such biscuit bakers still remaining. They produce a range of over a hundred products, most to traditional recipes, all made with healthy ingredients 'with only natural colourings, flavourings or additives where these are absolutely necessary'. Mr Keen told me, 'Our aim is to rely on the quality of our raw materials and our baking skills to provide an acceptable product for the customer.' Which they do – their biscuits are as near 'home-made' in taste as you can get, and their *Crunchy Bars* (a recent development which they see as an alternative to traditional chocolate and sugar confectionery) are delicious and fuel many long family car journeys. They market their products both under the 'Northumbrian' label, and, the largest proportion, under own-brand labels for Boots, Sainsbury's, Allinsons, Prewetts and the National Trust. Or you can go to their factory shop between 11.30a.m.–2.30p.m. any weekday and buy factory rejects, new product trials (always interesting) and surplus gift pack stocks.

Whitburn Moors Farm Yoghurt

R Holmes & Sons,
Whitburn Moors Farm, Sunderland Road,
Cleadon, Tyne & Wear SR6 7UN
Tel. Whitburn (0783) 293127

M F HOLMES

The Holmes family have been farming here since 1810 and have always produced and sold milk in Sunderland and South Shields. The *yoghurt* side of the business was started in 1984 when it was seen that there was a gap in the local market for such a product. It is *produced in the churn*, and the *four fruit flavours* are made with whole fruit. No artificial flavourings, colours or stabilisers are used. The milk from their herd of 220 Friesian cows is used for the yoghurt and for *double* and *whipping cream*. The *milk* itself is sold both pasteurised and untreated, skimmed and semi-skimmed. Retail outlets include a number of dairies in the Sunderland and South Shields area; Country Whole Foods, 290 Fulwell Road, Sunderland; Super VG, 222 Chester Road, Sunderland, and K & R Canter, 253 Chester Road, Sunderland. The farm shop is open from 9a.m.–5p.m., Monday to Friday, and on Saturday, 9a.m.–12p.m., and is just off the A1018 just north of Sunderland, between Sunderland and Cleadon village.

Eggleston Hall Cookery and Flower School

Talbot Gray Ltd,
Eggleston Hall, Barnard Castle,
Durham DL12 0AG
Tel. Teesdale (0833) 50378

MRS R H GRAY

Mrs Gray started her cooking school in this imposing house in 1972, and from it have sprung many offshoots of enormous benefit to the cause of good food in the area. The dishes cooked in the kitchens are supplied, fresh and frozen, to their shop, Partners, 26 Horsemarket, Barnard Castle; Tel. (0833) 38072. Wholefoods are used as far as possible, and recipes are Cordon Bleu, or their own. There is a wide range of dishes from classic soups like *Vichyssoise* to the wonderfully named and delectable *Gâteau Panache* (meringue alternately layered with chocolate and raspberry cream). The *Spinach Flan with Hollandaise* is a sophisticated and rich vegetarian dish much appreciated by unpersuaded meat-eaters. Partners also sells *Bradenham hams,* and the *local Cotherstone cheese,* still made at two nearby farms. This is a semi-soft naturally crusted cheese, which used to be made seasonally from May to the 'first frost' (which comes early in these northern hills), but is now made all the year round. Recently opened is Partners Flower Shop, 27 Horsemarket, Tel. (0833) 88847, which also sells vegetables, some of them grown organically in the Eggleston Hall gardens. The school also runs courses and demonstrations by famous chefs – ask to be included in their mailing list for advance notice of these. Partners is open from

9.30a.m.–5p.m., six days a week from July to Christmas. For the rest of the year, the hours are the same, but it is closed all day on Thursdays. The Flower Shop is open at the same times, but six days a week all year. Barnard Castle is on the A67 about 16 miles east of Brough.

SCOTLAND

Kippers, smoked salmon and Finnan haddock – all of these one expects to find in Scotland, and I did, in quality and abundance. What I hadn't realised was the quality and abundance of good cheese being made – I had felt that climate must of necessity produce a restricted range of cheese. But you only have to read Mrs Chalmers's* and Mrs Russell's* accounts of cheesemaking on Orkney to realise that the conditions are ideally suited for the production of excellent cheese. Reggie and Susannah Stone* make wonderful cheese up in Ross & Cromarty – Crowdie and Caboc, two of Scotland's oldest cheeses. Down in the balmier south, several newer cheeses are being made – John Curtis* is producing Bonchester and Teviotdale, near Annan, Carol Neilson* is making ewes' milk Barac, and in Lanarkshire, Humphrey Errington* is reviving the eighteenth-century tradition of ewes' milk cheeses in this area with his Lanarkshire Blue, made along the lines of Roquefort.

Oyster farming is a natural enterprise, too, for Scotland, and John Noble at Ardkinglas* and Iain Moody on Mull* are both finding markets for their oysters far south of the border, as well as in the good hotels and restaurants on the Scottish side.

I found Fergus Morrison's* bere milling on Orkney particularly interesting, since this ancient grain is now only grown there, and must frequently be threshed in a travelling threshing mill as communications, of necessity, depend on tides and winds.

Betinna, Lady Thomson's* apple growing at Priorwood Gardens, near Melrose, captures the imagination too, as she is carrying on a tradition started by the monks of Melrose Abbey in the twelfth century – finding that the shelter of the Tweed valley produces an abundance of fruit: medlars, pears, plums and gages as well as apples. The varieties themselves span the centuries, from Court Pendu Plat to some of the most recent cultivars.

Donald Maclean*, in Crieff, has supplied many potato enthusiasts with rare seed potatoes in his time – his collecting zeal began when he was a schoolboy, and fortunately he has never grown out of it. He can supply potatoes of at least 200 different varieties, and you can buy one or two, or a kilo or two, depending on whether you want something from his museum collection, or a more humdrum and useful crop, like King Edwards. He supplies the museum garden at Quarry Bank Mill, in Cheshire (see page 161) with varieties like Kepplestone Kidney, Early Market and Clovulrin.

My inclusion of no fewer than seven producers of smoked salmon explains the difficulty I had in deciding on quality. They varied more in flavour than anything else as the quality was consistently high amongst those listed. In one the flavour of juniper was faint but distinctive, in another – the Mermaid* smoked salmon from the Outer Hebrides – the peat flavour was pronounced although still subtle, in a third, bourbon wood chips gave enormous character. These are the 'rustic' flavours, which I enjoyed very much indeed, and found a welcome change from the more 'polite' flavour of the big brands. For these, champagne is the best accompaniment, for the others, single malt whiskies are the things to drink. The quality of the Finnan haddock demonstrated that here was another fish to be eaten raw, thinly sliced, with brown bread and butter and wedges of lemon. It is as good in its own right as smoked salmon, and deserves to be taken more seriously.

Arran Provisions Scottish preserves

The Old Mill, Lamlash,
Isle of Arran, KA27 8JU
Tel. Lamlash (077 06) 606/607/370
IAIN A RUSSELL

Iain and Janet Russell left Birmingham in 1973 to return to their family home on Arran. Using old family recipes they began making high quality Scottish products – marmalades, mustards, preserves, jellies and honeys. They do a range of very good jellies in particular, and curiously are the only people I came across who make, commercially, the traditional northern *rowan jelly* which is so good with lamb and game – even better than redcurrant jelly. Arran Provisions do an *Apple & Wild Rowan Jelly* (apple is necessary to make the rowans set, as they contain very little pectin) in their Savoury Jellies range. And *Port Wine*, and *Claret Wine* jellies, too, which I found delicious with *fromage blanc* as a dessert. The mustards are original too; the *Leek Mustard* is recommended for serving with Welsh lamb, of course, and the *Lemon Mustard* with fish instead of tartare sauce – it was certainly very good with grilled herring. These are available by mail order, wholesale, and to personal callers. Stockists 'are too numerous to list'. Personal callers are welcome between 9a.m.–5p.m., Monday to Friday all year round. Lamlash is only about 3 miles south of Brodick, where the car ferry from Ardrossan on the mainland docks.

Barac ewes' milk cheese

Windyknowe, Annan, Dumfries-shire
DG12 5LN
Tel. Annan (046 12) 4691
MICHAEL AND CAROL NEILSON

The Neilsons are making a very successful revival of a traditional cheese produced in the area until 1939. It is a *semi-soft, mild flavoured round cheese*, made from the unpasteurised milk of the farm's Friesland flock, and matured for at least two months. *Soft cheeses and yoghurt* are produced seasonally.

Barac is available (wholesale) by mail order and is stocked by many of the good cheese shops countrywide. Personal callers are welcome, but please telephone first. Annan is 9 miles west of Gretna on the A75.

Biggings farmhouse Orkney cheese

*Biggings Farm, Stenness,
Orkney KW16 3EY
Tel. Stromness (0856) 850314*

OLIVE CHALMERS

Mrs Chalmers makes the traditional *full fat soft Orkney cheese,* in 4-pound rounds, which was at one time in danger of vanishing altogether. Olive Chalmers' own words best describe Orkney cheese and butter making: 'Cheese has been made in these islands since cheese began. Every farmhouse had a milking cow and the surplus milk was made into cheese and butter. The cheese was dried, then stored in the meal girnel. The butter, if any was in surplus, was salted in big earthenware jars to be used in winter. The habit died out over the years as folk got more affluent but it has gradually come back again owing to the tourist trade; no two people make cheese the same way.' But she is bitter that EEC milk quotas limit her output of cheese; she can only make enough to sell from the farm gate, and that is a long way to go for most personal callers. However, they are welcome, but should obviously telephone first. A car ferry runs from Scrabster, just north of Thurso, to Stromness on the mainland of Orkney, and Loch of Stenness is only a mile or two further north.

Boardhouse Mill bere, pease and oatmeal

*Boardhouse Mill, Birsay, Orkney
Tel. Birsay (085 672) 363*

FERGUS AND ELEANOR MORRISON

Boardhouse Mill is now the only working water-powered mill in Orkney and Shetland, the most northerly in Europe, and the only source of *beremeal. Bere* is an ancient barley, grown throughout northern Europe since the Iron Age, but now grown only on Orkney. After drying the grain in a peat- and chaff-fired kiln, it is then cleaned and passed slowly through three separate pairs of millstones. The flour thus produced has a high fibre and protein content, and makes delicious bannocks and biscuits, and can be mixed with wheat flour for bread-making or with oatmeal for porridge. The mill also produces *pease* and *oat meals,* and *100% wholewheat flour.* The Morrisons run the mill without help, 'Although daughters Sarah (10) and Tessa (5) show potential,' wrote Fergus – but are nevertheless rapidly developing a thriving business despite the remoteness of Boardhouse.

Biggings Farm
STENNESS · ORKNEY
FULL FAT SOFT
CHEESE
*
made with
FULL CREAM JERSEY MILK

SCOTLAND

'Frequently grain brought to the mill has been cut with a binder, stooked, stacked and threshed in a travelling mill.' Sales are through wholesalers: A Bain Wholesale, Commercial Road, Lerwick, Shetland; Sutherland Bros, Gowrie Place, Wick, Caithness; J & T Roger, Rosebank Mill, Cupar, Fife; Green City Wholefoods, 23 Fleming Street, Glasgow; J Meff & Co., Aberdeen. Contact any of these for advice on retail outlets. Mail order is available also, and personal callers are welcome from mid-May to mid-September, between 1–5p.m. except on Saturdays. Loch of Boardhouse is on the north-western tip of the Mainland of Arran.

Bonchester Cheese

Easter Weens Enterprises, Easter Weens, Bonchester Bridge, nr Hawick, Roxburghshire TD9 8JQ
Tel. Bonchester Bridge (0450 86) 635
JOHN AND CHRISTIAN CURTIS

Bonchester is a Coulommiers-type cheese, soft, with a natural rind, and when mature has a flavour approaching Camembert. It is made from the unpasteurised milk from the Easter Weens herd of pedigree Jersey cows. *Teviotdale* is a dales-type hard cheese made from the same milk, during the autumn. Farming methods are semi-organic – some fertilizer is used, but no sprays. Sales are via wholesalers and to personal callers, and the cheeses can be sent by mail order. There is a long list of stockists, which includes good 'serious' cheese shops like Wells Stores, as well as smaller shops doing their best to promote knowledge of British farmhouse cheeses – please telephone

John Curtis for further details. Easter Weens also has holiday lodges to let, so personal callers are very welcome, on a trusting arrangement: 'Help yourself from the fridge at the back door and leave money in the tin.' Parties of up to forty can be shown round the dairy in the evenings (7–7.30p.m. approx) in spring and early summer, by prior arrangement. Bonchester Bridge is on the A6088 8 miles south-west of Hawick.

Breckan Rabbits

Upper Breckan, Sanday, Orkney KW17 2AZ
Tel. Sanday (085 75) 421
WILLIAM SICHEL

William and Elizabeth Sichel started their *rabbit breeding* enterprise in 1982, with grant aid from the Highlands & Islands Development Board, and the Orkney Islands Council. The islanders of Sanday initially regarded the venture with some scepticism, as the islands are overrun with wild rabbits anyway, but the Sichels have proved that there is a market for this tender meat, low in fat and cholesterol. They sell to local shops and to a wholesaler in Kirkwall, and are expanding into Aberdeen and the Shetlands. Personal callers are welcome, by appointment, between 9a.m. and 9p.m.

Messrs Cockburn and Skelton, goats' produce

*Ledlewan Farm, Killearn,
Glasgow G63 9LL
Tel. Killearn (0360) 50344*
EWEN L COCKBURN

Fresh and *frozen goats' milk, yoghurt* in both *plain* and *fruit flavours* (the fruit is organically grown), *soft* and *hard cheeses* are all made here. Sales are via wholesalers S L Neil, Balmore Industrial Estate, Glentanar Road, Glasgow. Retail outlets include: Killearn Store, Main Street, Killearn, Glasgow and The Granary, 24 Busby Road, Clarkston, Glasgow. Visitors are welcome at any time. Ledlewan Farm is 1 mile from the A81, 7 miles north of Milngavie, north of Glasgow, and is signposted after you leave the main road.

Hebridean Oysters Ltd

*Pennyghael, Isle of Mull, Argyll
PA70 6HD
Tel. Pennyghael (068 14) 232*
IAIN MOODY

Iain Moody rather ruefully feels that the main interest the public may have in his enterprise is in Patch, the retired milk horse who pulls the cart which transports the oysters to the sorting shed, and who earned Mr Moody some publicity in 1985. But the real aim is to raise Pacific oysters in the exceptionally clear waters off the west coast of Oban. Scallops, mussels and native oysters are also available. 95% of the sales are door-to-door delivery by Securicor, and the remaining 5% to personal callers. Hotels which serve his oysters include The Lygon Arms, Broadway, Worcestershire, and Tarn End Hotel, Talkin, nr Brampton, Cumbria. Visitors are welcome throughout the year at low tide (please either check the tide times, or telephone beforehand). From the Oban to Mull ferry, take the road to Iona (A849). The oyster beds are two miles beyond Pennyghael, at Killunaig Farm on the shores of Loch Scridain.

Highland Fine Cheeses Ltd

*Blarliath, Tain, Ross & Cromarty
IV19 1LZ
Tel. Tain (0862) 2034 and 2734*
MR AND MRS E R STONE

Susannah Stone has revived two traditional regional cheeses – *Crowdie* (a moist cottage cheese, thought to be Scotland's oldest cheese), and *Caboc* (made to a secret family recipe) which is a wonderfully rich soft fat cheese rolled in toasted oatmeal, and the one most often exported to England. Interesting variations include *Crowdie and cream* (made with double cream), and *Hramsa* (cream Crowdie flavoured subtly with chopped wild garlic) – if you can buy this, try stuffing wild trout with some before baking them in the oven. There is also *Crowdie flavoured with garlic*, and *Galic* (Caboc flavoured with garlic and rolled in oats and nuts). Mrs Stone told me that they supply their unsalted Crowdie to hospitals and patients on kidney machines all over Britain, 'because, for some reason – possibly the old recipe and method of manufacture – it is very low in magnesium, sodium and other elements which are bad for those on certain types of diets.' Scottish wholesalers include Messrs Crowson & Son, East Kilbride, Strachclyde (035 52 25647), and Highland Larder, Inverness (0463 226410). Personal callers are welcome between 9.30a.m.–5p.m., Monday to Friday. Tain is on the A9, on the Dornoch Firth. 'Go north through High Street, turn right down Shore Road, and turn left, parallel to the Firth, and down track to the Blarliath (Gray Moor in the Gaelic).'

Islay Tablet – Scottish goats' milk confectionery

Great Glen Foods Ltd,
Old Ferry Road, North Ballachulish, nr Fort William, Inverness-shire PH33 6RZ
Tel. Onich (085 53) 277

DOUGLAS AND TRICIA LOCKE

Islay Tablet is *fudge* made from goats', rather than cows' milk, and named after 'taiblet', a traditional Scottish sweet. I would not have been able to tell the difference between this and ordinary fudge if I had not been told – very good, and ideal for allergy sufferers. The milk, from a herd of Anglo-Nubian goats, is equivalent in richness to Jersey cows' milk, and *ice cream* and a *soft cheese* are also made. Islay Tablet comes in fourteen flavours, including *10-year-old Islay malt whisky, kirsch, lemon and orange*. For details of wholesalers, please telephone. Islay Tablet can be supplied by mail order, and there is a factory shop, open 9a.m.–6p.m., Monday to Saturday, and on Sundays as well in the tourist season. Old Ferry Road is a slip road off the A82 on the north side of Ballachulish Bridge.

Lanark Blue ewes' milk cheese

H J Errington & Co., Ogscastle,
Carnwath, Lanarkshire ML11 8NE
Tel. Dunsyre 089 981 257

HUMPHREY ERRINGTON

Lanark Blue is a mould-ripened ewes' milk cheese made according to the recipe for Roquefort, and ripened in an environment of humidity and temperature identical to that found in the Roquefort Caves. The Erringtons began marketing the cheese in small amounts in May 1985, and by early 1986 Lanark Blue had made such a name for itself that it was featured on Derek Cooper's *Food Programme* on BBC Radio 4. This area of Lanarkshire had a large sheep's cheese production in the eighteenth century, and this link gave the name to the Erringtons' cheese. The milk is all from their own ewes, unpasteurised, but stringently tested for cleanliness in their own laboratory. So enormous has been the demand for the cheese that at the time of writing only retail shops in Edinburgh are supplied: Rowlands, Howe Street; Valvona & Crolla, Leith Walk; Herby's, Raeburn Place;

Gourmet's Delicatessen, Morningside; Victor Hugo, Marchmont. Distribution round the British Isles should soon be established, as well as farm shop and mail order sales. Please telephone for further details.

Loch Fyne Oysters Ltd

Ardkinglas Estate Office, Cairndow, Argyll
Tel. Cairndow (049 96) 264/217
JOHN NOBLE, ANDREW LANE

John Noble returned home to Ardkinglas to run the family estate in the mid-70s, after working in the wine trade. Remembering the oyster shells he and his cousin used to pick up from the loch shore, and pulverise for hen-grit during the War, he looked into the idea of oyster farming on Loch Fyne, with the help of Andrew Lane, a marine biologist working in the area. They now raise not only *Pacific*, or *gigas oysters*, but *langoustines*, *lobsters*, *spiny lobsters*, and *mussels*, in large seawater tanks. They also act as agents for two creel boats fishing in the Sound of Jura. Salmon is smoked here, and cured for Gravadlax – Springbank malt whisky is included in the cure. *Loch Fyne herring* are *kippered*, and marinated in various ways, including a *'sweet' marinade* with a tomato and wine vinegar base, and a *cream sherry marinade*. The *rollmop herrings* in sherry are a revelation to all those who thought that malt vinegar must be involved in the making of rollmops. Sales are mainly to restaurants by Securicor and rail. The Ardkinglas shop is at the head of the loch, open from April to October. Callers are welcome at other times too. Cairndow is at the head of Loch Fyne, on the A83.

Maclean's potatoes

Dornock Farm, Crieff, Perthshire
Tel. Crieff (0764) 2472
DONALD MACLEAN

Luckily for us all, Donald Maclean started collecting potatoes when he was a boy, while the rest of us were collecting much less useful things like matchboxes and marbles. Without his enthusiasm, which has created the largest private collection in the world (over 350 varieties), we would know nothing of the culinary delights of Catriona (long, purple-eyed, introduced in 1920), or Belle de Fontenay (Brittany's speciality). I have been buying seed potatoes from Donald Maclean for as many years as I've had a garden, experimenting yearly with such varieties, old and new, as Ninetyfold, Edzell Blue and Wilja, and finally discarding Pink Fir Apple in favour of Aura – worth digging up the lawn for. He supplies *naturally* grown seed potato varieties by parcel post for interested amateur growers, and educational use, rural schools and museum gardens, such as that at Quarry Bank Mill, Styal (see page 161). He acts as potato consultant to gourmet hotels, collaborates with cookery book writers and appears on television and on radio. He serves on the Fruit and Vegetable Committee of the Royal Horticultural Society, and has won Gold Medal Awards at all the major shows for his displays of 200–300 varieties at a time. As potato hero of the British Isles, I, and all his admirers, feel he should receive greater appreciation for his work against *banalisation*. If you want to experiment with special potatoes, send for his list (stamped addressed envelope, please) at the beginning of October. There is no mailing list – you must remember to do this every year. Be prepared to order early, especially if you want a tuber or two from the 'Museum Collection', and be prepared, too, to accept substitutes, which are carefully chosen. Personal callers are welcome by appointment. Crieff is on the A85 17 miles west of Perth.

Macsween's haggis

Macsween's of Edinburgh,
130 Bruntsfield Place, Edinburgh
Tel. 031 229 1216
JOHN ANGUS MACSWEEN

This book would not be complete without one haggis-maker, and although many butchers in Scotland and the North of England make their own, Macsween's have been famous for their *haggis* for thirty years or more, and the quality is consistently high. I never serve haggis to anyone who categorically hates offal, since that is the flavour that haggis-lovers love, and offal-loathers loathe, although it is surprising what a dram of single malt whisky will do when drunk with it. John MacSween told me of their new venture – *vegetarian haggis*, made with nuts, mushrooms and lentils. He says 'it is already a winner with the vegi brigade' and I'm sure it is, but I can imagine Burns would have raised an eyebrow. MacSween's are also notable for other Scottish *charcuterie* – *Mealy Pudding*, *Mutton Pies* and *Black Pudding*. All can be supplied by mail order, thanks to vacuum packaging. The retail outlet list is very long; look in any good grocer's, or food hall, for MacSween's red tartan packing. The shop in Bruntsfield Place is open 7a.m.–5.30p.m. every weekday, but closes at 1p.m. on Wednesdays and 4.30p.m. on Saturdays.

A TRUE TASTE OF SCOTLAND

Priorwood Orchard

Priorwood Gardens, Melrose,
Roxburghshire
Tel. Melrose (089 682) 2493
PRISCILLA CAMPBELL

Lady Thomson has created an *Apple Walk* at Priorwood Orchard for the National Trust of Scotland, on land near Melrose Abbey, where the monks grew apples 700 years ago. It introduces visitors to more than forty British varieties ranging in date from those grown by the Romans in Britain, through 'The Golden Age' of the sixteenth to eighteenth centuries, to the present day. The modern varieties come as something of a shock – here are apples we never get the chance to see, let alone eat, so narrow is the range offered to us by the large commercial growers. The reason is not always clear: growing at Priorwood is the result of a cross between the Cox and the very ancient Court Pendu Plat, said to outcrop the Cox by fifty per cent, and to have an even more aromatic flavour than its delicious parent – surely a bestseller? Also here in this lovely orchard is Flower of Kent, reputed to be the apple which Sir Isaac Newton watched falling from a tree in his mother's garden in 1666, and Poma Costard, dated 1292, which gave costermongers their name. All these apples, rare and not so rare, prosper in the rich soil and sheltered conditions at Priorwood, and their heavy crops are turned into jams, jellies and chutneys, to be sold through the National Trust shop here. As for the apples themselves? 'We do not produce enough for wider distribution, nor do we have staff to pack up the products for postage, but we certainly are anxious to encourage visitors to our orchard and to buy personally,' Lady Thomson told me. The orchard contains other fruit trees – venerable pears, plums, gages, damsons, and a medlar. Priorwood Gardens and Orchard are open from April to Christmas, 10a.m.–6p.m. on weekdays, 1.30–6p.m. on Sundays. The best time to see the orchard is in the fruit season – July to Christmas. Melrose is 40 miles south of Edinburgh and 6 miles south-east of Galashiels, on the A6091.

Russell's farmhouse Orkney cheese

Breck & Myers, Shapinsay, Orkney
Tel. Kirkwall (0856) 71272

HUGH RUSSELL

Mrs Russell has made cheese all her long life, and her letter to me was full of the pleasures (and hard work) of cheesemaking on Shapinsay, which despite a population of 350, still manages to make 'quite a lot of cheese'. 'We have fifty-eight breeding cows and fifty year-olds and meantime we have got twenty-three calves but could have more by morning. We have about eight Friesians for milking and they are lovely. The grass up here in summer is green and lovely and the cheeses are put out in a shed to dry in the lovely fresh air.' Any cheese made under such idyllic conditions must be good, and this is the farmhouse Orkney which the Rances sell at Wells Stores. But Mrs Russell feels that while the future for the cheese is good, she and her husband Hugh are 'getting older, and hardly able to carry on with it', this despite their healthy diet of beremeal bannocks and good home-made butter and cheese, which enables them to go on working, Mrs

Russell, Brecks, Shapinsay, medium fat, Cheese.

Russell says, from 6a.m.–10p.m. in summer. We must hope that the Russells' daughter will carry on the cheesemaking. Meanwhile, personal callers are welcome 'anytime'. A few cheeses are posted to England (look for them in good cheese shops, marked 'Russell, Brecks, Shapinsay' on the handwritten label), and can be found in Flett's the Butcher, Stromness, Orkney.

St Michael's goats' dairy produce

St Michael's, Dryfesdale, Lockerbie, Dumfries-shire DG11 2RH
Tel. Lockerbie (057 62) 3386
KAY WAKEFIELD-RICHMOND

Milk, yoghurt, and a *Coulommiers* and a *semi-hard cheese* are all produced from Kay Richmond's herd of dairy goats. She is secretary of the Dumfries & Galloway Goatkeepers' Association, and is particularly fussy about dairy hygiene. She can also 'dowse allergies in a few minutes', and has therefore produced an alternative diet sheet for allergics. Sales are mainly by local delivery, and to personal callers, who are welcome at any time. St Michael's is 1½ miles out of Lockerbie on the B723 Boreland road.

SMOKED AND CURED FISH

One of Scotland's finest products is smoked and cured fish, whether it is smoked salmon, Loch Fyne kippers, or Finnan haddock. I found it very difficult to decide what was the best of any of them; one person liked a nationally famous brand, another found it dull, and so on; I had the same problem with kipper tastings. So I list several producers of all three – the only proviso was that none should use artificial colouring.

Cromack smoked mackerel, kippers

Cromack Ltd,
Bath Street, Fraserburgh, Aberdeenshire
Tel. Fraserburgh (0346) 27850
PETER DUTHIE

Locally landed fish are hand-filleted here and smoked over hardwood chips. Fish are dyed *only* to customers' requests, and no additives are used. Their *natural hot smoked mackerel* is very good indeed, and they are hoping to be able to persuade all their customers to do without dyes altogether, trusting that present media coverage on the disadvantages of dyeing will prevail. A new addition to their range is *Deli-Mack* – rolled fillets of mackerel with garlic and herbs, or with spices. They supply wholesale only, and their retail outlets include: Ark Fisheries, 51/52 Cliffe High Street, Lewes, East Sussex; Monks Seafoods, 31 Leys Avenue, Letchworth, Hertfordshire; B & A Roome, 43 Sadler Gate, Derby; D Woracker, High Street, Ryde, Isle of Wight, and many more. Personal callers are welcome, hours are '8 till late Monday to Saturday' or they can be contacted at home (telephone 03467 696).

Inverawe smoked salmon and trout

Inverawe Smokehouses, Inverawe House, Taynuilt, Argyll PA35 1HU
Tel. Taynuilt (086 62) 446
ROBERT CAMPBELL-PRESTON

Smoked Loch Etive trout is the speciality here; treated in the same way as salmon, these are large locally grown trout, about 1½lbs to a side. A good mail order service is available, to the USA as well as nationally in the UK, and there are retail and wholesale sales. Personal callers are welcome every day of the year between 9a.m.–6.30p.m., except at Christmas and the New Year. The Smokehouse is off the main A85 Glasgow to Oban road on Loch Etive, just north-east of Bridge of Aire. Their smoked venison is delicious, too.

Mermaid peat-smoked salmon

Mermaid Fish Supplies,
Clachan, North Uist, Outer Hebrides PA82 5ET
Tel. Lochport (087 64) 209
MR AND MRS GEORGE JACKSON

George Jackson 'found his niche and stopped to enjoy it' on North Uist in 1969 after three years of working his way around the world. Now he and his wife happily produce the most delicious peat-smoked salmon (one of my favourites). Peat smoking is very difficult, and took the Jacksons some time to master, until what seemed like a mistake turned out to be the best method. Sales are by mail order, retail, and 'we are always open to suggestions or requests – we do our own marketing'. Personal callers are welcome, usually 8a.m.–6p.m., but often until 10p.m., six days a week – closed on Sundays.

Mill Smokehouse smoked trout and salmon

Cessintully Mill, Thornhill,
Stirlingshire FK8 3QE
Tel. Thornhill (078 685) 348
MR AND MRS B C ROUTLEDGE

Another of my favourites – salmon and trout smoked over sawdust and chips from the local cooperage. The coopers rebuild American bourbon whisky barrels for storing Scotch whisky, and the flavour of bourbon is distinct but subtle. Salmon is smoked for local fishermen too. Sales are by mail order, to personal callers, and by delivery to a few local restaurants. Mrs Routledge has a market trailer and sells at Kildean Mart, Stirling, every Thursday from 9a.m.–3p.m. all year round. She also supplies Mrs Juliet Fellick, 18 Manor Close, Felpham, Bognor Regis, West Sussex (Tel. 0243 876138), who sells additive-free meat and fish. Callers to the smokehouse should telephone first, please. Thornhill is on the A76 14 miles north of Dumfries.

Pinneys smoked salmon

Pinneys of Scotland Ltd,
Brydekirk, Annan, Dumfries-shire
DG12 5LP
Tel. Ecclefechan (057 63) 401/8

DAVID STAPLETON

Pinneys are one of the largest salmon smokers in the country, and have a devoted following. They supply Waitrose, Marks & Spencer, Tesco, Fortnum & Mason, Harrods, Partridge's of Sloane Street, London SW1 and Leatham's Larder (see page 75) as well as outlets in France, Italy, Hong Kong and the USA. There is a mail order service for private customers, and a shop on the premises, open 9a.m.–5p.m., Monday to Friday, where prices are 5 per cent below the mail order prices. To find the shop and smokehouse, take the Eaglesfield turning from the A74 north of Gretna, and follow signs to Brydekirk (about 3 miles). Pinneys is just before Brydekirk on the left, and is signposted.

Ritchie's of Rothesay – Loch Fyne kippers, Finnan haddock

37 Watergate, Rothesay,
Isle of Bute
PA20 9AD
Tel. Rothesay (0700) 3012

NEIL RITCHIE

Ritchie's produce authentic 'bland cured' smoked wild Scotch salmon to a secret recipe; Finnan haddock ('haddies', whole smoked haddock, split down the belly); Loch Fyne kippers – all without additives or colouring. Sales are via mail order for the kippers and smoked salmon, wholesale for all the products, and at their shop in Rothesay, which is open from 8.30a.m.–5p.m. from Monday to Saturday. On arrival at Rothesay Pier, the shop is five minutes' walk up Watergate, straight ahead.

Scots Caught Seafoods Ltd – Arbroath Smokies

Lochside, Elliot, Arbroath, Angus
Tel. Arbroath (0241) 79791

ALAN AND ANNE SPENCE

Arbroath Smokies are whole smoked haddock, usually seen tied together in pairs. The Spences also produce Finnan haddock, smoked salmon, trout and Golden Fillets (skinned haddock smoked over whisky barrel chips). No dyes or additives are used.

Spinks smoked salmon and smokies

R R *Spink & Sons,*
35 Seagate, Arbroath, Angus DD11 1BZ
Tel. Arbroath (0241) 72023

R R SPINK JNR.

Spinks is an old-established family firm, by appointment to HRH The Queen Mother. Their salmon is cured traditionally, and in Drambuie; the Smokies are cured in the traditional way. No dyes or additives are used. Sales are mail order, through wholesalers, and retail through their own shop, open from 9a.m.–5.30p.m., Monday to Saturday.

Summer Isles smoked wild salmon

Summer Isles Foods Ltd,
The Smokehouse, Achiltibuie, Ullapool, Ross-shire IV26 2YG
Tel. Achiltibuie (085 482) 353

KEITH DUNBAR

Summer Isles' juniper smoked salmon has a very faintly medicinal flavour which we liked very much; the smoked haddock and kippers are also good. They also do a range of smoked meats – venison, Highland beef, mutton, and beer-cured hams. Their distribution is via their own company, Highland Larder, which supplies hotels, restaurants and shops with a wide range of Highland specialities – for further details telephone Keith Dunbar. Retail outlets in the Highland area include: Clifton Coffee House, Tyndrum; Peter MacLennon & Co., Fort William, Argyll; Rhinds Supermarket, Invergordon, Ross & Cromarty; Geo. Menzie, Auchterarder, Perthshire. The Smokehouse is north of Achiltibuie, at Altandhu. In Achiltibuie, turn right at the junction by Achnahaird Bay and follow the road past the campsite entrance and over the hill to Altandhu.

Sales are by mail order, through wholesale, for export, and to personal callers 9a.m.–5p.m., Monday to Friday.

BY APPOINTMENT TO
HER MAJESTY QUEEN ELIZABETH
THE QUEEN MOTHER
FISHMONGERS

R. R. SPINK & SONS
35, SEAGATE, ARBROATH, SCOTLAND

SPECIALIST CURERS SINCE 1915

Walkers shortbread

*Walkers Shortbread Ltd,
Strathspey Bakery, Aberlour,
Grampian AB3 9PB
Tel. Aberlour (034 05) 555*

JAMES N WALKER (SALES AND MARKETING)

I also have to include a shortbread baker in this book, and Walkers are without doubt the best, as well as one of the few still completely independent bakers, owned and run by the three grandchildren of the founder. This is real butter shortbread – the flavour is excellent – and they do an interesting range of products on the shortbread theme; *Highlander* is hand-made and rolled in demerara sugar, and there are *Petticoat Tails, Chocolate-Chip Shortbread*, and a *Wholemeal Shortbread* for the fibre-conscious. There is a range of Scottish biscuits, including the perfect accompaniment to Atholl Brose (that 'giant's drink' of cream, honey, whisky and oatmeal) – *Oatmeal and Honey Biscuits*, fruit cakes – *Scotch Bun* and *Dundee Cake*, and *oatcakes*. No artificial colourings, flavourings or additives are used in any of their products. Distribution is very wide, to good food shops nationally and internationally, and also through their own shop at 99 High Street, Aberlour, open 8a.m.–5p.m., Monday to Saturday.

Scottish Baking At It's Best

Walkers
pure butter
shortbread

FINGERS · PETTICOAT TAILS · HIGHLANDER

oatcakes
FINE AND HIGHLAND [2 VARIETIES]
Made in the Scottish Highlands

USEFUL ORGANISATIONS

The British Bee Keepers Association
National Agricultural Centre
Stoneleigh, Kenilworth
Warwickshire

British Deer Farmers Association
Cluanie
Teanassie by Beauly
Inverness-shire

British Goat Society
Rougham
Bury St Edmunds
Suffolk IP30 9LJ

The British Sheep Dairying Association
Wield Wood
Alresford
Hampshire SO24 9RU

Cheddar Farmhouse Cheese Federation
(also Lancashire and Cheshire cheese)
c/o S Thorpe
Crampway Ltd
Glastonbury
Wells
Somerset

Devon Fare Ltd
Symonds
Dunsford
Exeter
Devon EX6 7DR

Farm Holiday Bureau (see British Bee Keepers Association)

Farm Shop and Pick Your Own Association
Hunger Lane
Mugginton
Derby DE6 4PL

Farmhouse Cidermakers' Association
Burrow Hill
Kingsbury Episcopi
Martock
Somerset

Goat Producers' Association
c/o A G R I
Church Lane
Shinfield
Reading
Berkshire RG2 9AQ

Guild of Conservation Food Producers
Bedford Silo
Mile Road
Bedford MK42 9TB

Home Farm Magazine
Broad Leys Publishing Co
Widdington
Saffron Walden
Essex CB11 3SP

National Federation of Women's Institutes
– Market Department
39 Eccleston Street
London SW1W 9NT

The Real Meat Co. Ltd
East Hill Farm
Heytesbury
Warminster
Wiltshire BA12 0HR

Traditional Farm Fresh Turkey Association
Brecon
Chyngton Road
Seaford
East Sussex BN25 4HH

The Welsh Cookery Centre
Llangoedmor
Cardigan
Dyfed SA43 2LE

The South-West

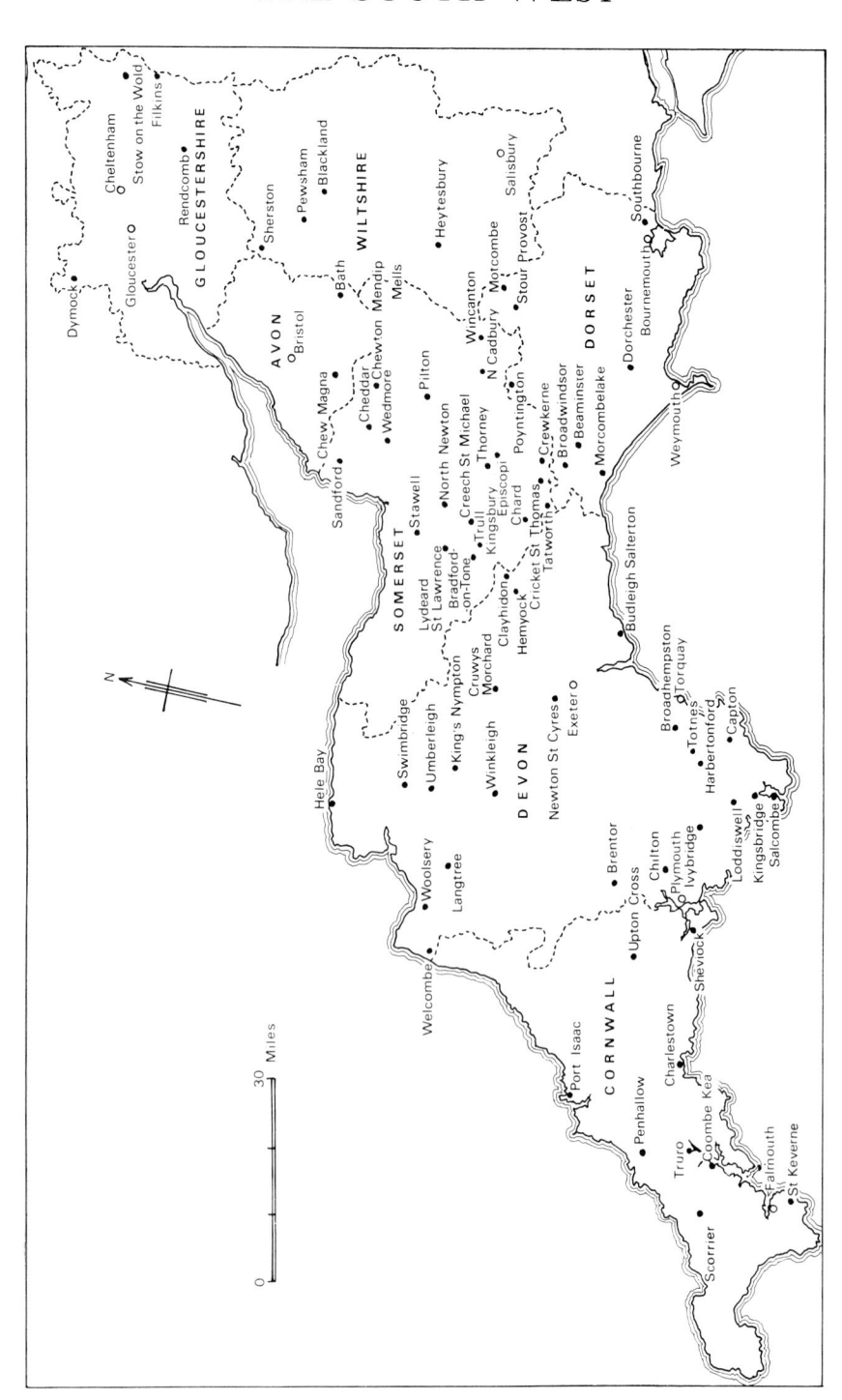

Southern England

London and the South-East

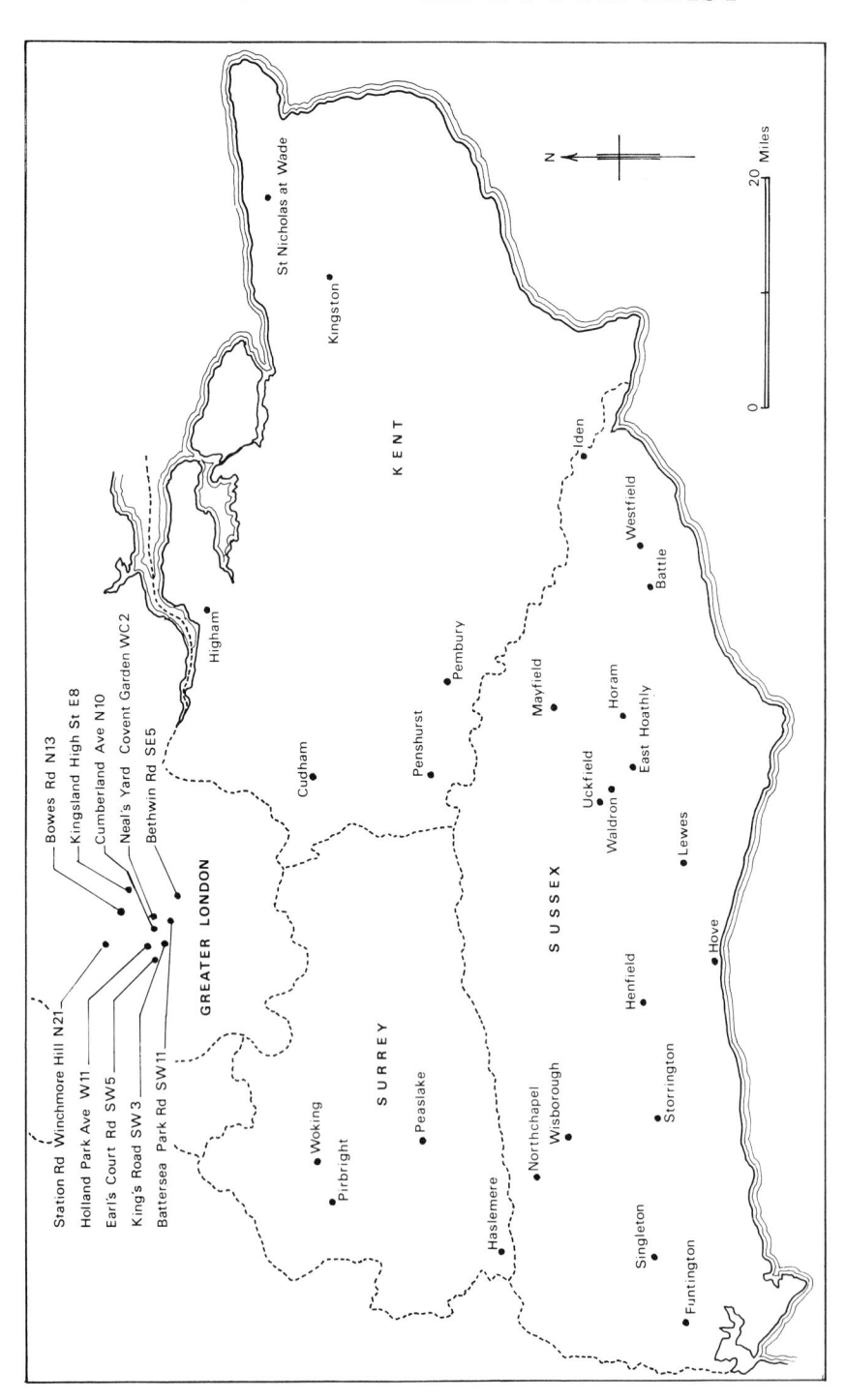

WALES

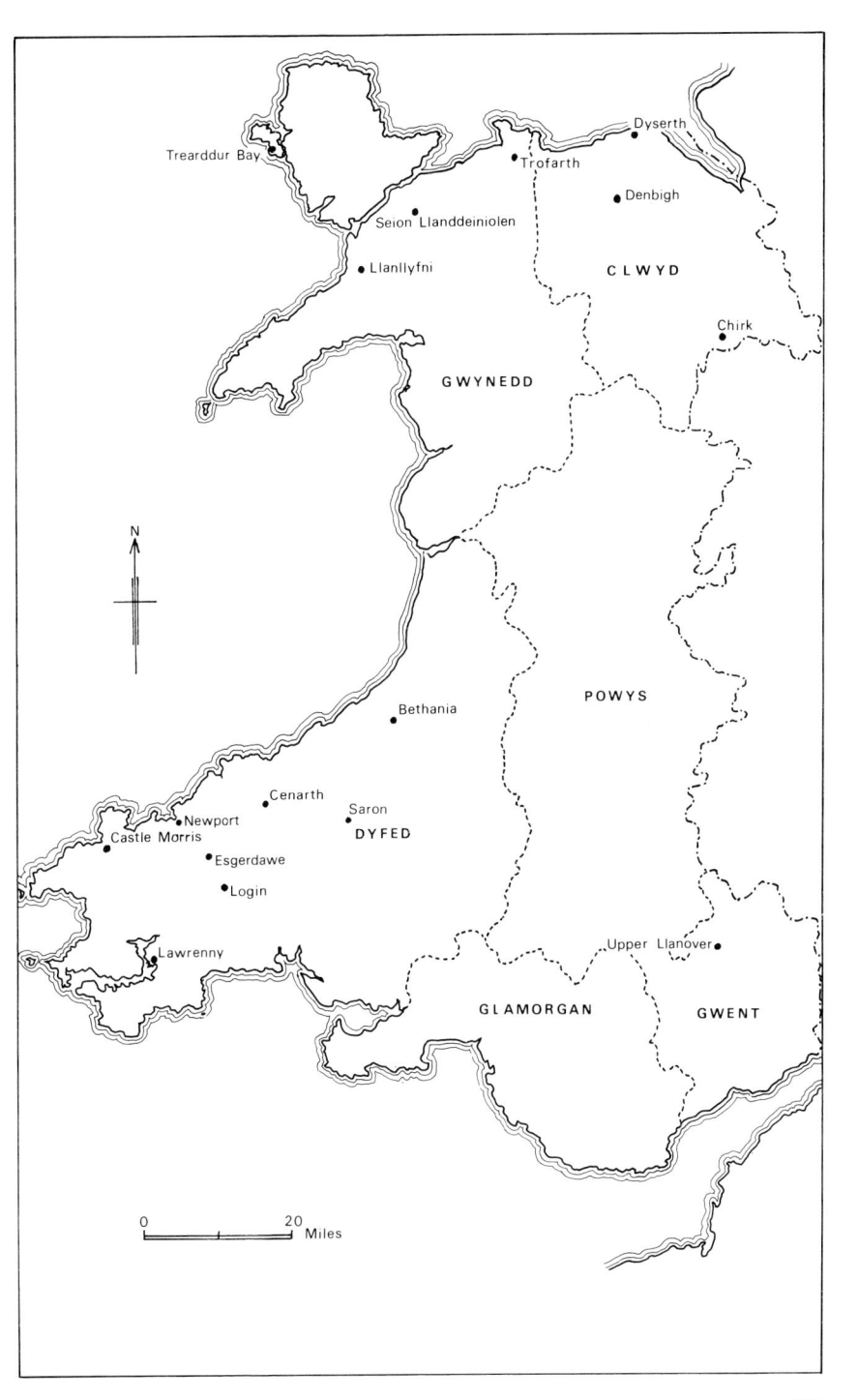

The West Midlands

THE EAST MIDLANDS

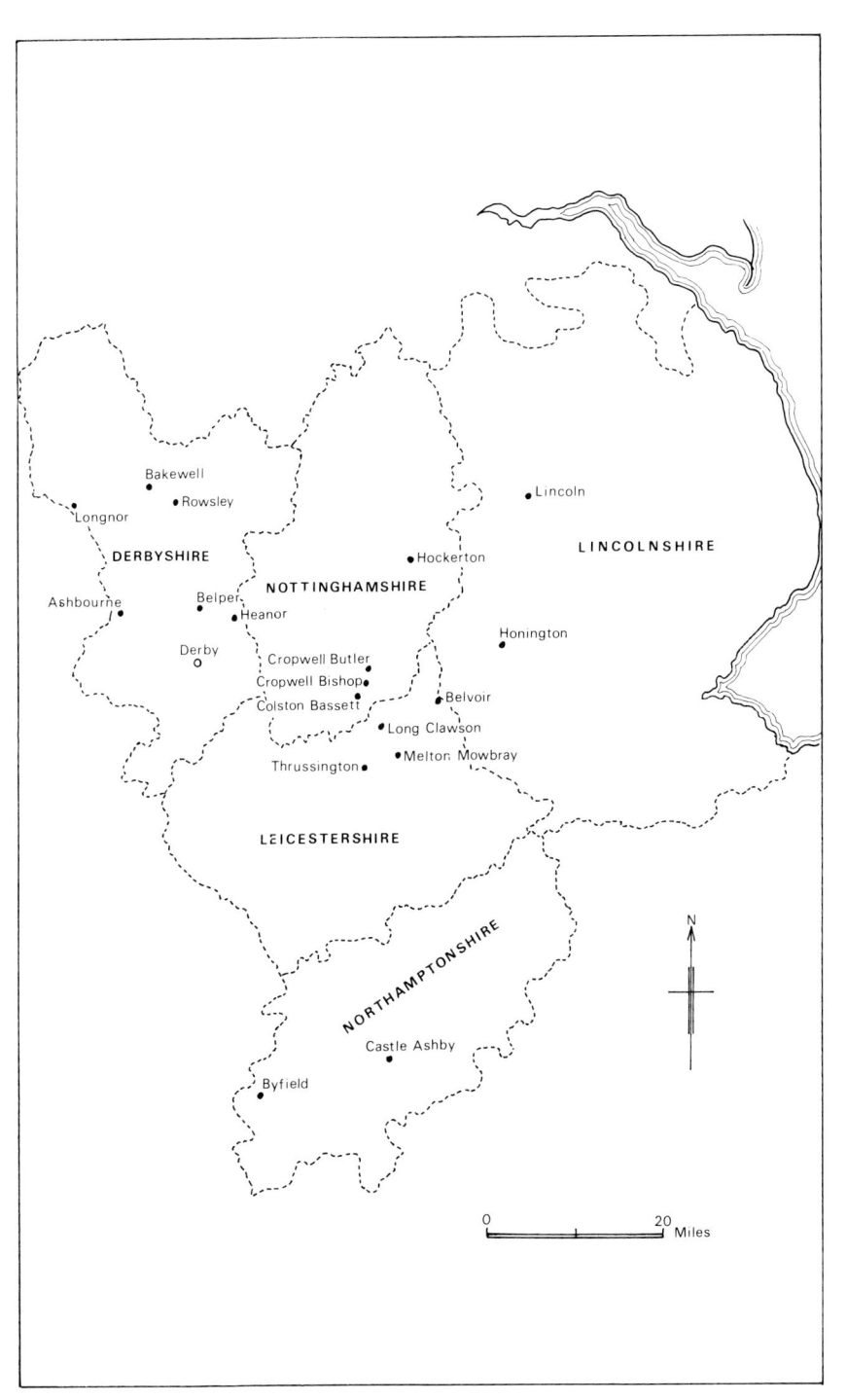

Eastern England

The North-West

The North-East

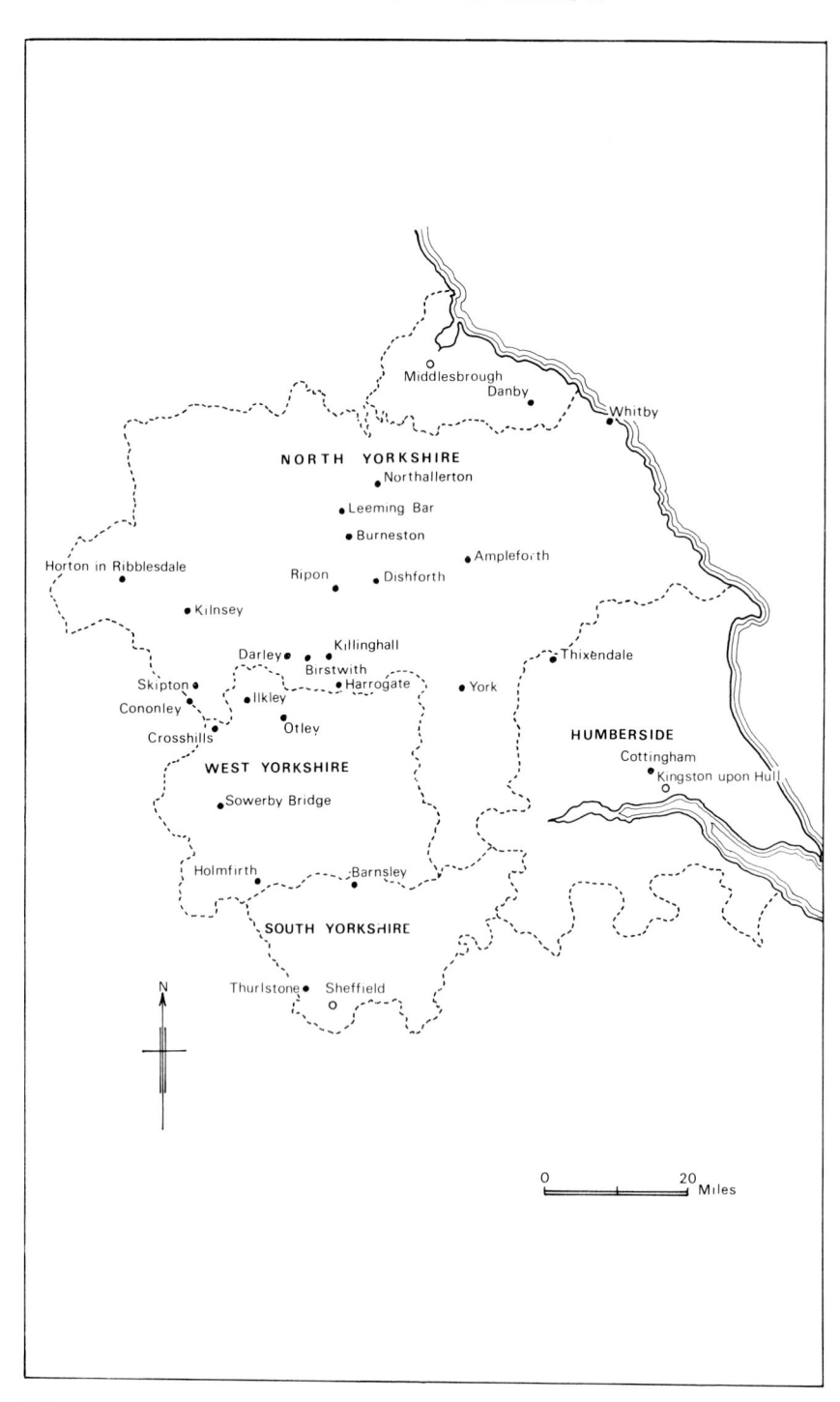

NORTHERN ENGLAND

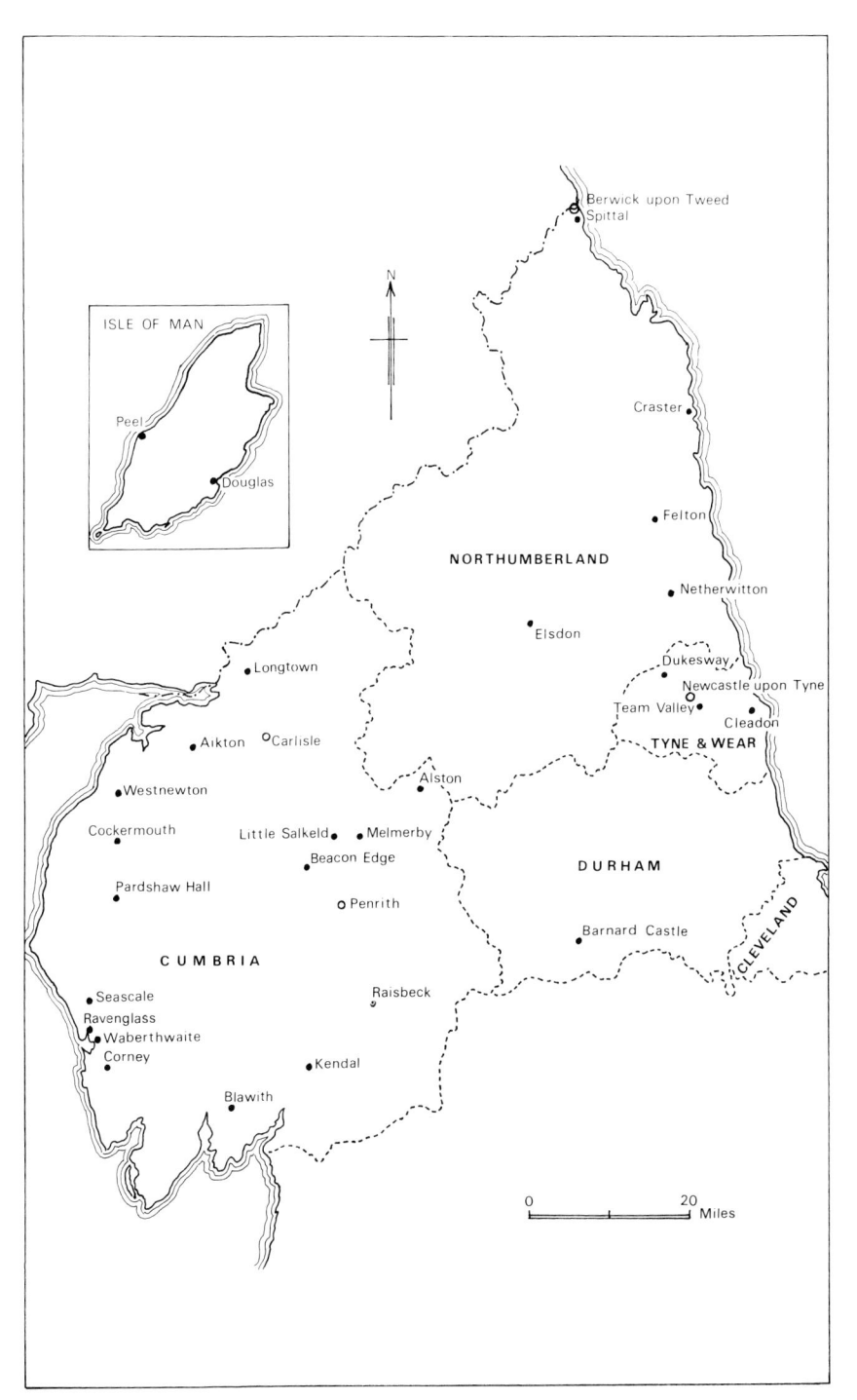

SCOTLAND

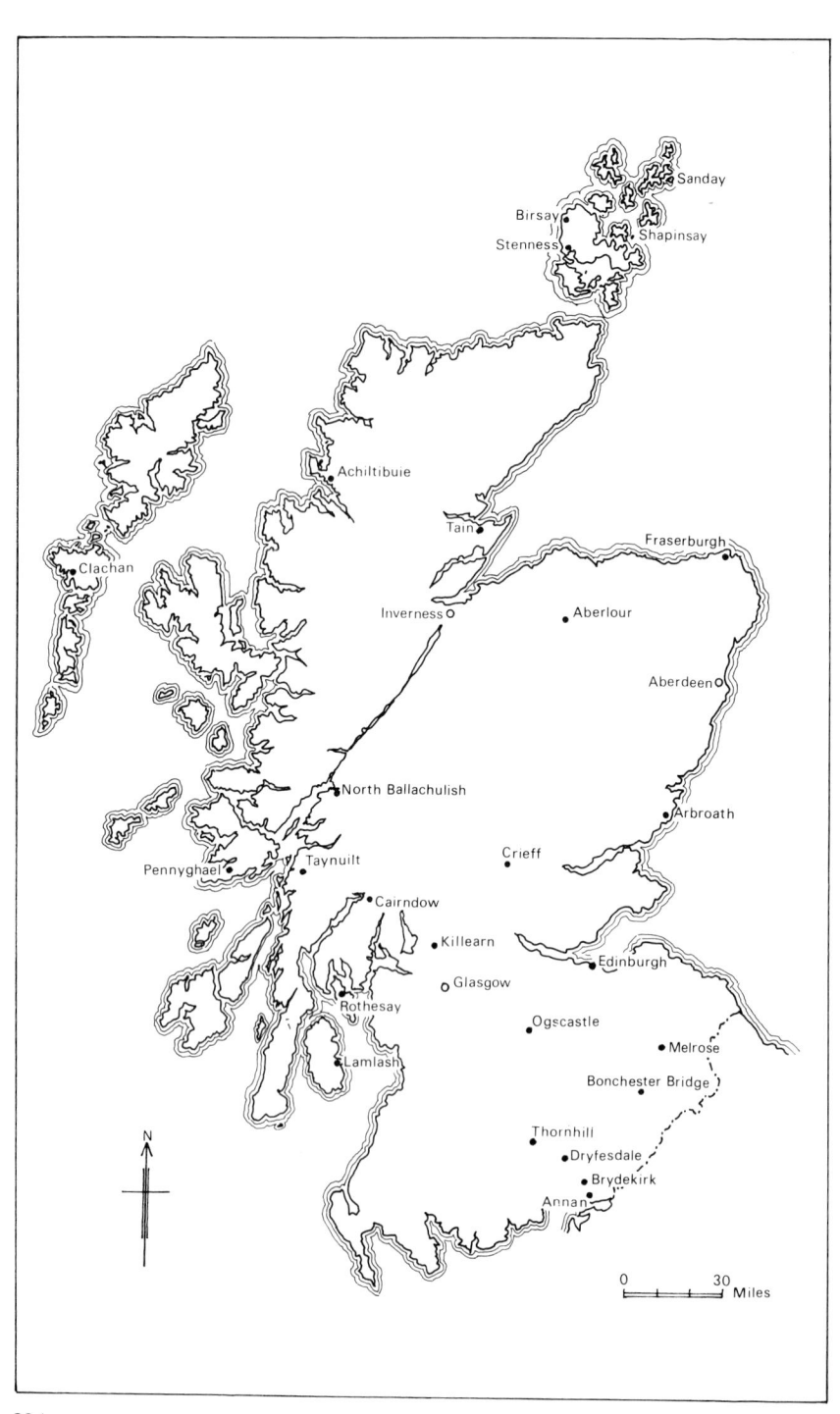

SHOPS

The following shops stock good regional produce. Those marked * are wholesalers.

BB's Deli, Mumbles, Swansea, Glamorgan, WALES
de Blank, Justin, 42 Elizabeth Street, LONDON SW1
Booth, E H, & Co, Victoria Street, Windermere, CUMBRIA
Bwyd-y-Byd, Station Road, Crymych, Dyfed, WALES

Captain Cook, Pembroke Dock, Dyfed, WALES
Chatsworth Farm Shop, Pilsley, nr Bakewell, DERBYSHIRE
Cheddar Gorge, Compton Street, Ashbourne, DERBYSHIRE
The Cheese Board, Twickenham, MIDDX
The Cheese Shop, 17 Kensington Gardens, Brighton, EAST SUSSEX
The Cheese Shop, 74 Beccles Road, Oulton Broad, SUFFOLK
The Cheese Store, Grove Street, Wilmslow, CHESHIRE
The Cheeseboard, 1 Commercial Street, Harrogate, YORKS.
The Cheesery, Regent Road, Altrincham, CHESHIRE
Cookery Nook, Church Street, Pershore, WORCS
Country Delicacies, Tarporley, CHESHIRE
Country Fayre, 83 Station Road, Redcar, CLEVELAND
*Crowson & Son, East Kilbride, Strathclyde, SCOTLAND
Curds & Whey, The Market, Swansea, Glamorgan, WALES

Dartington Farm Food Shop, Cider Press Centre, Dartington, Totnes, DEVON
*Duff & Trotter, 47 Bow Lane, LONDON EC4 and 13–15 Leadenhall Market, LONDON EC3

Edmond's Delicatessen, 33 Brentgovel Street, Bury St Edmunds, SUFFOLK
Electra's Delicatessen, 30 Westgate, Guisborough, CLEVELAND

Fruit & Spice Delicatessen, Shop No 2, 57 High Street, Yatton, AVON

Gibbs Food & Wine Shop, St Davids, Pembrokeshire, WALES

Gibson's Restaurant, 8 Romilly Crescent, Canton, Cardiff, WALES
Gloucesters Cheese & Wholefoods, 5 New Market, Otley, YORKS
Peter Gott, Sillfield Farm, Kendal, CUMBRIA
The Gourmet, School Hill, Lewes, EAST SUSSEX
J & J Graham, Market Street, Penrith, CUMBRIA
Green Door, 89 East Street, Hereford, HEREFORD & WORCS
The Guildford Cheese Shop, Guildford, SURREY

*Harvey & Brockless, 17–23 Linford Street, LONDON SW8
Hay Wholefoods, Hay-on-Wye, HEREFORD & WORCS
*Highland Larder, Inverness, SCOTLAND
Hobbs, South Audley Street, LONDON W1
Hobson's Choice, Queen Street, Bottesford, NOTTS
Humble Pie, Market Place, Burnham Market, NORFOLK

James, 188 Beckenham High Street, Beckenham, GREATER LONDON
Julia's Cook Shop, Cathedral Road, Cardiff, WALES

J O King, Helmsley, N YORKS

*J & P Langman Ltd, Perrots Brook Farm, Cirencester, GLOS
Larners, Market Place, Holt, NORFOLK
Lidgate's Kitchen, 110 Holland Park Avenue, LONDON W11
Locke's Delicatessen, Jewry Street, Winchester, HANTS

*Mendip Foods Ltd, Keward Farm, Glastonbury Road, Wells, SOMERSET
*Mollington Farm Cheese Co Ltd, Grange Farm, Mollington, CHESHIRE
Moor Cheeses, 14 Main Avenue, Moor Park, Northwood, MIDDX

Naturally British, 13 New Row, Covent Garden, LONDON WC2
Neal's Yard Dairy, Covent Garden, LONDON WC2

The Organic Shop, Neal's Yard, Covent Garden, LONDON WC2

Partners, 27 Horsemarket, Barnard Castle, CO. DURHAM
Partridges, 132 Sloane Street, LONDON SW1
Paxton & Whitfield, 93 Jermyn Street, LONDON SW1
*Porter, Alan, Bar Lane, Roecliffe, Boroughbridge, YORKS

The Real Cheese Shop, High Street, Barnes, LONDON SW13
Rosslyn Delicatessen, 56 Rosslyn Hill, LONDON NW5

Saltmarsh & Druce, Market Square, Witney, OXON
Shepherd's Purse, Church Street, Whitby, N YORKS
*Sullivan, Vin, 4 Frogmore Street, Abergavenny, Gwent, WALES

Taste Bud, High Street, Totnes, DEVON
Thoughts of Food, 60 Wellby Street, Grantham, LINCS

Valvona & Crolla, 19 Elm Row, Edinburgh, SCOTLAND

Wells Stores, Streatley-on-Thames, Reading, BERKS
With Relish, 1 Lacy Road, LONDON SW15

MAIL ORDER INDEX

The following offer a full or partial mail order service. For further details, see the main entry.

Adsdean Farm (hormone-free meat)   84
Alston Cheese   192
Arran Provisions (preserves)   210
Ashdown Smokers   192
Bakewell Pudding   129
Barac Cheese   210
Beamer Dairy Goats   179
Betty's Café Tea Rooms   177
Boardhouse Mill   211
Bonchester Cheese   212
Brown & Forrest (smoked eel)   38
Budleigh Salterton Pâté   24
Burrow Hill (cider mulling spices)   39
Cenarth Smokery   94
Clearwater Smoked Salmon   68
Cornish Smoked Fish   21
Culham Harvest Foods   66
The Curry Club   79
A W Curtis & Sons (Lincolnshire chine)   135
Dart Valley Foods (preserves)   27
Devon Fare   29, 30, 35, 223

235

PRODUCT INDEX

Devon Herbs 27
Dunkerton's Cider 104
Emmett's Stores (hams & bacon) 146
Fieldfare Mustard 96
Mary Ford Cake Artistry Centre 49
Gordon's Mustard 79
Head Mill Trout Farm 29
Heal Farm (pork products) 30
Hebridean Oysters 213
Highland Larder 221
Hockwold Manor (Norfolk Black turkeys) 155
Islay Tablet (goats' milk fudge) 214
Inverawe Smoked Foods 219
Lanark Blue cheese 214
Leatham's Larder 75
Levens Farm Products 180
Lighthorne Associates (Herbs, wholesale) 110
Little Acorn (ewes' milk products) 97
Ruth Liversedge (chocolates) 63
Llangloffan Cheese 98
Lune Smoked Foods 170
Lynher Valley Dairy 21–2
Donald Maclean (seed potatoes) 215
Macsweens (haggis) 216
Marianglas (goats' cheese) 99
Mermaid Smoked Salmon 219
Mill Smokehouse 219
Millers Damsel (Wheat Wafers) 64
Minola Smoked Foods 57
Moores' Dorset Knobs 50
Moorland Bacon 130
Murray's Meat 33
A R Paske & Co (seakale plants) 148
Michael Paske Farms (fresh asparagus) 136
Peartree Pork Products 144
Phillips Smoked Salmon 65
Pinneys Smoked Salmon 220
Ritchies of Rothesay (smoked salmon) 220
Meg Rivers (cakes) 68
Rock's Country Wines 67
A E Rodda & Son (clotted cream) 22
Rachel Roskilly (clotted cream) 23
Salcombe Smokers 35
Scots Caught Seafoods (Arbroath Smokies) 220
Scotwild Smoked Salmon 201
Sheppy's Cider 46
Slack's Cumberland ham 198
Spinks Smoked Salmon 221
Stapleton Farm (dairy products) 35
R Stiff & Sons (bacon) 149
Stoke Lacy Herb Garden 109
Sussex Smokehouse 89
Thornton's Chocolates 131

Threeshires Dairy 125
The Village Bakery 199
Welcombe Country Fayre (herbs) 36
Westmorland Smoked Foods 173
Bar Woodall (parma-style hams) 200
Woodnutts Ltd (chocolate couverture) 90

PRODUCT INDEX

Bakery & Cereal Products
Ashworth & Stannard, Norwich, Norfolk 156
Bakewell Pudding Shop, Bakewell, Derbyshire 129
W W Bellamy, Salford, Greater Manchester 163
Betty's Café Tea Rooms, Harrogate, Ilkley, Northallerton and York, Yorks 177
Boardhouse Mill, Birsay, Orkney 211
Botton Bakery, Danby, N Yorks 178
Caudwell's Mill, Rowsley, Matlock, Derbyshire 129
Charlecote Mill, Hampton Lucy, Warwick, Warks 110
Cheshire Wholefoods Ltd, Chester 162
Christy's Wholemeal, Grange Farm, Hockerton, Notts 133
Cobb & Co, Bath, Avon 41
Cressage Bakery, Cressage, Shropshire 114
Crowdy Mill, Harbertonford, Totnes, Devon 26
J Durig, Hale, Altrincham, Cheshire 164
Fitzbillies, Cambridge 150
Mary Ford Cakes, Southbourne, Bournemouth, Dorset 49
Furniss & Co, Truro, Cornwall 21
Green Dragon Bakery, Ashbourne, Derbyshire 130
Hele Mill, Hele Bay, Ilfracombe, Devon 31
Hoskens' Mill, Blacklands, Calne, Wilts 53
'Elizabeth King', Cropwell Butler, Notts 134
The Krusty Loaf, Market Drayton, Shropshire 116
Lurgashall Mill, Weald & Downland Museum, Singleton, W. Sussex 87
The Mill Oven, Storrington, W. Sussex 88
Millers Damsel, Newbridge, Yarmouth, Isle of Wight 64

S Moores, Morcombelake, Bridport, Dorset 50
Muncaster Mill, Ravenglass, Cumbria 196
North Staffordshire Oatcakes, Newcastle under Lyme, Staffs 120
Over Mill, Over, nr St Ives, Cambs 150
'Pimhill' Flour, Harmer Hill, Shrewsbury, Shropshire 117
Raywell Flours, Raywell, Cottingham, E Yorks 186
Meg Rivers, Lower Brailes, Banbury, Oxon 68
St Nicholas Court Farms Ltd, nr Birchington, Kent 83
Shaws Biscuits Ltd, Team Valley Trading Estate, Gateshead, Tyne & Wear 204
Springhill Farm Foods Ltd, Aylesbury Bucks 70
Stanleys Crumpets, Barnoldswick, Lancs 171
Stapleton Farm, Langtree, nr Torrington, Devon 35
The Village Bakery, Melmerby, Penrith, Cumbria 199
Matthew Walker (Derby) Ltd, Heanor, Derby 132
Walkers Shortbread, Aberlour on Spey, Grampian 222
The Watermill, Little Salkeld, Penrith, Cumbria 199
G Weinholt, Alderley Edge, Cheshire 167
Yates & Son, Low Petergate, York 187

Beverages
Aspall Cyder, Stowmarket, Suffolk 144
Belvoir Fruit Farms Ltd, Grantham, Lincs 135
Burrow Hill Cider, Kingsbury Episcopi, Martock, Somerset 39
Cavendish Manor Vineyards, Cavendish, Sudbury, Suffolk 145
Copella Fruit Juices, Boxford, Suffolk 146
Cornish Cider Co, Coombe Kea, Truro, Cornwall 20
Cornish Scrumpy Co, St Dennis, nr St Austell, Cornwall 20
Decantae Spring Water, Trofarth, Clwyd 125
Dittisham Fruit Farm, Capton, nr Dartmouth, Devon 25
Dorset Spring Water, Stoke Abbott, Beaminster, Dorset 49
Dunkerton's Cider Co, Luntley, Pembridge, Hereford 104
Duskin Farm Ltd, Kingston, Canterbury, Kent 81

236

PRODUCT INDEX

C J Hartley Ltd, Swanmore, Southampton, Hants 62
Inch's Cider Co., Winkleigh, Devon 31
Island Country Foods, Ashey, Ryde, Isle of Wight 63
Knight's Cider, Storridge, nr Malvern, Worcs 105
Merrydown Plc, Horam, East Sussex 87
Norbury's Cider Co, Leigh Sinton, nr Malvern, Worcs 105
Norfolk Punch, Upwell, Norfolk 157
Penshurst Vineyards, Penshurst, Kent 82
Pippins Cider Co, Pembury, Kent 83
Revells Farm, Linton, Ross-on-Wye, Hereford 108
Rock's Country Wines, Twyford, Berks 67
St George's English Wine, Heathfield, East Sussex 89
R J Sheppy, Three Bridges, Bradford-on-Tone, Somerset 46
Sherston Earl Vineyards, nr Malmesbury, Wilts 54
Thatcher's Cider, Sandford, Bristol, Avon 48
Yearlstone Vineyards, Bickleigh, Tiverton, Devon 37

Cheeses – G denotes goats' cheese, E, ewes' milk cheese.
Alston Cheese, Alston, Cumbria 192
Appleby's Hawkstone Cheese, Prees, Shropshire 112
G Battle Abbey Farm, Battle, East Sussex 85
G Beamer Dairy Goats, Thixendale, Malton, N Yorks 179
E G Beenleigh Blue Cheese, Ashprington, Totnes, Devon 24
Biggings Farm, Stenness, Orkney 211
Blue Cheshire Cheese, Whitchurch, Shropshire 113
Bonchester Cheese, Easter Weens, Bonchester Bridge, Roxburgh 212
Botton Creamery, Danby, N Yorks 178
Breck & Myres, Shapinsay, Orkney 217
T & J M Butler, Inglewhite, Lancs 168
E Carolina Cheese, Chard, Somerset 39
E Cedaridge Farm, Henfield, Sussex 86
Chewton Farms Ltd, Chewton Mendip, Bath 40
E Coleford Blue Cheese, Coleford Water, nr Lydeard St Lawrence, Somerset 43
Colston Bassett & District Dairy, Colston Bassett, Notts 133
The Dairy House, Weobley, Herefordshire 106
E G Dalton's Farmhouse Country Delicacies, Pott Shrigley, Macclesfield, Cheshire 162
Dorset Blue Cheese, Farmer Bailey's Cheese Centre, Motcombe, Dorset 48
R A Duckett, Wedmore, nr Wells, Somerset 42
E H J Errington & Co, Ogscastle, nr Carnwath, Lanark 214
G S & G Fowler, Arkholme, Carnforth 169
R & J Fuller, Sible Hedingham, Halstead, Essex 142
E Furzehill Farm, Pirbright, Surrey 80
H & E J Grant Ltd, Trull, Taunton, Somerset 43
G Hadari Cheese Ltd, Chirk, Clwyd 97
Highland Fine Cheeses Ltd, Blairliath, Tain, Ross & Cromarty 213
S & G Keen, Wincanton, Somerset 44
G Levens Farm Products, Killinghall, Harrogate, N. Yorks 180
E Little Acorn Products, Bethania, Llanon, Dyfed 97
Llanboidy Farmhouse Cheese, Whitland, Login, Dyfed 98
Llangloffan Cheese, Castle Morris, nr Haverfordwest, Dyfed 98
Long Clawson Dairy, nr Melton Mowbray, Leics 127
G Lubborn Cheese Ltd, Crewkerne, Somerset 45
Lynher Valley Dairy, Upton Cross, Liskeard, Cornwall 21–2
G Marianglas Cheese, Llanllyfni, Caenarfon, Gwynedd 99
C & M Martell, Dymock, Glos 56
G Miracle Dairy Herd, Westfield, Hastings, E. Sussex 88
J & E Montgomery, North Cadbury, Somerset 45
G Moorlands Cheese, Rushton Spencer, nr Macclesfield, Cheshire 165
Neal's Yard Dairy, Covent Garden, London WC2 76
G Paradise Goats' Cheese, Holt, Wimborne, Dorset 51
Park Farm Cheeses, Umberleigh, Devon 33
J G Quicke & Partners, Newton St Cyres, Exeter, Devon 34
E Redesdale Dairy, Elsdon, Otterburn, Northumberland 203
G Ribblesdale Goats' Cheese, Horton-in-Ribblesdale, Settle, N Yorks 180
G Robrock Dairy Goats, Thurlstone, Sheffield, S Yorks 181
E G Roundoak Dairy, Cheddar, Somerset 45
G St Michael's Dairy Produce, Lockerbie, Dumfries 218
E Sheviock Cheese, Torpoint, Cornwall 19
Somerset Creameries, Cropwell Bishop, Notts 134
Staffordshire Organic Cheese, Acton, Newcastle-under-Lyme, Staffs 120
Thornby Moor Dairy, Aikton, Wigton, Cumbria 198
G Threeshires Dairy, Castle Ashby, Northants 125
Ty'n Grug Cheese, Esgerdawe, Llandeilo, Dyfed 100
G Vulscombe Devon Goats' Cheese, Cruwys Morchard, Tiverton, Devon 36
E Wackley Farm, Burlton, Shrewsbury, Shropshire 118
G K & E Wardle, Blawith, nr Ulverston, Cumbria 195
Webster's Dairy Ltd, Saxelby, nr Melton Mowbray, Leics 127

Chocolates & Confectionery
Cromwells Chocolates, Bath 41
Knutsford, Cheshire 162
Upton-on-Severn, Worcs 106
Dorchester Chocolates, Poundbury, Dorchester, Dorset 48
J Durig, Hale, Altrincham, Cheshire 164
Fitzbillies, Cambridge 150
Furniss & Co, Truro, Cornwall 21
Geoffroi, Winchmore Hill, London N21 74
The Golden Fudge Co, West Pimbo, Skelmersdale, Lancs 169
Islay Tablet, North Ballachulish, nr Fort William, Inverness 214
Jon's Toffee, Sowerby Bridge, Halifax, W Yorks 181
Ruth Liversedge, Beaulieu, Hants 63
Norfolk Delight, Upwell, Norfolk 157
Rococo, 321 Kings Road, London SW3 77
Rowena's Fudge, Penkridge, Stafford, Staffs 120

237

PRODUCT INDEX

Sarah's Lakeland Fudge, Cockermouth, Cumbria 197
Stapleton Farm, Langtree, nr Torrington, Devon 35
Thornton's Chocolates, Belper, Derbyshire 131
G Wienholt, Alderley Edge, Cheshire 167
Wiper's, Kendal, Cumbria 295
Woodnutts, Hove, East Sussex 90

Dairy Products – and see *Cheese* producers. Ice-cream producers are included in this section.
E Abbey House Farm Products, Goosey, Faringdon, Oxon 67
G Adam's Rib Farm, Ulting, nr Maldon, Essex 140
E Ashdale Products, Monyash, nr Bakewell, Derbyshire 128
G Beechenlea Dairy Goats, Pewsham, Chippenham, Wilts 52
G Blackdown Farm, Loddiswell, Kingsbridge, Devon 24
G Bowyers Court Farm, Wisborough Green, W Sussex 85
G Cerin House Products, Dishforth, N Yorks 180
G Messrs Cockburn & Skelton, Killearn, Glasgow, Lanark 213
Cricketer Farm Foods, Chard, Somerset 41
E Jane Croswell-Jones, Mells, Frome, Somerset 42
G Custance Goats, Hainford, Norwich, Norfolk 153
G Deaward Farmhouse, Byfield, Daventry, Northants 125
Denbigh Farmhouse Ice-cream, Denbigh, Clwyd 95
Denton Dairy Farm Shop, Lambourne, Berks 66
G The Elms Farmhouse Produce, Lower Westholme, Pilton, Somerset 43
English Ice-creams, Staveley, nr Kendal, Cumbria 194
Eshott Dairy Produce, Felton, Morpeth, Northumberland 202
Eveleigh Jersey Produce, Cruwys Morchard, Tiverton, Devon 28
E 'Ewe Tree Farm', Embley Park, Romsey, Hants 61
G Fir Tree Farm, Darrow Green, Nr Harleston, Norfolk 154
E Foxfire dairy products, Clayhidon, nr Cullompton, Devon 29
G Ghyllside Herd, Westnewton, Aspatria, Cumbria 195
Hadley Park Farm, Leegomery, Telford, Shropshire 114
G Horn Park Farm, Beaminster, Dorset 50

'Kettle's Farm', Llanddeinoilen, Caernarfon 97
J & P Langman, Perrotts Brook Farm, nr Cirencester, Glos 56
Leworthy Mill, Woolsery, Bideford, N Devon 33
Longley Farm, Holmfirth, nr Huddersfield, W Yorks 182
G Lyneve Dairy Goats, Ladbroke, Leamington Spa, Warks 111
Manor Farm Dairy Products, Thrussington, Leics 126
'Meadow Cottage' Ices, Headley, Bordon, Hants 64
G Morrelhirst Dairy Goats, Netherwitton, Morpeth, Northumberland 202
G Noblestone Goats, Longtown, Carlisle, Cumbria 195
E Ostler Dairy Sheep, Horringer, Bury St Edmunds, Suffolk 147
Ray's Farm, Billingsley, Bridgnorth, Shropshire 117–18
A E Rodda & Son, Scorrier, Redruth, Cornwall 22
Rachel Roskilly, St Keverne, Cornwall 23
Salcombe Dairy Ice-cream, Salcombe, Devon 34
Stapleton Farm, Langtree, nr Torrington, Devon 35
G Thorncliff Goats, Dyserth, Clwyd 100
Whitburn Moors Farm Yoghurt, Cleadon, Tyne & Wear 205
E Wield Wood Dairy, nr Winchester, Hants 65
Yorkshire Dales Ice-cream, Cononley, Keighley, W Yorks 187
G Zorapore Goat Herd, Peterchurch, Herefordshire 109

Fresh Fish – and see *Smoked Products*
Anglesey Oysters, Trearddur Bay, Anglesey 93
The Ark, Lewes, E. Sussex 84
Andrew Athill, Morston, Holt, Norfolk 151
Berwick Salmon Fisheries, Spittal, Berwick-on-Tweed 201
Brown & Forrest, Thorney, Langport, Somerset 38
The Butley-Orford Oysterage, Orford, Suffolk 145
Clearwater Products, East Hendred, Wantage, Oxon 68
F. Cooke, London E8 73
Garron Foods Ltd, Lawrenny, Dyfed 96
Head Mill Trout Farm, Umberleigh, N Devon 29
Hebridean Oysters, Pennyghael, Mull 213

Kilnsey Trout Farm, Kilnsey via Skipton, N Yorks 182
A J Leggett, Beccles, Suffolk 147
Loch Fyne Oysters, Ardkinglas, Cairndow, Argyll 215
R Phillips, Quarr Hill, Binstead, Isle of Wight 65
Riversdale Farm, Stour Provost, Gillingham Dorset 52
Tern Fisheries Ltd, Peatswood, Market Drayton, Shropshire 118

Fruit, Herbs and Vegetables
Ampleforth Abbey Orchard, Ampleforth, Yorks 177
Arne Herbs, Limeburn Hill, Chew Magna, Avon 37
Belvoir Fruit Farms, Grantham, Lincs 135
Blackmoor Estate Ltd, Liss, Hants 61
Bryn Saron Farm Produce, Saron, Llandysul, Dyfed 94
Charlton Orchards, Creech St Michael, Taunton, Somerset 40
Crape's Fruit Farm, Aldham, Colchester, Essex 141
Deaward Farm, Daventry, Northants 125
Dentons Farm Shop, Lambourne, Berks 66
Devon Herbs, Brentor, Tavistock, Devon 27
Dittisham Fruit Farm, Capton, nr Dartmouth, Devon 25
S & G Fowler, Carnforth, Lancs 169
Frome Organic Growers, Canon Frome Court, nr Ledbury, Hereford 107
Hill Farm Orchards, Swanmore, Southampton, Hants 62
Island Country Foods, Ashey, Ryde, Isle of Wight 63
Jack's Produce, Kimbolton, Leominster, Hereford 107
D & S Jenkins, Dinmore, Hereford 107
Kingcob Garlic, Newchurch, Sandown, Isle of Wight 63
K & S C Knight, Storridge, nr Malvern, Worcs 105
Lighthorne Associates Ltd, Moreton Morrell, Warks 110
D Maclean, Crieff, Perthshire 215
Mayall Organic Farm, Harmer Hill, Shrewsbury, Shropshire 117
Mockbeggar Farm, Higham, nr Rochester, Kent 82
Morrelhirst Produce, Netherwitton, Morpeth, Northumberland 202

238

PRODUCT INDEX

Muttons Organic Growers, Thornbury, Bromyard, Hereford 108
A R Paske & Co Ltd, Kentford, Newmarket, Suffolk 148
Michael Paske Farms Ltd, Honington, Grantham, Lincs 136
Priorwood Gardens, Melrose, Roxburgh 216
Snitterfield Fruit Farm, Stratford-on-Avon, Warks 111
Stawell Fruit Farm, Bridgwater, Somerset 47
R & G Stevens, West End, Woking, Surrey 80
Stoke Lacy Herbs, Bromyard, Hereford 109
The Strawberry Farm, Birstwith, Harrogate, N Yorks 186
Tatworth Fruit Farm Ltd, Chard, Somerset 47
Welcombe Country Fayre, Welcombe, nr Bideford, Devon 36
York Grounds Farm, Cottingham, E Yorks 186

Prepared Foods – see also *Bakery & Cereal Products* and *Smoked Foods*
The Budleigh Salterton Pâté Co, Budleigh Salterton, Devon 24
Cheshire Larders, Eccles, Manchester 162
Clearwater Products, East Hendred, Wantage, Oxon 68
A J Cole & Sons, Saffron Walden, Essex 140
Country Cooks, Tretire, St Owens Cross, Hereford 106
Culham Harvest, Hurley, Maidenhead, Berks 66
Devon Larder Recipes (Country Larders), Hemyock, Devon 27
J Durig, Hale, Altrincham, Cheshire 164
Eggleston Hall, Barnard Castle, Co Durham 205
Elstones, Knutsford, Cheshire 164
Essex Larders, Hounslow Green, Dunmow, Essex 142
Fordhall Farm, Market Drayton, Shropshire 114
Garron Foods Ltd, Lawrenny, Dyfed 96
Mrs Gill's Indian Kitchen, London N21 74
Kilnsey Park & Trout Farm, Kilnsey via Skipton, N. Yorks 182
Lidgate's Kitchen, Holland Park Avenue, London W11 75
Linden Lea English Pâté, Longton, Stoke-on-Trent, Staffs 118
La Maison des Sorbets, Battersea Park Road, London SW11 76

The Pasta Factory, Kings Road, London SW3 77
Prospero Fine Ices, Wiveton, nr Holt, Norfolk 157
'Puddings', Poynington, nr Sherborne, Dorset 51
St Nicholas Mill, nr Birchington, Kent 83
Smythes, Altrincham, Cheshire 165
Somerset Ducks, North Newton, Bridgwater, Somerset 47
Whole Earth Natural Foods, Park Royal Road, London NW10 78

Fresh Meat and Meat Products
Adsdean Farm, Funtington, Chichester, W Sussex 84
T Appleton & Sons, Ripon, N Yorks 183
J F Bishop Ltd, Uckfield, E Sussex 85
Black Sheep Marketing Ltd, Ingworth, Norwich, Norfolk 151
Bowyers Court Farm, Wisborough Green, W Sussex 85
Andy Callwood & Son, Ledbury, Hereford 104
Chiltern Beef, Marlow Bottom, Bucks 69
H H Collins (Broadway) Ltd, Broadway, Worcs 105
A W Curtis & Sons Ltd, Lincoln, Lincs 135
Custance Goats, Hainford, Norwich, Norfolk 153
Dalton's 'Farmhouse Country Delicacies', Pott Shrigley, Macclesfield, Cheshire 162
John Dixon, Quendon, Saffron Walden, Essex 141
Dorset Farms, Broadwindsor, Dorset 49
Emmett's Stores, Peasenhall, Saxmundham, Suffolk 146
Fir Tree Farm, Darrow Green, Denton, Norfolk 154
Flintan Enterprises, Mayfield, E Sussex 86
Fordhall Farm, Market Drayton, Shropshire 114
Sam Gosling, Longton, Stoke-on-Trent, Staffs 119
A H Griffiths, Leintwardine, nr Craven Arms, Shropshire 115
Harris – Leeming Bar, Northallerton, N Yorks 184
Heal Farm, King's Nympton, Umberleigh, Devon 30
Albert Hirst, Barnsley, S. Yorks 181
Hopetown House, Bedale, N Yorks 183
Island Country Foods, Ashey, Ryde, Isle of Wight 63

Johnsons of Whitby, Whitby, N Yorks 184
'Elizabeth King', Cropwell Butler, Notts 134
W G Lough & Son, Jesmond, Newcastle-upon-Tyne 203
Charles Macsween & Son, Edinburgh 216
R May, Ditton Priors, Brignorth, Shropshire 116
Metcalfe Parket, King's Road, Harrogate, N Yorks 186
Moorland Farm Bacon, nr Longnor, Buxton, Derbyshire 130
Murray's Meat, Ashprington, Totnes, Devon 33
J H Nelson & Sons, Bakewell, Derbyshire 131
Norfolk Porkers, Bressingham, nr Diss, Norfolk 156
Peartree Pork Products, Weeley Heath, nr Clacton-on-Sea, Essex 144
M & C Provis, Port Isaac, Cornwall 22
The Real Meat Co., Heytesbury, Warminster, Wilts 53
Clive Sadd, Dorrington, nr Shrewsbury, Shropshire 116
Michael Slack, Raisbeck, Penrith, Cumbria 198
J Stanforth, Skipton, N Yorks 184
R Stiff, Kersey, Suffolk 149
C D Stone, Lower Westholme, Pilton, Somerset 43
G P Stonehouse & Son, York 185
Thornley & Son Ltd, Heath Charnock, Chorley, Lancs 172
G E Thornton & Sons, Crosshills, Keighley, Yorks 185
J Titterton & Sons Ltd, Reddish, Greater Manchester 166
Weegmann's, Otley, N Yorks 185
A T Welch, Nantwich, Cheshire 166
Bar Woodall, Waberthwaite, Millom, Cumbria 200

Game and Poultry
Breckan Rabbits, Sanday, Orkney 212
Callwood & Son, Ledbury, Hereford 104
Cottage Farm Turkeys, Cudham, Sevenoaks, Kent 81
Fayre Game, Lytham, Lancs 168
Fordhall Farm, Market Drayton, Shropshire 114
Hockwold Manor Black Turkeys, Thetford, Norfolk 155
Kelly Turkeys, Danbury, Essex 142
Kilnsey Park & Trout Farm, Kilnsey via Keighley, Yorks 182

239

PRODUCT INDEX

A J Leggett & Sons, Beccles, Suffolk 147
W G Lough & Sons, Jesmond, Newcastle-upon-Tyne 203
Nether Winchendon Farms, nr Aylesbury, Bucks 70
Peartree Pork Products, Weeley Heath, nr Clacton-on-Sea, Essex 144
R Phillips, Quarr Hill, Binstead, Isle of Wight 65
Roundthorn Farmhouse Foods, Beacon Edge, Penrith, Cumbria 197
Sherston Quail, Malmesbury, Wilts 54
Somerset Ducks, North Newton, Bridgwater, Somerset 47

Condiments and Preserves

Arran Provisions, Lamlash, Isle of Arran 210
Aspall Cyder, Stowmarket, Suffolk 144
Blackmoor Estate Ltd, Liss, Hants 61
Dorothy Carter Preserves, Iden, Rye, E Sussex 86
Cartwright & Butler, Wells-next-the-Sea, Norfolk 152
L Chirnside, Upper Llanover, Abergavenny, Gwent 96
Clare's Kitchen, Rendcomb, Cirencester, Glos 55
A J Cole & Sons, Saffron Walden, Essex 140
Culham Harvest, Hurley, Maidenhead, Berks 66
Cumberland Mustard, Alston, Cumbria 194
Dart Valley Foods, Lee Mill, Ivybridge, Devon 27
J Durig, Hale, Altrincham, Cheshire 164
Elstones, Knutsford, Cheshire 164
The English Provender Co, Aldreth, Ely, Cambs 149
Farmhouse Fare, Great Haywood, Staffs 119

Farmhouse Preserves, Darley, Harrogate, N Yorks 179
Fieldfare Mustard, Newport, Dyfed 96
S & G Fowler, Carnforth, Lancs 169
Gordon's Mustard, Peaslare, Surrey 74
Humble Pie Foods, Burnham Market, Norfolk 155
Maldon Crystal Salt Co Ltd, Maldon, Essex 143
Martin & Grafton, Golborne, Warrington, Lancs 171
Michaelmas Fare, Swimbridge, nr Barnstaple, Devon 32
Mockbeggar Farm, nr Rochester, Kent 82
Ostler Dairy Sheep, Horringer, Bury St Edmunds, Suffolk 147
Otter Vale Products, Budleigh Salterton, Devon 25
Oxbridge Selected Products, Oxford 68
Penshurst Vineyards, Penshurst, Kent 82
Priorwood Gardens, Melrose, Galashiels 216
The Proper Food Co, London SW5 77
Roundthorn Farmhouse Foods, Beacon Edge, Penrith, Cumbria 197
St George's English Wine, Heathfield, Sussex 89
Suffolk Farm Produce, Weybread, Diss, Norfolk 158
Matthew Walker (Derby) Ltd, Heanor, Derby 132
Wiltshire Tracklements, Calne, Wilts 55

Smoked Products

Ashdown Smokers, Corney, Millom, Cumbria 192
Brown & Forrest, Thorney, Langport, Somerset 38
The Butley-Orford Oysterage, Orford, Suffolk 145

Cenarth Smokery, Cenarth, Newcastle Emlyn, Dyfed 94
Cley Smokehouse, Cley-next-the-Sea, Norfolk 152
The Cornish Smoked Fish Co, Charlestown, St Austell, Cornwall 21
Cromack Ltd, Fraserburgh, Grampian 218
John Curtis Ltd, Douglas, Isle of Man 196
George Devereau & Son, Douglas, Isle of Man 196
Inverawe Smokehouses, Taynuilt, Argyll 219
Leatham's Larder, Bethwin Road, London SE5 75
A J Leggett, Beccles, Suffolk 147
Lune Smoked Foods, Kendal, Lancs 170
Mermaid Fish Supplies, Clachan, North Uist 219
The Mill Smoke House, Thornhill, Stirling 219
Minola Smoked Foods, Filkins, Lechlade, Glos 57
T Moore & Sons Ltd, Peel, Isle of Man 196
R Phillips, Quarr Hill, Binstead, Isle of Wight 65
Pinney's, Annan, Dumfries 220
L Robson & Sons, Craster, Alnwick, Northumberland 204
Salcombe Smokers, Kingsbridge, S Devon 35
Scots Caught Seafoods Ltd, Arbroath, Tayside 220
Smythes, Altrincham, Cheshire 165
R R Spink, Arbroath, Tayside 221
Summer Isles Foods Ltd, Achiltibuie, Ullapool, Ross-shire 221
Sussex Smoked Foods Ltd, North Chapel, W Sussex 89
Tern Fisheries Ltd, Peatswood, Market Drayton, Shropshire 118
Westmorland Smoked Foods Ltd, Kirkby Lonsdale, Lancs 173